Palgrave Series in Asia and Pacific Studies

Series Editors
May Tan-Mullins
University of Nottingham
Ningbo, Zhejiang, China

Adam Knee
Lasalle College of the Arts
Singapore

Filippo Gilardi
University of Nottingham Ningbo China
Ningbo, China

The Asia and Pacific regions, with a population of nearly three billion people, are of critical importance to global observers, academics, and citizenry due to their rising influence in the global political economy as well as traditional and nontraditional security issues. Any changes to the domestic and regional political, social, economic, and environmental systems will inevitably have great impacts on global security and governance structures. At the same time, Asia and the Pacific have also emerged as a globally influential, trend-setting force in a range of cultural arenas. The remit of this book series is broadly defined, in terms of topics and academic disciplines. We invite research monographs on a wide range of topics focused on Asia and the Pacific. In addition, the series is also interested in manuscripts pertaining to pedagogies and research methods, for both undergraduate and postgraduate levels. Published by Palgrave Macmillan, in collaboration with the Institute of Asia and Pacific Studies, UNNC.

More information about this series at
http://www.palgrave.com/gp/series/14665

Hing Kai Chan · Faith Ka Shun Chan ·
David O'Brien
Editors

International Flows in the Belt and Road Initiative Context

Business, People, History and Geography

Editors
Hing Kai Chan
University of Nottingham Ningbo
China
Ningbo, China

Faith Ka Shun Chan
University of Nottingham Ningbo
China
Ningbo, China

David O'Brien
Ruhr University Bochum
Bochum, Germany

Palgrave Series in Asia and Pacific Studies
ISBN 978-981-15-3132-3   ISBN 978-981-15-3133-0   (eBook)
https://doi.org/10.1007/978-981-15-3133-0

Cover illustration: Contributor: Lok Yiu Cheung/Alamy Stock Photo

This Palgrave Macmillan imprint is published by the registered company Springer Nature Singapore Pte Ltd.
The registered company address is: 152 Beach Road, #21-01/04 Gateway East, Singapore 189721, Singapore

CONTENTS

LIST OF CONTRIBUTORS

Faith Ka Shun Chan School of Geographical Sciences, University of Nottingham Ningbo China, Ningbo, China;
Water@Leeds, School of Geography, University of Leeds, Leeds, UK

Hing Kai Chan Nottingham University Business School China, University of Nottingham Ningbo China, Ningbo, China

Julie Yu-Wen Chen Department of Cultures, University of Helsinki, Helsinki, Finland

Neil Collins Nazarbayev University, Astana, Kazakhstan

Li Cui School of Business, Dalian University of Technology, Panjin, China;
China Business Executives Academy, Dalian, China

Jing Dai Nottingham University Business School China, University of Nottingham Ningbo China, Ningbo, China

Marina Glushenkova Nottingham University Business School China, University of Nottingham Ningbo China, Ningbo, China

Saileshsingh Gunessee Nottingham University Business School China, University of Nottingham Ningbo China, Ningbo, China

Rongxing Guo Capital University of Economics and Business, Beijing, China

Zhimei Lei College of Mechanical Engineering, Chongqing University, Chongqing, China

Pengfei Li College of Geomatics, Xi'an University of Science and Technology, Xi'an, China

Jia Jia Lim Nottingham University Business School China, University of Nottingham Ningbo China, Ningbo, China

Jianmin Liu Nottingham University Business School China, University of Nottingham Ningbo China, Ningbo, China

Nancy Xiuzhi Liu School of Education and English, University of Nottingham Ningbo China, Ningbo, China

Christian Müller University of Nottingham Ningbo China, Ningbo, China;
Visiting Research Fellow, Rothermere American Institute, University of Oxford, Oxford, UK

David O'Brien Faculty of East Asian Studies, Ruhr-University Bochum, Bochum, Germany

Christopher B. Primiano KIMEP University, Almaty, Kazakhstan

Zhiyu Sun School of Business, Dalian University of Technology, Panjin, China

Juanle Wang Institute of Geographic Sciences and Natural Resources Research, Chinese Academy of Sciences, Beijing, China

Shuojiang Xu Nottingham University Business School China, University of Nottingham Ningbo China, Ningbo, China

Kaizhong Yang Chinese Academy of Social Sciences and Peking University, Beijing, China

Yuzhe Zang College of Geomatics, Xi'an University of Science and Technology, Xi'an, China

Fangli Zeng Nottingham University Business School China, University of Nottingham Ningbo China, Ningbo, China

LIST OF FIGURES

LIST OF TABLES

CHAPTER 1

Recent Trends on Belt and Road Initiative (BRI) Research

Hing Kai Chan, Faith Ka Shun Chan and David O'Brien

1.1 Introduction to BRI Research

The Belt and Road Initiative (BRI) is an enormous development strategy initiated by the Chinese Government in 2013. It refers to the Silk Road Economic Belt (SREB), which links China with Europe through Central and Western Asia, and the twenty-first Century Maritime Silk Road (MSR), which connects China with Southeast Asian countries, Africa and

H. K. Chan (✉)
Nottingham University Business School China, University of Nottingham Ningbo China, Ningbo, China
e-mail: hingkai.chan@nottingham.edu.cn

F. K. S. Chan
School of Geographical Sciences, University of Nottingham Ningbo China, Ningbo, China
e-mail: faith.chan@nottingham.edu.cn

D. O'Brien
Faculty of East Asian Studies, Ruhr University Bochum, Bochum, Germany
e-mail: David.OBrien@ruhr-uni-bochum.de

© The Author(s) 2020   1
H. K. Chan et al. (eds.), *International Flows in the Belt and Road Initiative Context*, Palgrave Series in Asia and Pacific Studies,
https://doi.org/10.1007/978-981-15-3133-0_1

Europe (Rolland 2017). With the BRI strategy, it is projected that China will further integrate itself into the world economy and strengthen its influence across three continents.

This hugely ambitious project aims at transnational collaboration with countries not only in Asia Pacific but also extending to Europe, Africa and beyond. The BRI will change the shape of international trade due to the huge scale of infrastructural development. In addition, due to the involvement of inter-country activities, the BRI will significantly affect the current political equilibrium. This initiative has already and will continue to alter the geopolitical balance in East Asia, Central Asia and on into Europe. Realities which have existed since the end of the Cold War are being called into question by the scope and scale of this project.

While the People's Republic of China (PRC) strongly rejects claims that the project is neo-colonial in aim, it is a reality that it brings a substantial Chinese economic and political presence into parts of the world long considered Russia's sphere of influence. While relations between Russia and China currently appear better than at any time in their recent history, these two huge nations have often existed in a state of mutual suspicion and BRI has the potential to once again destabilise this relationship.

In its early manifestation, China has done a good job of convincing its neighbours that the BRI is a positive and a mutually beneficial project, which could signify a new and more fairly balanced world order. Yet these are uncertain times across the whole world and while China's neighbours currently view the BRI in a mostly favourable light, it is not hard to conceive of a situation where the optics might change and perceptions of China as trying to gain an upper hand in a region not considered its own historically, could develop. There are obvious parallels here with the nineteenth-century Great Game when Russia and Britain engaged in a fierce rivalry for influence in the same region. While China may not face a competing great power in Central Asia for now, it is not hard to conceive of a situation arising where a competing narrative to that espoused by the PRC develops.

Furthermore, the infrastructure projects are directly related to geographical issues along the BRI route. BRI is engaged mainly with infrastructure and planning on the overland and maritime trade routes. Therefore, multinational cooperation between BRI countries is vital and lessons must be learned from the past to understand the historical, social-cultural and environmental issues of BRI to avoid potentially disastrous outcomes.

Large geospatial transnational trade partnerships with Central Asia, Southeast Asia, Middle East, Europe, Japan and Korea, etc., have long been part of China's economic strategy, with huge success in the last few decades since the "Open Door Policy" was established in 1978. Chinese transnational trade routes have existed since the Tang Dynasty (618–907 CE), understanding historical, social-cultural and environmental factors is vital when it comes to informing stakeholders, policy- and decision-makers aiming to establish long-term and sustainable ideas for further developments.

This volume focuses on the shifting nexus between global infrastructures due to the BRI and emerging issues in the political, international relations and geographical fields. Building on recent theoretical and conceptual advances in the study of infrastructure, large technical systems and technoscience in science and technology studies and innovation studies, this volume aims to bring together a broad understanding of the key issues.

1.2   The Three Distinctive Research Areas

1.2.1   Business

BRI involves a lot of bilateral infrastructure projects between China and the BRI partner countries. On the one hand, these projects generate a lot of business opportunities; on the other hand, they also demand lots of business and project management skills. Traditional business theories may not be perfectly applicable in the BRI context in practice. First, it is because the coverage of the BRI is extremely wide, and is possibly the widest regional initiative ever. In addition, it involves far more external factors, such as national security, cross-cultural issues, among others, than the other alliances or collaborations between countries. To master these projects well is not easy. Second, the ultimate objective of the BRI is to improve international trade, and consequently, new business models are needed. Therefore, the business context of BRI cannot be underestimated. Notwithstanding this, research and development in this area is surprisingly limited because currently studies are very much focusing on the high-level national issues regarding BRI. Business context is more hands-on and relates to relatively more practical issues.

More specifically, current studies in business and management domain mainly discuss the economic benefits of the BRI (Huang 2016; Zhai 2018; Li et al. 2019), optimisation of the infrastructural projects to logistics network (Shao et al. 2018; Sheu and Kundu 2018; Kuzmicz and Pesch 2019) and sustainability (Shaikh et al. 2016; Solmecke 2017; Liu and Xin 2019). Borrowing concepts from a recent review conducted by Thürer et al. (2019), the BRI will affect global business, particularly in supply chain management, in two aspects: business entities and flow.

Business entities refer to the companies in supply chains. The major aim of the BRI is to improve regional connectivity. In a business sense, this is to improve the linkage between the business entities, or companies. This requires the integration of business processes between companies in different nations. For instance, cross-border e-commerce systems aim to achieve this integration. The BRI plays an irreplaceable role in connecting the physical logistics and supply chain activities along the BRI routes in view of this integration. Otherwise, merely developing the logistics infrastructure in different BRI countries cannot achieve the intended efficiency. Nevertheless, the economic benefits or economic efficiency of introducing the BRI-related projects are still unclear. There is a pressing need to first understand how, economically, the BRI can be beneficial to the countries involved. Multi-method approaches may be required (Chan et al. 2019).

The second aspect, flow, focuses more on the linkage of the physical BRI activities or countries by emerging, and in particular, digital technologies. One potential research area in this regard is the digital Silk Road (Jia and Shuang 2015; Shen 2018). The notion of the *"Digital Silk Road"* or *"Digital Belt and Road"* (Guo et al. 2018) resonates with research on the interplay of logistics and supply chain management, the international economy and the Internet. Digital industries and infrastructures are an integral part of the BRI (Kozłowski 2018). Flow here also includes the financial flow rather than just the flow of physical goods. The integration of financial flow will lead to market integration. However, the mechanism of such market integration warrants investigating. Digital connectivity is the counterpart of the infrastructural connectivity in the physical Silk Road. Digital connectivity in the digital Silk Road is a natural extension of the evolution of the digital economy (Fishwick 2017) and is of vital importance in creating various participatory digital platforms (Fung et al. 2018; Seele et al. 2019). The development of standard information systems along the BRI is therefore of vital importance to accommodate the flow along the BRI countries. This will further promote and enhance trade and economic development along the BRI countries.

To master the above issues, it is very clear that the current talent development programmes, which normally do not take such a wide scope into consideration, are insufficient to train management personnel to deal with all challenges. There is a need to reshape talent development programmes in relation to BRI. Since BRI is international in nature, such programmes cannot be tailored to just one country or region. This will indirectly address the issues surrounding politics such as diversity in culture which may compromise national security risks.

1.2.2 Politics

A detailed exploration of the political impact of such a huge project is beyond the scope of this volume. What is intended instead is to provide a snapshot of some of the key political narrative flows taking place at this time and their potential impact in some of the regions the BRI will impact.

Of course, Central Asia is a key to BRI and any examination of the political context of the initiative must pay close attention to this huge, diverse region. It is a region of complex identities, rich in natural resources, occupying a key strategic position between Asia and Europe. The importance of Central Asia generally and to the BRI specifically cannot be in doubt, as Vakulchuk and Overland (2019, p. 116) write *"Central Asia, while a culturally and historically homogenous region, remains one of the least integrated regions in the world"*. It is interesting to examine the dilemma facing Central Asian states to explore what strategies are available to maximise the benefits of the BRI.

The PRC is adamant that BRI is a mutually beneficial "win-win" situation for any country willing to join it. Yet China is keenly aware of political narratives and will use the full extent of its soft and hard power to achieve its aims. The recent unprecedented security clampdown in the Xinjiang Uyghur Autonomous Region (XUAR) in China's northwest has demonstrated the extent to which China will go to ensure its narratives are not challenged. The XUAR is one of the key areas of development for the BRI project. Long described as the Pivot of Asia (Lattimore 1950). Xinjiang is perhaps China's most sensitive region, comprising as it does a complex ethnic makeup, vast mineral resources, and bordering eight of its neighbours in often-uneasy relation. Given that Xinjiang is the place where several of the BRI "economic corridors" start and it is from Xinjiang where Chinese trains reach Western Europe, it is a springboard for several of the BRI's main routes. Due to the monumental role that Xinjiang plays in determining the success of the BRI, having stability in Xinjiang is of utmost importance. Addressing the uneven development in the western part of China is also a central objective of the BRI.

Politically BRI is of course a Chinese narrative, which does matter because it is inherently concerned with causality, recognising that from the historical perspective specific events can yield a multiplicity of equilibria. But narrative alone is insufficient since many questions relate to events that did not take place (or have not yet taken place) or are concerned with the motivations behind why certain behaviour or events have not occurred. The disputes in the South China Sea is a good demonstration despite China's best efforts to control the narrative, events have a tendency to develop in unpredictable ways. Over the course of human history, boundary and territorial disputes have often stemmed from historical and cultural claims; they may have also resulted from fundamental geopolitical changes. China's activities in the South China Sea, on the one hand, and its huge, "Belt-and-Road Initiative"-related investment, on the other, will raise profound global and regional implications.

In aim, BRI extends well beyond Asia such as Northern European countries rather than the commonly mentioned Eastern European countries. It could have political and economic impacts in some unexpected contexts and regions. For example, Finland "might" be able to construct very concrete transportation links with the support of Chinese funding and that these routes can be counted as an extension of the BRI initiative, thus the so-called Polar Silk Road. One can conceive the BRI as a conceptual framework that awaits interested parties to give it substance and inject real meaning. China frequently portrays the BRI as contributing to peace and development. This often leads scholars to examine its influence in developing countries, such as those in Central Asia and Africa (Chen and Günther 2019; Chen and Jiménez-Tovar 2017). However, China is also interested in developed countries where the impact of BRI will also be felt, economically, culturally and politically.

1.2.3   History and Geography

From the historical perspective, the relationship between modern China and the European countries during eighteenth to nineteenth century is vital. China underwent a period of tremendous change during the Qing dynasty (1636–1912), gradually developing reforming its governance system as it came more into contact with "western" civilisation (Zhao 2015). The implications from the recent past, such as during that period in the late Qing Dynasty, provide a useful context to understanding current BRI policy.

A core aim of BRI is the further development of cities and metropolitans within the "Belt" and "Road" routes and economic corridors. This volume explores current approaches by the BRI which will see Asian cities (located in China, Southeast Asia, South Asia and Middle East) expand further and become metropolitan regions, some of these will transform to megacities (with populations of over 8 million). However, currently there is a lack of understanding of how BRI may influence these cities in China and in BRI countries. We expect further developments on infrastructures and socio-economic activities will enhance employment opportunities that attract younger generations to settle in these cities (Insch and Bowden 2016), thus some cities will transform into "megacities" in the future. This volume aims to explore how city branding and positioning, which is important in attracting more talent and investments will impact on the developments of these cities.

BRI covers large geographical spatial areas across continents involving multinationals and transnational cooperation. For example, the BRI programme has designated several transnational economic corridors across regions between China, Southeast Asia, South Asia, Central Asia, Russia, and Middle East and extensively to Europe. It is projected these activities and practices will encourage further infrastructure developments (e.g. construction of transnational highways, railways, ports, buildings, etc.) and enhance international financial and trade cooperation (Lechner et al. 2018). It is expected the BRI will initiate huge socio-economic benefits, but equally these developments may compromise and deteriorate environments, ecosystems and bio-diversity (Li et al. 2014).

In fact, many BRI involved countries on the terrestrial areas are located in semi-arid or arid (dry) areas which face challenges from desertification, for example countries in Central Asia, Middle East and Southern and

Southeastern Europe. Further development will lead to substantial land-use changes, deforestation and de-vegetation. There is a need to address these issues and offer recommendations new solutions to reduce and control desertification.

1.3   CHAPTERS IN THIS VOLUME

We have collected 11 recent research articles that are allocated to three sections. These articles present contemporary research that in line with above review. Below is a list of the chapters featured in this volume:

Chapter 2: Gunessee, S., and Liu, J., The Economics of the Belt and Road Initiative.

Chapter 3: Xu, S., Zeng, F., and Chan, H.K., New Research Direction of the Joint Sea-and-Land Transportation of the Ningbo Port Under the Belt and Road Initiative.

Chapter 4: Glushenkova, M., International Market Integration in the Context of the Belt and Road Initiative.

Chapter 5: Cui, L., Dai, J., Lei, Z., Lim, J.J., and Sun, Z., Innovative Talent Development in Chinese Universities Under the Belt and Road Initiative.

Chapter 6: O'Brien, D., and Primiano, C. B., Opportunities and Risks Along the New Silk Road: Perspectives and Perceptions on the Belt and Road Initiative (BRI) from the Xinjiang Uyghur Autonomous Region.

Chapter 7: Collins, N., Players or Spectators? Central Asia's Role in BRI.

Chapter 8: Guo, R., and Yang, K., China's Belt and Road Initiative and the South China Sea Disputes: Toward a New Mutual Deterrence Equilibrium.

Chapter 9: Chen, J.Y.-W., The Making of the Finnish Polar Silk Road: Status in Spring 2019.

Chapter 10: Mueller, C., Between Adoption and Resistance: China's Efforts of 'Understanding the West', the Challenges of Transforming Monarchical Legitimacy and the Rise of Oriental Exceptionalism, 1860 to 1910.

Chapter 11: Liu, N., Port City on the Maritime Silk Road: Ningbo's City Branding under the Theme of Intellectuals.

Chapter 12: Li, P.-F., Zang, Y.-Z., Chan, F.K.S., and Wang, J.-L., Desertification and Its Prevention Along the Route of China's Belt and Road Initiative.

The contributions of each chapter are summarised as follows:

Section 1: Business
This section aims to bring out 4 distinctive studies regarding the development in the business domain from the BRI perspective. They are summarised as follows:

- One important discipline of business study is economics. Since the BRI involves international trade between BRI partner countries, and will influence other countries as well, there is a need to understand the "economics" of the BRI. Gunessee and Liu in Chapter 2 examine the economic drivers, impacts and challenges of the BRI. They identify five economic drivers that lead to the development of the BRI. Subsequently, the BRI will facilitate the raising of bilateral trade across BRI economies. Although the drivers and hence benefits mentioned above are obvious, the BRI is not without challenges. In this chapter, Gunessee and Liu explain above in more detail.
- Logistics and transportation is the main favourable industry from the BRI projects. It is because the BRI aims to improve connectivity between the BRI countries. Sea and rail transportation are among the most important transportation modes in the BRI context. It is because the BRI consists of the Silk Road Economic Belt (SREB), which links China with Europe through Central and Western Asia by rail, and the twenty-first Century Maritime Silk Road (MSR), which connects China with Southeast Asian countries, Africa and Europe (Rolland 2017) by sea. In this connection, joint sea-and-rail transportation method plays a vital role to connect the SERB and MSR of the BRI. Xu et al. in Chapter 3 investigate the factors that affect the adoption of such a joint system at the organisational level. They reviewed the current practices regarding such joint method, and propose a one-stop electronic booking and tracking platform for joint sea-and-land transportation.
- Integration is almost a pre-requisite of good connectivity, which is the main focus of the BRI. Therefore, another business research opportunity regarding BRI is to study how the countries can be integrated. In this sense, there are many aspects that can be integrated. Among those, international market integration fits nicely with the BRI. In Chapter 4, Glushenkova studies how international market

integration has been evolving from the BRI perspective. She measures market integration by price dispersion across countries. If a market is more integrated, the price dispersion between the countries in the market is expected to fall. Therefore, the evolution of market integration can be examined by relevant panel data. Empirical results showed that China has become more integrated with the BRI partner countries in terms of price convergence. The BRI can enhance the global market convergence process and be beneficial for all partner countries. Successful implementation of the BRI can reduce barriers to international trade from business perspective.

- One critical success factor of running a good business is all about talents, i.e. human capability. This is equally important to the successful implementation of BRI infrastructural projects. Obviously, the higher education sector plays a dominating role in this area. Such talents are not limited to technical experts, but general business talents. In Chapter 5, the final chapter in this section, Cui et al. stress the need of cultivating business talents for BRI and identify different patterns in so doing in China from a qualitative interview study. Content analysis reveals that all the studied universities focus more on academic research activities (e.g. setting up research centres, academic conferences, etc.) rather than developing talents in the context of the BRI. Although they pay attention on general employability, only fast and convenient approaches are adopted to help develop talents who are capable to deal with international issues surrounding the BRI.

Section 2: Politics

This section presents 4 chapters that relate to the issues surrounding political environment and international relations:

- In Chapter 6, O'Brien and Primiano explore the seeming contradiction of Xinjiang being both a central conduit of the new Silk Road and China's most rigidly controlled and restricted region. Given that Xinjiang is the place where several of the BRI "economic corridors" start and it is from Xinjiang where Chinese trains reach Western Europe, it is a springboard for several of the BRI's main routes. Due to the monumental role that Xinjiang plays in determining the success of the BRI, having stability in Xinjiang is of utmost importance.

Addressing the uneven development in the western part of China is also a central objective of the BRI. O'Brien and Primiano argue that since 2017 Uyghurs who are in contact with people from abroad are increasingly viewed with suspicion by the Government who have launched an unprecedented campaign which has seen up to 1 million people interned without trial. A campaign which the Chinese government insist is a vocational education programme designed to help poor Uyghurs gain better jobs. If the Chinese government develops Xinjiang in terms of infrastructure on the one hand, and on the other brutally represses the Uyghur population the potential for instability and conflict in Xinjiang and beyond is very real.

- The BRI has the potential to deeply impact international relations in the regions it passes through. Much like the ancient Silk Road, BRI is not just a route where goods are transmitted but also where ideas, cultures and ideologies meet and are exchanged and sometimes come into conflict. It could have a lasting impact on China's relationship with its neighbours and while there is much potential for economic growth concerns too exist. Comparisons to the Great Game of the nineteenth century when Britain and Russia competed intensely for influence in Central Asia may not be exaggerated. Collins in Chapter 7 projected that the countries of BRI will be impacted in different ways. China's giant neighbour of Kazakhstan which is rich in natural reserves stands to gain the most but historical, cultural and religious tensions exist. In this chapter, Collins writes that China is building more infrastructure in Central Asia than any other country or international agency, but the long-term question remains as to who will benefit and who will not. Much of the BRI-related funding is going to the oil, coal and gas sectors and is aimed primarily at harnessing the supply line of fossil fuels to the PRC. The continued need to differentiate themselves for purposes of home consumption delimits the extent to which the five former Soviet republics can act in harmony. Added to these dynamics have been tensions over water resources, ageing Soviet-era infrastructure and tax and other impediments to cross-border trade. The BRI is a signature project for President Xi and may be both a vehicle for Chinese values and the PRC's alternative political model. Both Russia and China have strong geopolitical interests in Central Asia and, to an increasing extent, are accommodating each other's interests even if they eschew formal agreement. Their facilitating approach has increased since the Russian invasion of Crimea and China's trade disputes with the United States.

- Politically BRI is of course a Chinese narrative and as Guo and Yang argue in Chapter 8, narrative matters because it is inherently concerned with causality recognising that from the historical perspective specific events can yield a multiplicity of equilibria. But narrative alone is insufficient since many questions relate to events that did not take place (or have not yet taken place) or are concerned with the motivations behind why certain behaviour or events have not occurred. Over the course of human history, boundary and territorial disputes have often stemmed from historical and cultural claims; they may have also resulted from fundamental geopolitical changes. China's activities in the South China Sea, on the one hand, and its huge, "Belt-and-Road Initiative"-related investment, on the other, will raise profound global and regional implications.
- BRI of course extends well beyond Asia and as Chen in Chapter 9 shows that the BRI could have political and economic impacts in some unexpected contexts and regions. Finland is the focus of this study because it seems that Finland "might" be able to construct very concrete transportation lines with the support of Chinese funding and that these routes can be counted as an extension of the BRI initiative, thus the so-called Polar Silk Road. Chen in Chapter 9 writes that one can conceive the BRI as a conceptual framework that awaits interested parties to give it substance and inject real meaning.

Section 3: History and Geography

This section aims to bring out 3 distinctive studies regarding history, geography and environmental concerns from the BRI perspective (Chapters 10–12). This section offers insights and recommendations to stakeholders of BRI to achieve social-economic and environmental sustainability. They are summarised as here:

- Mueller in Chapter 10 provided understanding between the West and the East that addressed with European political thought and the implication of European concepts on legislations, statehood and "human rights" during the late Qing Dynasty in China during 1870–1910. Many readers have only focused on the international trade and foreign collaboration and investment after the "Open Door Policy" established in 1978, but there were substantial influences from the "West" in the early nineteenth century in the late Qing Dynasty enhanced by European countries. Mueller then focused on the active adoptions within cultural transfers and indicated China reached out to the Western countries between 1870 and 1910, in prior to identify concepts of law, statehood and "human rights" and modernised itself to a Europeanised global normative standard of successful structures of statehood. The chapter argued the diplomatic missions to the European courts and the international public and private law associations, then further discussed the exchange of ideas between scholars of public law and the influence on early humanitarianism from Europe to China a century ago to modernise the Chinese Empire at home. That highlighted on the foundations of statehood with which contemporary China operates to pursue an outward looking mission of foreign investment with the garments of humanitarian help which is obliging for the current and future BRI trade developments on legislations and international trade laws.

- Cities, branding and marketing are one of the core value to promote BRI further. In Chapter 11, Liu describes the development of cities and metropolitans, and how cities are branding themselves by all means in order to stand out for the benefits from socio-economic development. The study investigates the Southern City of Ningbo, being an important hub in the ancient Maritime Silk Road, and famous in historical heritage and modern intellectuals. During 2017, the municipal government in Ningbo decided to brand the city on three themes: (1) The city of Intellectuals, (2) The city of Music, (3) The city of Films. This study by using in-depth semi-structured interviews with stakeholders and discussed with their own stories concerning whether the intellectuals fits in with the city branding. The chapter ended and concluded with providing recommendation to policy-makers and stakeholders to develop more specific contents under the branding and more integration of higher educational institutions.

- Environmental impacts, especially Desertification is a crucial issue that most of BRI involved countries of the semi-arid and arid countries such as in the Mid-West and North West of China, Central Asia, Middle East and Eastern Europe. Li et al. in Chapter 12 look at the desertification circumstances in these BRI countries, in prior to provide solutions and recommendations to control and mitigate desertification in the context under BRI policy. The chapter has indicated the problems and issues at the countries that have been suffered along the BRI by using geographical features via a map that demonstrated the distribution of desertification areas that currently affected these countries, included the impacts on eco-environment and economic impacts, etc. The chapter further discussed the existing solutions and recent progresses on the desertification control and ended by providing recommendations from a perspective of balancing future developments sustainably in these BRI countries that are at risk of desertification.

Despite the broad coverage of these interdisciplinary chapters, which incorporate a wide variety of perspectives to understand BRI and the issues associated with it, each chapter contributes to the issues and debates significantly. BRI itself is very broad, and impossible to study from a narrow perspective. For example, the business section of this book reflects that a unified system (economics, financial markets, information systems, talent development and so on) is required to make BRI activities more standardised. Readers can also learn from the politics in different regions in view of the development of BRI across different locations. Looking at bilateral political issues is not sufficient from the wider BRI perspective. This also links to the long development of the traditional Silk Road and trading relationship between China and her partners, both historically and geographically.

By assembling these chapters in this volume, it is hoped that the BRI activities can be facilitated and implemented smoothly, and that this volume serves as an important reference book in the field for researchers and practitioners. The organisation of this volume will follow the structure of this chapter. The last chapter will conclude the implications from these studies.

References

Chan, H. K., Dai, J., Wang, X., & Lacka, E. (2019). Logistics and supply chain innovation in the context of the Belt and Road Initiative (BRI). *Transportation Research Part E: Logistics and Transportation Review, 132,* 51–56.

Chen, Y. W., & Günther, O. (2019, in press). Back to normalization or conflict with China in Greater Central Asia? Evidence from local students' perceptions. *Problems of Post-Communism.* https://doi.org/10.1080/10758216.2018.1474716.

Chen, Y. W., & Jiménez-Tovar, S. (2017). China in Central Asia: Local perceptions from future Elites. *China Quarterly of International Strategic Studies, 3*(3), 429–455.

Fishwick, O. (2017, December). China in the fast lane on digital Silk Road. *China Daily.*

Fung, K. C., Aminian, N., Fu, X., & Tung, C. Y. (2018). Digital Silk Road, silicon valley and connectivity. *Journal of Chinese Economic and Business Studies, 16*(3), 313–336.

Guo, H., Liu, J., Qiu, Y., Menenti, M., Chen, F., Uhlir, P. F., et al. (2018). The digital belt and road program in support of regional sustainability. *International Journal of Digital Earth, 11*(7), 657–669.

Huang, Y. (2016). Understanding China's Belt & Road Initiative: Motivation, framework and assessment. *China Economic Review, 40*, 314–321.

Insch, A., & Bowden, B. (2016). Possibilities and limits of brand repositioning for a second-ranked city: The case of Brisbane, Australia's "New World City", 1979–2013. *Cities, 56*, 47–54.

Jia, L., & Shuang, G. (2015, July). China, EU to promote digital Silk Road. *China Daily.*

Kozłowski, K. (2018, in press). BRI and its digital dimension: Twists and turns. *Journal of Science and Technology Policy Management.* https://doi.org/10.1108/JSTPM-06-2018-0062.

Kuzmicz, K. A., & Pesch, E. (2019). Approaches to empty container repositioning problems in the context of Eurasian intermodal transportation. *Omega, 85*, 194–213.

Lattimore, O. (1950). *Pivot of Asia: Sinkiang and the inner Asian frontiers of China and Russia.* Boston: Little Brown.

Lechner, A. M., Chan, F. K. S., & Campos-Arceiz, A. (2018). Biodiversity conservation should be a core value of China's Belt and Road Initiative. *Nature Ecology and Evolution, 2*, 408–409. https://doi.org/10.1038/s41559-017-0452-8.

Li, J., Liu, B., & Qian, G. (2019). The Belt and Road Initiative, cultural friction and ethnicity: Their effects on the export performance of SMEs in China. *Journal of World Business, 54*(4), 350–359.

Li, Z., Wang, J., Zhao, Z., Dong, S., Li, Y., Zhu, Y., et al. (2014). Eco-environment patterns and ecological civilization modes in the Sile Road Economic Zone. *Resouce Science, 36*(12), 2476–2482 (in Chinese with English abstract).

Liu, Z., & Xin, L. (2019). Has China's Belt and Road Initiative promoted its green total factor productivity? Evidence from primary provinces along the route. *Energy Policy, 129,* 360–369.

Rolland, N. (2017). China's "Belt and Road Initiative": Underwhelming or game-changer? *The Washington Quarterly,* 40(1), 127-142.

Seele, P., Jia, C. D., & Helbing, D. (2019). The new Silk Road and its potential for sustainable development: How open digital participation could make BRI a role model for sustainable businesses and markets. *Asian Journal of Sustainability and Social Responsibility,* 4(1), 1.

Shaikh, F., Ji, Q., & Fan, Y. (2016). Prospects of Pakistan-China energy and economic corridor. *Renewable and Sustainable Energy Reviews, 59,* 253–263.

Shao, Z. Z., Ma, Z. J., Sheu, J. B., & Gao, H. O. (2018). Evaluation of large-scale transnational high-speed railway construction priority in the belt and road region. *Transportation Research Part E: Logistics and Transportation Review, 117,* 40–57.

Shen, H. (2018). Building a digital Silk Road? Situating the Internet in China's Belt and Road Initiative. *International Journal of Communication, 12,* 2683–2701.

Sheu, J. B., & Kundu, T. (2018). Forecasting time-varying logistics distribution flows in the One Belt-One Road strategic context. *Transportation Research Part E: Logistics and Transportation Review, 117,* 5–22.

Solmecke, U. (2017). Multinational enterprises and the 'One Belt, One road' initiative: Sustainable development and innovation in a post-crisis global environment. *The Copenhagen Journal of Asian Studies,* 34(2), 9–27.

Thürer, M., Tomašević, I., Stevenson, M., Blome, C., Melnyk, S., Chan, H. K., & Huang, G. Q. (2019, in press). A systematic review of China's Belt and Road Initiative: Implications for global supply chain management. *International Journal of Production Research.* https://doi.org/10.1080/00207543. 2019.1605225.

Vakulchuk, R., & Overland, I. (2019). China's Belt and Road Initiative through the lens of Central Asia. In F. M. Cheung & Y. Y. Hong (Eds.), *Regional connection under the Belt and Road Initiative: The prospects for economic and financial cooperation* (pp. 115–133). London: Routledge.

Zhai, F. (2018). China's Belt and Road Initiative: A preliminary quantitative assessment. *Journal of Asian Economics, 55,* 84–92.

Zhao, S. (2015). Rethinking the Chinese world order: The imperial cycle and the rise of China. *Journal of Contemporary China,* 24(2015), 961–982.

PART I

Business

CHAPTER 2

The Economics of the Belt and Road Initiative

Saileshsingh Gunessee and Jianmin Liu

2.1 Introduction

China's recent economic rise in the global economy has been through many phases. It started with the 'Open Door Policy' of the late 1980s that ushered in the first wave of 'opening up' in modern times. The key goals during this first phase of opening up were to absorb technology and skills from abroad through foreign direct investment (FDI) and encourage export-led industrialisation. This dual strategy of attracting FDI and promoting exports fuelled economic growth; hence, shaping initial Chinese economic development (Bramall 2009, pp. 360–361; Lin 2012, pp. 3–4).

Fuelled by the 'Going Global Policy' of the early 2000s, the second phase of China's economic rise was grounded in an outward-oriented strategy, pushing Chinese firms to invest abroad. Simultaneously, the overall engagement with global markets was propelled further through China's World Trade Organization (WTO) accession in 2001. It is argued that the principal aims of the second phase of opening up was to meet the

S. Gunessee (✉) · J. Liu
Nottingham University Business School China,
University of Nottingham Ningbo China, Ningbo, China
e-mail: saileshsingh.gunessee@nottingham.edu.cn

© The Author(s) 2020
H. K. Chan et al. (eds.), *International Flows in the Belt and Road Initiative Context*, Palgrave Series in Asia and Pacific Studies,
https://doi.org/10.1007/978-981-15-3133-0_2

19

resource needs at home and access foreign technology through acquisitions. This was a shift from China being an attractor of FDI to a source of FDI to the world; where in recent years, Chinese outward FDI has caught up and even outweighed inward FDI into China (China Policy 2017; Naughton 2018, pp. 439–440).

The third phase of China's economic rise has taken a new guise: the 'Belt and Road Initiative', which was proposed in 2013. It has been dubbed as one of the largest supranational initiatives in recent decades and likened to the 'Marshall Plan', both in terms of its reach and ambition (Chaisse and Matsushita 2017). Seen as a huge infrastructure and cooperation project with 'geopolitical' and 'geo-economic' ramifications, it has generated a new phase of internationalisation and has been labelled as 'Going Global 2.0' (China Policy 2017).

Yet, the Belt and Road Initiative (BRI hereafter) is more than an infrastructure project. While infrastructure has played, and is playing, a fundamental role in the initial stage, BRI is much more than that. It has been depicted to have five main goals: development strategies and policies coordination, infrastructure and facilities connectivity, 'unimpeded' trade that enables trade facilitation, financial integration, and people-to-people bonding and exchange (Baker Mackenzie 2017; Bastos 2018; Huang 2016). It is portrayed as motivated by several factors that include furthering global and regional cooperation (China Policy 2017; Gao 2018); while from a Chinese viewpoint, the 'deeper' motivations include sustaining economic growth and asserting greater presence in the international economic architecture (Huang 2016).

Not surprisingly as an on-going initiative, BRI has attracted widespread attention since it was proposed in 2013. Whether it is through popular press, reports, or scholarly articles, a lot have been written on BRI (Anwar 2018; Baker Mackenzie 2017; Hillman 2018; Kuo and Kommenda 2018; Lu et al. 2018; Zhang et al. 2018; Zheng 2017).

This chapter adds to this burgeoning literature in a distinct way. It provides an 'economic' perspective on the BRI. Though we do not completely eschew the 'political' stance in our discussion, our focus is predominantly on the 'economics of BRI'. Thus, we look at its relevance, drivers, impact, and challenges more specifically from an economic perspective. In this chapter, we accomplish this in two ways. First, we provide a descriptive analysis and statistical overview to document stylised economic facts about BRI (mostly for the 'economic overview' part); second, we adopt a narrative approach that draws from the extant literature, synthesise, and add to it (for the remaining parts).

There are two merits of taking an 'economic' lens. First, the existing literature is somewhat vast (see Anwar 2018); this implies that what we want to achieve—literature narrative and synthesising—has to be constrained. Second, an economic viewpoint, given its 'positivist domain', allows us to narrow in on 'facts and evidence', instead of the 'rhetoric' that has come to define some of the literature on BRI.

This chapter is organised as follows. The next section provides facts on BRI through a statistical overview of foreign economic cooperation in BRI economies. In particular, it draws out some key economic facts and shows the economic relevance of BRI. Then Sect. 2.3 offers a summative review of the economic drivers behind BRI, followed by the economic impact in Sect. 2.4, and politico-economic challenges surrounding BRI in Sect. 2.5. A final section then outlines some implications through a synthesised overview of these three facets of BRI.

2.2   ECONOMIC OVERVIEW

This section provides a statistical overview on BRI and documents key facts therefrom. To start with, Appendix Table 2.7 shows the geographical distribution of the participating countries in BRI. It is clear that most of these countries are from Asia and Europe. In fact, of the 71 BRI economies to date, 64 countries that joined before 2015 were mostly Eurasian. The seven countries that joined from 2015 are South Korea, New Zealand, Panama, South Africa, Morocco, Ethiopia, and Madagascar, predominantly African countries.

Table 2.8 classifies these economies in terms of their income (see Appendix). It shows that there are roughly similar numbers of countries in the first three income categories. A key feature of this grouping is the overall heterogeneity across BRI economies. In an empirical study by Hu et al. (2018), where they measure and assess the 'overall development' level of BRI countries, they find that of the 18 high-income economies in their sample, 12 ranks among the top 16 in their overall comprehensive development assessment. According to them, 'good economic development contributes directly to developments in other aspects' (p. 219).

Table 2.1 Comparison of BRI to the world and OECD countries (average value) 2013, 2015, and 2017

	2013			2015			2017		
	World	*OECD*	*BRI*	*World*	*OECD*	*BRI*	*World*	*OECD*	*BRI*
Global Competitiveness Index (GCI)									
Institutions	4.044	4.795	3.918	3.979	4.742	3.878	4.095	4.836	4.017
Public institutions	3.967	4.73	3.855	3.878	4.669	3.774	4.031	4.794	3.95
Private institutions	4.274	4.989	4.107	4.282	4.963	4.188	4.289	4.96	4.219
Infrastructure	3.959	5.363	3.866	4.004	5.369	3.983	4.056	5.333	4.034
Transport infrastructure	3.797	4.959	3.612	3.773	4.926	3.674	3.772	4.857	3.701
Electricity and telephony infrastructure	4.12	5.767	4.119	4.234	5.813	4.293	4.339	5.81	4.366
Macroeconomic environment	4.689	4.953	4.822	4.757	5.049	4.873	4.684	5.276	4.776
Health and primary education	5.424	6.268	5.636	5.476	6.319	5.685	5.554	6.337	5.719
Health	6.023	6.843	6.351	6.1	6.86	6.343	6.112	6.856	6.354
Primary education	4.825	5.692	4.92	4.852	5.779	5.027	4.996	5.818	5.083
Higher education and training	4.146	5.25	4.184	4.203	5.346	4.239	4.314	5.398	4.382
Quantity of education	4.395	6.103	4.682	4.469	6.327	4.716	4.589	6.37	4.936
Quality of education	3.997	4.821	4.005	4.056	4.906	4.058	4.123	4.88	4.12
On-the-job training	4.046	4.827	3.866	4.085	4.805	3.943	4.229	4.945	4.09
Goods market efficiency	4.278	4.755	4.27	4.345	4.8	4.379	4.377	4.879	4.406
Foreign competition	4.66	5.165	4.611	4.495	5.02	4.492	4.524	5.162	4.511
Prevalence of trade barriers	4.337	4.877	4.303	4.338	4.552	4.365	4.334	4.722	4.371
Burden of customs procedures	4.088	4.835	3.955	4.063	4.939	4.054	4.14	4.97	4.129
Labour market efficiency	4.33	4.64	4.303	4.191	4.486	4.164	4.248	4.651	4.18
Flexibility	4.489	4.557	4.582	4.45	4.503	4.507	4.508	4.638	4.559
Efficient use of talent	4.171	4.722	4.024	3.931	4.468	3.82	3.989	4.663	3.801
Financial market development	4.087	4.567	4.019	4.019	4.56	4.019	4.001	4.532	3.962
Efficiency	3.552	4.033	3.498	3.546	4.065	3.558	3.725	4.294	3.749

	2013			2015			2017		
	World	*OECD*	*BRI*	*World*	*OECD*	*BRI*	*World*	*OECD*	*BRI*
Trustworthiness and confidence	4.621	5.102	4.541	4.491	5.055	4.481	4.278	4.771	4.175
Technological readiness	4.000	5.389	3.896	3.961	5.434	3.9	4.178	5.607	4.141
Technological adoption	4.79	5.49	4.672	4.665	5.39	4.613	4.578	5.361	4.534
ICT use	3.21	5.288	3.121	3.257	5.477	3.187	3.777	5.852	3.748
Market size	3.677	4.714	3.824	3.785	4.727	3.894	3.857	4.652	3.943
GDP (USD billion)[a]	2409	1371	194	2579	1433	218	2850	1451	239
GDP per capita (USD)[a]	13,617	38,978	10,624	13,659	40,557	10,987	13,489	41,172	11,498
Business sophistication	4.021	4.846	3.902	4.06	4.833	3.958	4.061	4.849	3.959
R&D innovation	3.401	4.51	3.207	3.449	4.457	3.317	3.566	4.514	3.454
Average overall pillars of GCI	4.171	5.004	4.171	4.186	5.01	4.191	4.249	5.072	4.248
Worldwide Governance Indicators (WGI)	0.000	1.179	−0.243	0.000	1.159	−0.178	0.000	1.119	−0.175
Voice and accountability	0.000	1.162	−0.445	0.000	1.132	−0.382	0.000	1.098	−0.393
Political stability	0.000	0.722	−0.332	0.000	0.648	−0.304	0.000	0.614	−0.282
Government effectiveness	0.000	1.322	−0.095	0.000	1.308	0.005	0.000	1.259	0.000
Regulatory quality	0.000	1.291	−0.075	0.000	1.288	−0.019	0.000	1.304	−0.002
Rule of law	0.000	1.295	−0.223	0.000	1.327	−0.143	0.000	1.249	−0.14
Control of corruption	0.000	1.284	−0.286	0.000	1.248	−0.224	0.000	1.191	−0.231

[a] *Notes* (1) GDP and GDP per capita use data from the World Development Indicators; (2) the Average Overall Pillars of GCI, uses the 12 original pillars of the Global Competitiveness Index, and the value ranging from 1 to 7 to denote worst to best; (3) The individual WGI lie between −2.5 and +2.5, denoting weak to strong governance

Data Sources World Economic Forum, The World Bank

Table 2.1 offers a comparison of BRI economies to countries world-wide and OECD (Organisation for Economic and Co-operation and Development) member nations on the basis of average value of several indicators over three years, drawn from the World Economic Forum's *Global Competitiveness Index (GCI)*, the World Bank's *World Development Indicators (WDI)*, and *World Governance Indicators (WGI)*. For example, it displays the various components or pillars that make up the GCI or competitiveness of countries. Although, as expected, the BRI countries' 'average overall GCI' is well below the OECD average (as with most indicators and pillars), Table 2.2 shows six countries among the top 10 BRI economies that have an overall GCI average higher than the OECD average in 2017. Not surprisingly, these six countries include five high-income economies (Singapore, New Zealand, Qatar, Israel, and South Korea).

The 'average overall GCI' in Table 2.1 shows that the BRI average is close to the world average over the three reported years (2013, 2015, and 2017). This is intriguing as BRI economies consist of only a few low-income economies. Of the components that can account for this fact are institutions, infrastructure, labour market efficiency, financial market

Table 2.2 Top 10 BRI countries' Global Competitiveness Index (average value), 2017

Rank	Country name	Global Competitiveness Index
1	Singapore	5.8664
2	New Zealand	5.4743
3	Qatar	5.3711
4	Israel	5.1691
5	South Korea	5.1466
6	Malaysia	5.1357
7	Estonia	4.9879
8	Czech Republic	4.8694
9	Saudi Arabia	4.7903
10	Lithuania	4.6736

Data Source World Economic Forum

development, technological readiness, business sophistication, and R&D innovation.[1]

The fact that the institutional pillar is lower than the world average, including the sub-components of public and private institutions, poses a challenge for the development of BRI countries and perhaps future development of the BRI. Lin (2012) identifies institutions as a key ingredient for economic growth (p. 10). Hu et al. (2018) also highlight political stability and good governance as a premise for development and thus, emphasise its importance in the success of the BRI. This is discussed in greater detail in Sect. 2.5 as a politico-economic challenge to BRI (along with giving more meaning to the *WGI*).

Next, the 'market size' component is shown to be higher than the global average among the BRI economies, though *GDP (gross domestic product) per capita* is interestingly lower. One explanation for this is the notion that the GCI captures market size as both a domestic and export market of a specific economy. This means that market scope permeates beyond national boundaries and envisions how an economy is connected to the global market, where a large market—domestic and foreign—allows firms to exploit economies of scale (Schwab and Sala-i-Martín 2017, p. 36). In the optic of BRI, establishing a large regionally and globally connected market for member countries is a core goal; thus, this can be seen as promising (see Sect. 2.3 on large market opportunities as one of the key 'economic drivers' of BRI).

Table 2.1 is also revealing when we look at 'connectivity', especially given that two of BRI's strategic goals are to establish 'facilities connectivity' and 'unimpeded trade' (see Baker Mackenzie 2017, p. 2). The relevant components to consider are 'infrastructure' and its sub-components, and goods market efficiency's sub-components, 'prevalence of trade barriers' and 'burden of custom procedures'. In a globalised world where ICT and innovation play a key role (see Baldwin 2016, p. 1), the technology-related pillars, 'technological readiness', 'business sophistication', and 'R&D innovation' are salient for our purposes.

At the outset, it can be seen that BRI economies have a lower average in the technology and innovation domain, especially when it comes to

---

[1] Note that the GCI scale ranges from 1 to 7, with 1 being the absolute worst and 7, the absolute best. A higher value implies a high score in the said category and indicates its distance to the best. Any comparison would provide a 'relative' sense of how well a country or group of countries are doing.

'ICT use' and 'technological adoption'. Furthermore, the administrative burden at customs and the prevalence of trade barriers are relatively low, though improving relative to the world average (see Table 2.1). When it comes to infrastructure, it is lower than the global average, mainly due to transportation infrastructure being poor from a comparative lens. This suggests that BRI as a means to foster cooperation and connectivity is saddled with subpar infrastructure, administrative trade burden, and lack of innovativeness. We see this as a challenge to be discussed later in Sect. 2.5.

The next set of statistical overview depicts China's foreign economic cooperation with other BRI economies. Tables 2.3 and 2.9 highlight the various forms that these foreign economic engagements take: trade, outward FDI, engineering/contracting projects, and labour services (see Appendix for Table 2.9). This can be further decomposed as shown in both tables.

As such, the economics of BRI is multi-faceted as it fosters all these forms of economic cooperation; this highlights the importance of seeing BRI beyond one dimension. In turn, this can be linked with Lin and Wang's (2017) suggestion of going beyond economic assistance (aid) as economic cooperation. Such economic cooperation would also include trade, equity investment, and non-equity infrastructure investment. They also argue that economic development leading to structural transformation must encompass these elements. BRI, being a multi-faceted cooperative initiative comprising of these elements, goes beyond economic assistance, in spite of the role played by the Asian Infrastructure Investment Bank (AIIB). Consequently, BRI goes beyond the notion of the 'Marshall Plan', as dubbed by some analysts and scholars (Yu 2017).[2]

Table 2.3 reveals that only two forms of foreign economic cooperation with BRI economies have risen consistently post-2013: 'FDI stocks' and 'turnover of engineering projects'. While Chinese FDI outflows to BRI economies fell in 2016, it bounced back in 2017. However, this mirrors the fact that worldwide Chinese OFDI (outward FDI) flows rose in 2016 but contracted in 2017.[3] Table 2.9 discloses the top-ten-ranked BRI countries in terms of Chinese foreign economic cooperation. Singapore, Malaysia, Vietnam, and Indonesia are the 'most' engaged, at least

---

[2] The Marshall Plan was a US initiative of 'economic assistance' to Western European economies to rebuild post-World War II.

[3] FDI flows contracting in 2016 and 2017 is the result of the tightening of regulation surrounding capital outflows, somewhat affecting labour flows as well in 2016.

Table 2.3 China's foreign economic cooperation post-2013

	2014		2015		2016		2017	
	All	*BRI*	*All*	*BRI*	*All*	*BRI*	*All*	*BRI*
Trade (USD billion)								
Exports	2342.293	773.718	2273.468	752.062	2097.631	706.977	2263.371	771.770
Imports	1959.235	729.878	1679.565	600.719	1587.926	556.035	1843.793	666.994
Outward FDI (USD billion)								
Flows	123.120	14.670	145.667	21.094	196.149	18.560	158.288	22.103
Stocks	882.642	103.735	1097.865	127.171	1357.390	144.984	1809.037	173.764
Engineering projects (USD billion)								
Turnover	142.411	72.835	154.074	77.319	156.417	81.867	168.587	92.958
Labour services (person)								
Personnel abroad for engineering projects	408,851	189,965	408,565	190,247	372,880	189,262	376,827	212,032
Personnel abroad for labour services	596,881	178,324	618,295	189,284	595,976	181,908	602,342	180,697

Data Source China Trade and External Economic Statistical Yearbook

across these economic dimensions and in terms of ranking; while of the 71 BRI economies, only 21 appear in the top ten. The latter fact shows a concentrated and less diversified Chinese foreign economic engagement, which lends support to the argument of the 'need' for the BRI as a coordination mechanism to broaden economic cooperation.

Considering Table 2.3 with Figs. 2.1 and 2.2 are revelatory about trade. Although Chinese trade, with all its trading partners and BRI partners, contracted in 2016, it recovered in 2017. While post-2013, when BRI came into effect, exports seemed to have been channelled

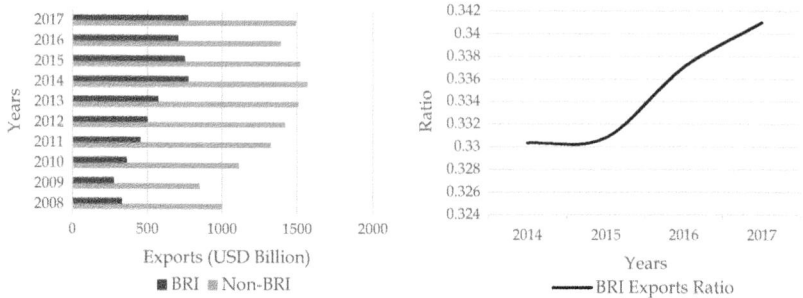

Fig. 2.1 Comparison of BRI and non-BRI countries' exports (*Data Source* China Trade and External Economic Statistical Yearbook & China Statistical Yearbook)

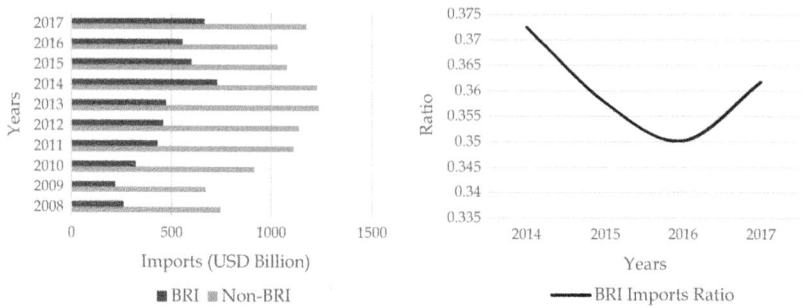

Fig. 2.2 Comparison of BRI and non-BRI countries' imports (*Data Source* China Trade and External Economic Statistical Yearbook & China Statistical Yearbook)

Table 2.4 Top 20 countries of China's outward FDI, 2017 (USD billion)

Rank	Country name	OFDI flows	OECD/BRI
1	Hong Kong China	91.15	–
2	The British Virgin Islands	19.30	–
3	Switzerland	7.51	OECD
4	United States	6.42	OECD
5	Singapore	6.31	BRI
6	Australia	4.24	OECD
7	Germany	2.72	OECD
8	Kazakhstan	2.07	BRI
9	United Kingdom	2.07	OECD
10	Malaysia	1.72	BRI
11	Indonesia	1.68	BRI
12	The Russian Federation	1.55	BRI
13	Luxembourg	1.35	OECD
14	Sweden	1.29	OECD
15	Laos	1.22	BRI
16	Thailand	1.06	BRI
17	France	0.95	OECD
18	Vietnam	0.76	BRI
19	Cambodia	0.74	BRI
20	Pakistan	0.68	BRI

Data Source China Trade and External Economic Statistical Yearbook

more towards BRI economies, as shown by the second panel of Fig. 2.1, imports only saw such trend after the 2016 trade contraction (see Fig. 2.2). Table 2.9 reports Korea, Malaysia, Thailand, Vietnam, and Indonesia as China's major trading partners.

With regard to Chinese OFDI, Tables 2.4 and 2.5 and Figs. 2.3–2.7 provide more information. Table 2.4 reports the top 20 economies receiving Chinese OFDI in 2017, where we can see a balance between developed economies and Asian BRI economies.[4] While investments to the developed world can be explained by the 'strategic asset-seeking motive',

[4] The investments channelled via British Virgin Islands and Hong Kong (China) normally have ultimate destination in Asia, Europe, or the United States. These have been termed as 'pass-through locales' or 'conduit jurisdictions' (Shambaugh 2013, p. 180).

Table 2.5 Sectoral distribution of China's outward FDI stocks, 2005–2017 (USD billion)

Sectors	BRI OFDI stocks	Worldwide OFDI stocks	Ratio (%)
Energy	129.42	354.77	36.48
Metals	22.52	123.9	18.18
Transportation	20.61	95.05	21.68
Real Estate	18.4	86.21	21.34
Logistics	12.69	32.98	38.48
Technology	8.81	50.91	17.31
Agriculture	8.69	79.48	10.93
Finance	7.66	75.2	10.19
Entertainment	6.95	38.81	17.91
Consumer	4.64	14.75	31.46
Construction	4.42	12.12	36.47
Others	3.75	17.1	21.93
Chemicals	2.22	11.73	18.93
Tourism	1.73	36.29	4.77
Public services	1.67	4.83	34.58
Medical	1.32	9.67	13.65
Education	0.19	0.31	61.29

Data Source The China Global Investment Tracker

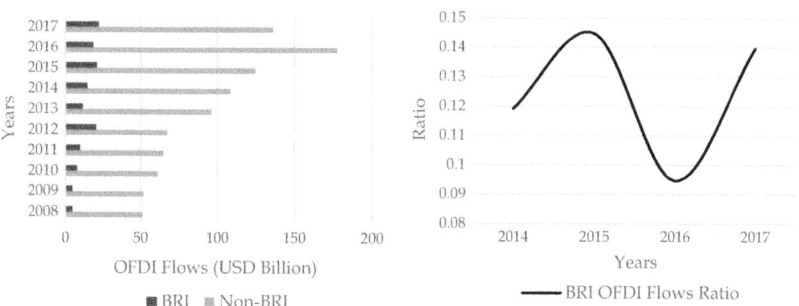

Fig. 2.3 Comparison of BRI and non-BRI countries' OFDI flows (*Data Source* Statistical Bulletin of China's Outward Foreign Direct Investment)

investments in Asia can be explained by geographical and cultural proximity (Buckley et al. 2018).

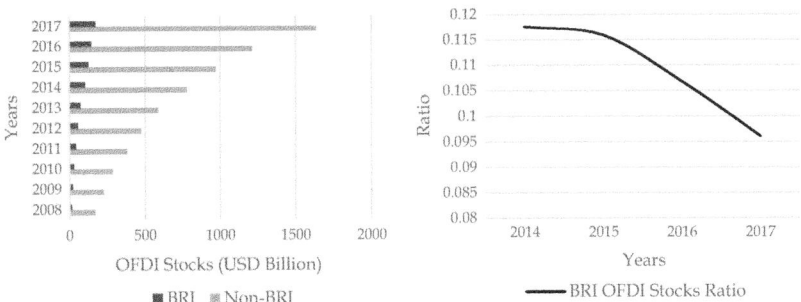

Fig. 2.4 Comparison of BRI and non-BRI countries' OFDI stocks (*Data Source* Statistical Bulletin of China's Outward Foreign Direct Investment)

The sectoral composition of Chinese OFDI stocks is documented in Table 2.5. This uses the sectoral categorisation of the *China Global Investment Tracker* by the American Enterprise Institute, which should be interpreted with care as it only monitors investments of $100 million and above.[5] With this statistical caveat in mind, we can infer that BRI economies are recipients of 'large' investments in the logistics, energy, and construction industries.

Figures 2.3 and 2.4 respectively show the flows and stocks of FDI from China to BRI and non-BRI economies, with the second panel of each figure depicting the post-BRI period. While OFDI flows do not reveal any post-2013 redirection of equity investments, OFDI stocks' graphs show a falling trend of BRI OFDI stocks relative to non-BRI OFDI stocks, despite the fact that OFDI stocks in BRI economies have increased in absolute terms over time, as shown in Table 2.3 and the first panel of Fig. 2.4. When considering the 'largest' investments as sourced from the *China Global Investment Tracker*, shown in Figs. 2.5–2.7, we see a similar pattern to the broader-sourced and documented Chinese OFDI flows (see Fig. 2.3). A split of FDI into mergers and acquisitions (M&As) and

---

[5] The implication is that the database focuses on 'large' investments and eschews smaller investments that can be numerous. As such, there may be a bias towards sectors where investments are few in numbers but large in value. Unfortunately, the China Trade and External Economic Statistical Yearbook and the Statistical Bulletin of China's Outward Foreign Direct Investment, which are our preferred sources for the statistical overview, do not have a sectoral decomposition by country.

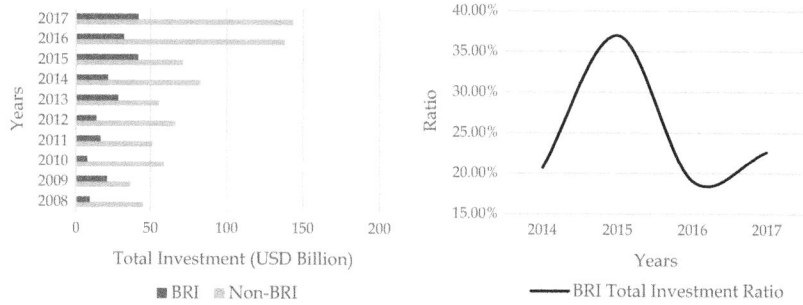

Fig. 2.5 Comparison of BRI and non-BRI countries' total investments (*Data Source* The China Global Investment Tracker)

greenfield investments, as shown in Figs. 2.6 and 2.7 respectively, also tell the same story.

It is worth noting that *Going Global 1.0* is often associated with *Chinese Companies Going Global* (Bellabona and Spiragelli 2007). Yet, when it comes to *Going Global 2.0* as BRI is depicted (China Policy 2017), it appears there is no relative predilection among Chinese companies' decision to invest in BRI economies.

Shifting our attention towards construction and engineering projects, we noted the increase in turnover in Table 2.3. As BRI aims to enhance interconnectivity and promote trade, the number of contracted infrastructure projects to be delivered under the aegis of BRI by 2017 is reported

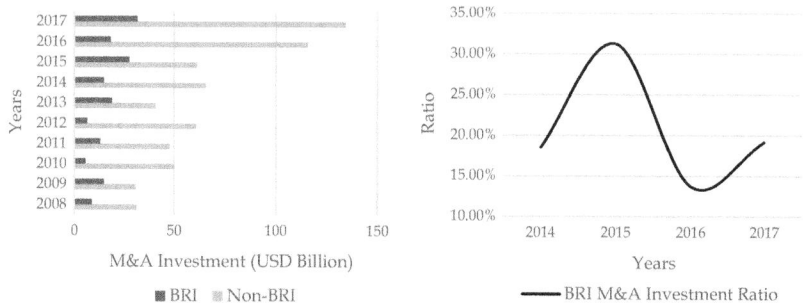

Fig. 2.6 Comparison of BRI and non-BRI countries' M&A investments (*Data Source* The China Global Investment Tracker)

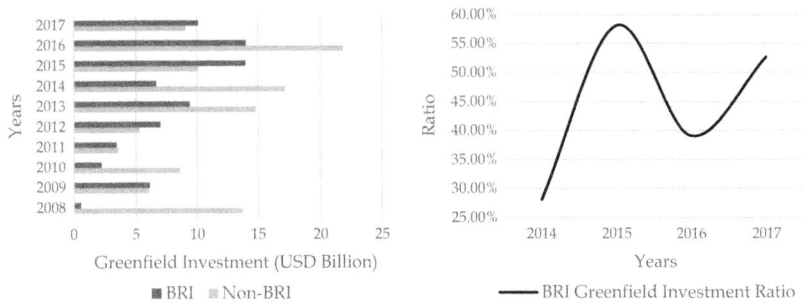

Fig. 2.7 Comparison of BRI and non-BRI countries' greenfield investments (*Data Source* The China Global Investment Tracker)

to be close to 1700 (Zhou and Esteban 2018). The 'largest' contracted construction investments by Chinese contractors are revealed to be in chemicals, metals, education, and energy in BRI economies relative to all economies (see Table 2.6).

Table 2.6 Sectoral distribution of China's construction contracts 2005–2017 (USD billion)

Sectors	BRI construction contracts	Worldwide construction contracts	Ratio (%)
Energy	205.01	308.39	66.48
Transportation	101.83	230.06	44.26
Construction	39.81	70.04	56.84
Metals	24.39	32.35	75.39
Chemicals	13.04	14.31	91.13
Agriculture	10.51	16.7	62.93
Public services	10.13	18.73	54.08
Technology	7.82	15.63	50.03
Others	4.98	6.92	71.97
Tourism	3.73	6.6	56.52
Education	3.12	4.44	70.27
Logistics	1.18	4.53	26.05
Medical	1.08	3.08	35.06
Entertainment	0.79	2.01	39.30

Data Source The China Global Investment Tracker

Figure 2.8 shows a comparison between BRI and non-BRI countries for engineering projects by turnover. It divulges a pattern of increased reallocation towards BRI economies post-2014. 'Personnel' supporting these contracting/engineering projects also seem to have increased during this period (see Fig. 2.9), unlike the general use of personnel (see Fig. 2.10). Yet, the 'largest' non-equity construction contracts do not seem to mirror contracted engineering projects (see Figs. 2.11 vs. 2.8).

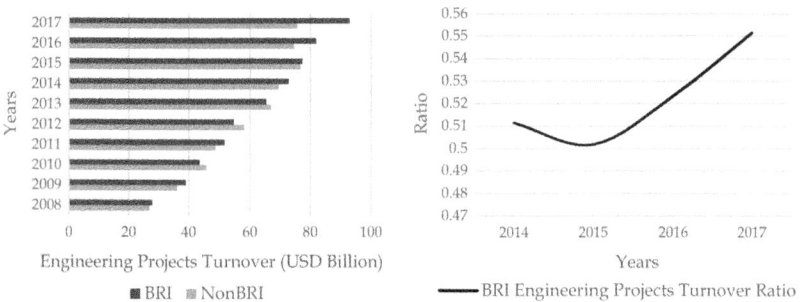

Fig. 2.8 Comparison of BRI and non-BRI countries' engineering projects turnover (*Data Source* China Trade and External Economic Statistical Yearbook & China Statistical Yearbook)

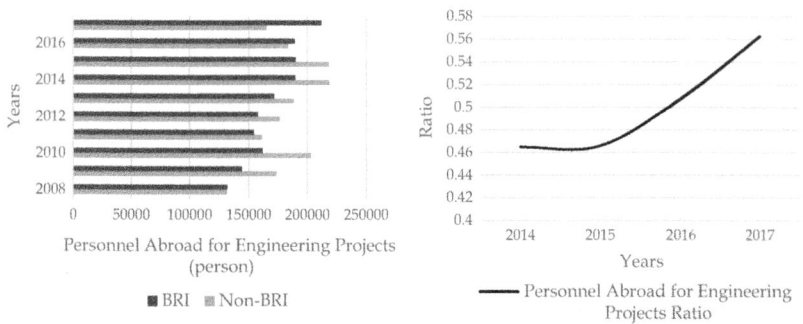

Fig. 2.9 Comparison of BRI and non-BRI countries' personnel abroad for engineering projects (*Data Source* China Trade and External Economic Statistical Yearbook & China Statistical Yearbook)

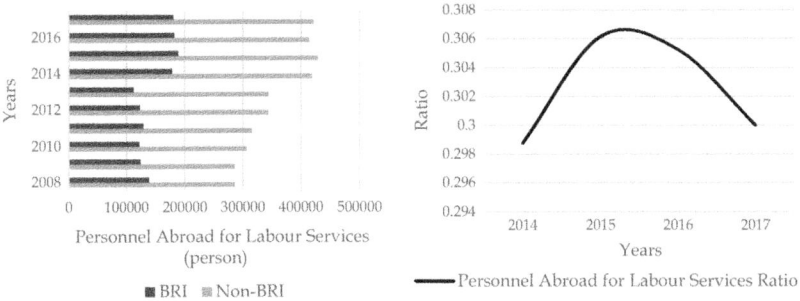

Fig. 2.10 Comparison of BRI and non-BRI countries' personnel abroad for labour services (*Data source* China Trade and External Economic Statistical Yearbook & China Statistical Yearbook)

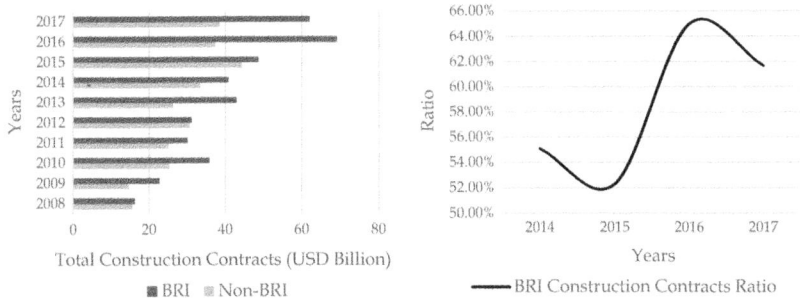

Fig. 2.11 Comparison of BRI and non-BRI countries' total construction contracts (*Data Source* The China Global Investment Tracker)

Table 2.9 shows Malaysia, Pakistan, and Saudi Arabia as the biggest beneficiaries for engineering projects. Pakistan ranking first in such non-equity investment is not surprising given that the 'China-Pakistan Economic Corridor' is part and parcel of BRI's six 'economic corridors' and is one of two that is very active. Thus, it has seen substantial infrastructure investment, particularly through the Gwadar Port (Baker Mackenzie 2017).

In summary, this section reveals some interesting facts about the BRI as related to the BRI economies and China's cooperation with these foreign economies. Two main economic facts are:

1. BRI economies represent a large market with opportunities and potential but with significant governance risks, administrative burden to trade, and technological impediment to connectivity;
2. China's post-BRI foreign economic cooperation with BRI countries has increased but without a systematic capital reallocation towards BRI economies, except for exports and contracted engineering projects (e.g. infrastructure investments).

2.3   Economic Drivers

We have highlighted some broad goals of *Going Global 2.0* via BRI. Still, there are several factors that have shaped and are motivating this on-going initiative. We outline a few key ones as follows.

Need for 'Going Global'. China has gone through various phases of 'outward orientation' of its economy, from the 'open door policy' to the 'going global policy' (Bellabona and Spiragelli 2007). The Going Global 1.0 started gaining momentum in the late 1990s before being officially announced in 1999 and the early 2000s; it ushered in a new wave of opening up for the Chinese economy (Shambaugh 2013). Its goal was to promote the internationalisation of Chinese companies (Bellabona and Spiragelli 2007; China Policy 2017).

Instead, the latest phase of 'going out', the so-called Going Global 2.0, has taken the shape of the BRI. It is noted that among its broad strategic goals, there is the goal to 'accelerate the internationalisation of Chinese firms and create world-class multinationals and supply chains' (Baker Mackenzie 2017, p. 6). In short, it is an extension of the original 'Go Global' policy, but reoriented and targeted.

Therefore, with continued 'internationalisation' being a broad goal, the internationalisation of Chinese companies and contractors and that of the Chinese currency are likely to be prioritised. Unlike Going Global 1.0, which was mostly motivated by the acquisition of resources and strategic assets, Going Global 2.0 is seen to be driven by the need to safeguard a return on investment, enhance world demand, and switch to portfolio investment (China Policy 2017). The rationale behind this shift is to address some of the shortcomings of the previous wave of going out, such as to 'ensure firms invested abroad more wisely, with greater concern for local sensibilities and China's image' (p. 4).

In a similar vein, there is a need to reinvigorate non-OECD economies' demand to allow Chinese companies to further internationalise. BRI offers them an opportunity to do so, which is somewhat linked with the aim to gain sustainable profits, as they expand global business operations. Infrastructure investment, particularly contracted engineering projects, tend to pave the way for Chinese multinationals' FDI (Yu 2017).

The internationalisation of the Chinese currency, the RMB, is one of China's strategic priorities (Baker Mackenzie 2017; Cheng 2016), while also being a natural outcome of the fact that China has become the world's largest trading nation (Kroeber 2016, p. 145).[6] Pre-BRI China has already gone through experimental efforts to achieve this (Aizenman 2015; Kroeber 2016, pp. 144–145). Thus, BRI's goal is to further strengthen the global role of the RMB, whereby it would be used in construction contracts or acquisitions. However, to date there is little evidence of transactions related to BRI being funded in RMB (Baker Mackenzie 2017). See Sect. 2.5 for more on this challenge.

Need for industrial restructuring. The industrial structure of an economy is a key determinant to economic growth (Lin 2012, p. 10). To sustain steady economic growth, Chinese industries need to reinvent themselves by upgrading and moving up the value chain, while having to deal with excess capacity. Undeniably, the economy is suffering from overcapacity or a supply glut across several industries (Chaisse and Matsushita 2017; Tekdal 2018). With domestic consumption insufficient to absorb such excess industrial capacity, exports have acted as a means to absorb this overcapacity in the past. However, with the contraction in world trade after the global financial crisis, the issue of oversupply came to the fore (Cai 2017; Wuttke 2017). Coupled with an ageing population and rising labour costs, this had the effect of dampening the profit margins of Chinese firms (China Policy 2017).

Solving the overcapacity problem is not just about increasing exports, which BRI facilitates, but also about shifting entire production operations abroad (Cai 2017; Wuttke 2017). Exporting to BRI economies can only partially absorb Chinese-manufactured products, such as aluminium, steel, cement, and flat-panel glass (Yu 2017). It is necessary for Chinese

---

[6]Though not always, it would seem logical for companies to be willing to conduct their trade in RMB, as they ship more and more goods to and from China (Kroeber, p. 145).

firms to move whole production facilities abroad to attain a comprehensive solution (Chaisse and Matsushita 2017; China Policy 2017). There are two added merits of moving production out of China and into neighbouring countries. First, it would deal with concerns on increasing labour costs; second, it would confront the current environmental pollution issue plaguing China, as it enables the offshore shifting of energy-intensive heavy industries (Tekdal 2018).

An added feature to industrial restructuring entails the need for industrial upgrading. While China has developed into the 'world factory', the erosion of competitiveness due to rising unit labour costs implies the need to move up the value chain or capture the higher end of the global value chain to stay competitive (Cai 2017). To achieve this, Chinese industries have to be upgraded. As such, the 'Made in China 2025' strategy, which is benchmarked on Germany's Industry 4.0 plan, was initiated to espouse an innovation-driven manufacturing sector (Wuttke 2017). The notion is that as Chinese firms venture abroad, they could be better prepared to lead the innovation charge globally, whereby Chinese standards are exported as well (China Policy 2017).

Indeed, BRI could be a first step to help promote this 'industrial upgrading' objective, as Chinese technological products and innovation make their way abroad (Baker Mackenzie 2017). Yet, the aim is not just to export high-end goods, but to promote the acceptance of Chinese standards and have a voice in setting global standards. Hence, BRI is used 'to promote [the] high-tech sector, as well as Chinese technical and engineering standards' (Cai 2017, p. 11). An example of Chinese standards making an impact within BRI economies is through the 'high-speed rail technology'. It is argued that upgrading and standards-setting go hand in hand, with the objective of delivering world-class multinationals (Cai 2017; China Policy 2017).

Sub-national inter-provincial development & cooperation with central control. China's economic growth has been greatly unbalanced, with growing regional economic disparities across its provinces and the 'Western Development Strategy' of the 2000s not delivering the anticipated effect (Chaisse and Matsushita 2017; Chan et al. 2008). Consequently, the central government has been looking at different alternatives to prop up the flagging inland provinces. In this optic, BRI is seen as an opportunity and solution towards sub-national development in China (Cai 2017; Tekdal 2018). Since the 'Belt' of the BRI cuts across vast parts of China's hinterland, the initiative is expected not only to foster cross-country connectivity, but also to facilitate the connectivity of inland provinces, such as Xinjiang and Yunnan, to the world (Yu 2017).

For instance, the China–Pakistan Economic Corridor—one of the flagship corridors under BRI—connects Kashgar in Xinjiang with the Gwadar Port (Cai 2017). Similarly, Yunnan borders Laos, Myanmar, and Vietnam (Association of Southeast Asian Nations (ASEAN) countries), while also being close to Bangladesh and India (South Asia), and Cambodia and Thailand (Southeast Asia). As such, Yunnan can become an important gateway to these economies from within China (Yu 2017). In short, BRI offers cross-border links and connectivity for these inland provinces with neighbouring countries and in turn, is likely to be a key ingredient in driving their transformation and development (Chaisse and Matsushita 2017; Tekdal 2018; Yu 2017).

A lesser-discussed, but related motivation of BRI, we argue, is that it can foster inter-provincial cooperation that had been undermined by fiscal competition and local protectionism, emanating from the fiscal reform of the 1990s. This reform led to fiscal decentralisation, leaving local cadres responsible for their own budgetary expenditure and having to generate revenue to fund it (Zhang 2012).

Critics argue that though the fiscal reform may have led to positive competitive pressures, it also led to regional protectionism and costly duplicative investments. This had the effect of restricting inter-provincial trade, which was not conducive to sub-national inter-provincial cooperation and growth (Chan et al. 2008). Henceforth, as a top-level administered initiative, BRI is geared to stimulate inter-provincial interactive cooperation and additionally, to re-focus economic power back to the centre (Chaisse and Matsushita 2017). That is, BRI has reinforced 'central control' because provincial-level projects that are part of the initiative have to be centrally approved and for which funding support is received (Yu 2018).

Need for economic cooperation. BRI can play a key role in developing regional economic integration and cooperation. Through its effort to facilitate infrastructure and facilities connectivity and development, BRI can circumvent costs of production associated with geographical conditions. Greater connectivity is expected to enhance bilateral trade and economic integration among BRI economies (Yu 2017). This inter-country

connectivity could be achieved through the seven economic corridors proposed under BRI (Zhou and Esteban 2018), which includes the New
Eurasian Land Bridge and the China-Pakistan Economic Corridor, as currently 'active' corridors (Baker Mackenzie 2017).

The BRI has given China the chance to consolidate various regional
cooperation agreements that it is part of and thus, further regional economic integration. These agreements include the ASEAN-China Free
Trade Area (ACFTA), the Asia-Pacific Economic Cooperation (APEC),
the Greater Mekong Sub-Region Economic Cooperation (GMS), and
the Shanghai Cooperation Organization (SCO). Given its links to these
agreements, China is actively trying to gain support from other member countries to participate in BRI, with the possible long-term aim of
integrating these numerous regional cooperation agreements (Yu 2017).
From the perspective of BRI economies, BRI as a 'regional integration'
initiative is also welcomed. For example, ASEAN countries have enormous infrastructure investment needs, especially to assuage the infrastructure divide between maritime ASEAN and mainland ASEAN (Jetin
2017).

It is noteworthy that from a Chinese stance, one 'deeper' motivation
for exploring this new international economic cooperation is to sustain
its economic growth, in that BRI is a blueprint to explore new economic
partnerships and new destinations for Chinese FDI and exports (Huang
2016). This is also echoed by Yu (2018), who argues that there is a
'supremacy of domestic interests' that dictates affairs in China, whether
it is about looking for a new engine of economic growth or resolving
China's excess production capacity.

Another way to think about the need for economic cooperation can
be seen through the politico-economic lens. Such lens portrays BRI as an
'Eastern model' of regional cooperation, as opposed to a Western model.
This emanates from developing nations' idea about having to tolerate an
inflexible Western model of international cooperation that places a 'constraining' emphasis on participation in the international economic order
conditional on institutional reform. Thus, opting into an Eastern model
of cooperation that is more flexible and less constraining is likely to be
embraced by BRI economies (see Shichor 2018).

In addition, the 'soft balancing' theory contends that a secondary
power would apply soft balancing to a hegemon by seeking to initiate
its own cooperative agreement, if it is left out of a cooperative agreement
(Zhou and Esteban 2018). The Trans-Pacific Partnership (TPP) was an

initiative led by the United States as a means to counterbalance China's geo-economic and geopolitical spheres of influence in the region, through its exclusion (Cheng 2016). Henceforth, BRI was considered as a balancing act to the United States' attempt of creating a regional trading bloc that excluded China (Cai 2017; Zhou and Esteban 2018).[7]

From both perspectives, it can be stipulated that China's economic rise and the manifestation of its rise through the BRI represent an alternative *strategic partner* to BRI economies. This can be further linked to the 'deeper' motivation for BRI, where 'China's intention is clear—to assert greater influence on international economic governance, starting from a specific regional trade and investment initiative' (Huang 2016, p. 318). Consistent with its desire to have a voice in setting global standards, China is seen as keen to have a say in the international economic architecture. This is best exemplified by the 'New Development Bank', the BRICS initiative that was established in 2014 as an alternative to the IMF and the World Bank (Tekdal 2018; Zhou and Esteban 2018).

Market opportunities. As argued above, the motivation behind attaining a large market is related to the need for Chinese firms to expand internationally, and the need for economic cooperation to establish a large market beyond national boundaries. With respect to the former, it is argued that Chinese companies are entering a new phase of their internationalisation process where they need to seek out new markets beyond their traditional markets in the developed world and thus, there is a need to explore demand for their products in non-OECD economies (China Policy 2017). It is natural then that this market expansion that stimulates demand would come from the region in the guise of economic cooperation, and BRI enables this through its strategic goal of facilitating connectivity across countries in the Eurasian region (Huang 2016).

However, this opportunity of a large market is not only for Chinese companies. BRI economies represent market opportunities to *all* BRI-resident companies given its 'tremendous size and scope' and 'large unexploited potential', where it is argued that BRI countries account for

---

[7] As a fascinating follow-up to this 'story' is how after the United States cancelled the TPP in 2017 it left a vacuum, which one could interpret as likely to further fuel the salience of BRI for the region; considering the retrenchment occurring through isolationist and protectionist positions and policies taken by the United States and the United Kingdom (Gao 2018).

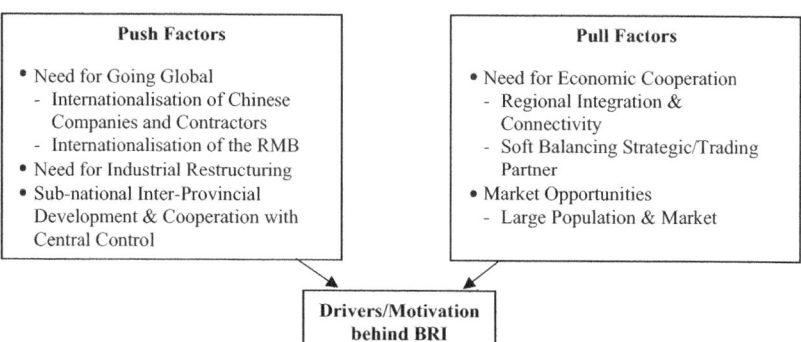

Fig. 2.12 Economic drivers of BRI

almost two-thirds of the world population (Ruta 2018). In Sect. 2.2, we highlight the fact that BRI economies possess 'market size' average higher than the world average, and a large domestic and export market should enable firms to exploit economies of scale. Yet, there is untapped potential due to subpar infrastructures and poor connectivity. BRI can help unlock this potential and help indigenous or international BRI-located firms to grab such market opportunities and potential.

Summary. Figure 2.12 summarises the key factors that have motivated and driven the BRI so far. These are classified as 'push' and 'pull' factors, in that they are driven respectively by motivating factors *within* China 'pushing' for internationalisation and by factors *outside* China acting as a 'lure' to go out (from the viewpoint of both China and other BRI countries). The push factors can be seen as three sub-factors, namely, the need for going global, the need for industrial restructuring, and sub-national regional development and cooperation. The pull factors comprise of two sub-factors, the need for economic cooperation and market opportunities.

2.4   Economic Impact

Scholarly works have discussed the effects of BRI in a 'broad' sense, mostly of its 'expected' and 'potential' impact (see Anwar 2018). Gao (2018) argues that BRI is likely to drive a new wave of globalisation given that the number of signatory countries who agreed to partake in the initiative is around 70. This takes special significance given the retrenchment observed in the West, with America First Policies and Brexit in the United States and the United Kingdom, respectively.

A *2017 Baker Mackenzie Report* outlines how BRI is creating and will create opportunities both for Chinese private firms and international firms. It highlights how BRI could benefit Chinese smartphone manufacturers, equipment suppliers, and property developers, given the significant demand for smartphones in BRI countries and as supply chains internationalise. Moreover, international companies can benefit as partners and suppliers, and importantly, global professional service firms and international financiers may find opportunities as well.

It might still be early to quantify and ascertain the economic impact of BRI, especially since it is an ongoing initiative. But one could look at trends, as we did in Sect. 2.2, or study short-term impacts. There have been some recent attempts, in this vein, to empirically study some 'specific' impact of BRI. Some studies have looked at the investment impact and others at the trade impact. The former is not surprising, as one key motivation of BRI is to promote the internationalisation of Chinese firms and contractors.

Du and Zhang (2018) quantitatively study the effects of BRI on Chinese companies' outbound M&A activities, using a difference-in-difference estimation methodology to determine the 'effect'.[8] They find that Chinese outward acquisitions in BRI economies increased post-BRI. In particular, both state-owned enterprises (SOEs) and non-SOEs channelled their investments towards BRI countries. SOEs made significantly more acquisitions in infrastructure, while non-SOEs acquired targets mostly in non-infrastructure sectors. They rationalise these findings on the basis that the former was 'part of the infrastructure investment plan embedded in the [Belt and Road] Initiative' (Du and Zhang, p. 190), so as to enhance infrastructure connectivity. In the case of non-SOEs, their actions could be motivated 'by the expected improvements in infrastructure' (p. 190), and expected policy coordination.

---

[8]The difference-in-difference method enables the researcher to separate countries (unit of observation here) into control and treatment groups and thus allows one to make 'causal inference'. One issue with studying economic 'impact' is establishing and inferring such casual effect. This is the issue that plagues most of the extant BRI 'impact' studies that make broad sweeping generalisation and claims about 'impact', when they are just gauging correlation at best. This also goes back to our motivation of focusing on 'economic' works and the 'economics of BRI' in this chapter.

Lv et al. (2018), also using difference-in-difference estimation, examine how BRI affected Chinese OFDI for business-group-affiliated firms and their independent counterparts. They find that BRI increased the probability of both types of firms to engage in OFDI, though the effect is stronger for group-affiliated enterprises than independent ones. One explanation, according to them, as to why independent firms are lagging behind business-group-member firms is the fact that the latter can rely on business group support and resources. This acts as 'insurance', given such investment is being made in risky overseas business environments, which BRI economies are noted for (see Sects. 2.2 and 2.5).

The trade impact is also an expected outcome of BRI since it is expected to promote foreign economic cooperation and foster regional trade. A study by Zhang and Wu (2018) investigates trade facilitation between China and some BRI economies from the period of 2011 to 2014. They use a gravity estimation model to examine how trade is impacted by a trade facilitation index, captured by port efficiency, customs environment, regulatory environment, electronic commerce, and financial environment. Though we have to be careful about interpreting anything pertaining to a BRI effect, given the sample period and absence of a 'comparative' group of countries, the findings can still be useful to understand how the trade regime within a region works and its effect. They find that trade facilitation (among other variables) have the most significant effect on trade between China and the sample of BRI countries. In particular, port efficiency is seen as a key facilitator, which means infrastructure has a significant role to play in facilitating bilateral trade flows.

It is noted that Eurasia accounts for more than 25% of global trade, and that trade flows among BRI countries are sensitive to trade costs and dependent on where trade costs fall (Konings 2018). Using econometric estimates from a gravity estimation of trade flows, both Konings (2018) and Boffa (2018) construe how falling trade costs could impact trade among BRI nations. Asserting trade costs falling by half, Konings' estimates predict that trade could increase by 12% for all BRI countries, with Central Asia and Eastern Europe seeing the largest increase. Meanwhile, the study by Boffa reports a rise in bilateral trade ranging from 1.3 to 1.7%, following a reduction in trade costs. All these effects are conditional on the fall of trade costs, an absence of which would lead to only small significant trade gains. One means through which trade costs can decline significantly is through transport and trade facilitation, reflecting the findings of Zhang and Wu (2018) on the role of trade facilitation for boosting trade and our own reported fact in Sect. 2.2 that BRI economies face relatively higher trade impediments. Henceforth, BRI has a crucial role in delivering trade facilitation.

However, it is worth noting that such trade effects from 'regional-integration-driven and trade-facilitated' BRI would not necessarily have a homogenous effect across all countries and be costless. The former is in fact highlighted in the study by Konings when she computes individual country effects. In a study that uses disaggregated trade data, Bastos (2018) notes that economies with export structure similar to China, such as Hong Kong (China), Vietnam, Malaysia, and the Philippines, are more likely to be affected by import competition from mainland China when regionally integrated. Nevertheless, there would also be mutual gains from trade for consumers (wider product range) and firms (efficiency gains from competition). Other BRI economies that have dissimilar production and export structures to China would be less exposed to such trade shocks from regional integration, while also benefitting as they could leverage their respective comparative advantages.

Furthermore, Bastos contends that though 'deeper economic integration typically generates gains at the country-level, it also imposes adjustment costs within countries. These costs are associated with reallocations of workers across sectors, regions, and occupations triggered by sector-specific competition and demand trade shocks' (p. 39). In short, this is the so-called 'Stolper-Samuelson' trade effect story of winners and losers from international trade theory.

Though it might be early to gauge the 'growth' effect of BRI, a study by Xiao et al. (2018) deploys a difference-in-difference estimation technique to examine whether BRI had an impact on sustainable development. Their results reveal an insignificant impact, but one that is positively signed across all indicators of sustainable development. They suggest various explanations for this finding, but the obvious one being that BRI is still in its early stage.

In summary, BRI has had a direct impact on *encouraging* Chinese OFDI and has the potential impact of raising bilateral trade across BRI economies, though this is dependent on trade facilitation and reduced trade costs. This is nuanced by the notion that trade shocks may have a distortionary effect within these economies depending on the (dis-)similarity of their trade structure.

2.5   Politico-Economic Challenges

So far we have documented what drives BRI and its (potential) impact. Several challenges facing the BRI have been documented in the extant literature (see Anwar 2018; Zhang et al. 2018). Here, we outline four politico-economic challenges facing BRI. These are the challenges of managing a megaproject, of navigating through an uncertain BRI world replete with risk and governance issues, of integration in the face of administrative and trade constraints, and of going beyond rhetoric and perception.

The first politico-economic challenge is the challenge of managing a large-scale project. It is often argued that megaprojects are hard to manage for the simple reason that they involve enumerable factors that are too complex to fathom and keep in check. These include the number of stakeholders involved and the different types of projects to manage (Flyvbjerg 2014). Huang (2016), for example, groups some of the cross-border BRI projects as high-speed railroads, oil and gas pipelines, and electricity and telecom links, and lists several projects under way for each category. Yet BRI is more than just these projects magnified. Apart from involving many stakeholders[9] (countries and organisations within those countries) and different project types, it has great 'aspiration', which is another defining feature of a megaproject (Flyvbjerg 2014). It also has a 'long-time' execution horizon, in that it is a multi-decade initiative (Baker Mackenzie 2017).

What makes this a challenge is the fact that such a megaproject is highly likely to have cost overruns (over budget), be delayed (rarely delivered on time), and more often than not, does not deliver the anticipated benefits (benefits shortfall). It is reported that nine out of ten large-scale projects face this challenge of being over budget, over time, and having a benefit shortfall (Flyvbjerg 2011).[10] Megaprojects that have faced this challenge include well-known projects in several countries. Examples include the Suez Canal (1900% cost overrun), Sydney Opera House (1400% over

---

[9] Yu (2018) highlights how the decision-making process about BRI within China is intricate and complex, where it can involve many stakeholders.

[10] There are three types of explanations behind megaprojects' cost overruns and benefits shortfall: technical, psychological, and politico-economic. The first relates to inadequate data for computing things through; the second, to optimism bias; and the third, to strategic misrepresentation (Flyvbjerg 2017). It would not be surprising that a grand project like BRI could be affected by all three.

budget), Panama Canal (200% over budget), Euro-Tunnel between UK and France (80% cost overrun) (see Flyvbjerg 2011, 2017). It is interesting to note that in the 1990s, Japan, motivated by excess industrial capacity at home and a slowing-down of its economy, initiated a somewhat similar proposal to the BRI, which was to finance and build infrastructure projects across Asia. This project ultimately failed (Holland 2016).

With this in mind, the question arises as to whether BRI-related projects will face a similar challenge in the future. A challenging outcome is if BRI and its projects do not deliver benefits and suffer budget overruns and delays, then China may suffer reputational damage (Hillman 2018).

The second challenge is one of managing risks and governance issues. While it provides significant opportunities for all BRI-participating economies including China, the BRI is not without risks and uncertainties, primarily geopolitical risks, with legal and macroeconomic risks also prevalent (Baker Mackenzie 2017; Ruta 2018).[11] Table 2.1 and our discussion in Sect. 2.2 outline how institutions—private and public—were far from the global average in BRI economies in 2017. In addition, the six WGIs in Table 2.1 portray BRI countries as encumbered with weaker than world-average institutional governance. Whether it is political stability, rule of law, regulatory quality, or control of corruption, BRI economies lag behind non-BRI economies. Critics argue that good governance and strong institutions are the foundation for economic development and thus, emphasise how BRI's success can hinge on this factor (Hu et al. 2018; Lin 2012, p. 10).

There are also macroeconomic risks, such as how to manage a country's debt burden and simultaneously recoup a return on investment (Ruta 2018).[12] It is argued that without projects that are clearly successful, BRI countries would be reluctant to invest if their returns are uncertain. This means that there is a need for 'model' projects showcasing success to convince partner countries (Cai 2017).

---

[11] Baker Mackenzie (2017) lists eight types of risks that projects related to BRI could face: project selection, project financing, project life cycle, legal and regulatory risk, political and security, M&A due diligence, financial exposure, and labour and corporate social responsibility.

[12] An example of this risk was the inability of Sri Lanka to service the debt made by China in building the Hambantota Port, which later turned into a debt-to-equity swap (Hillman 2018).

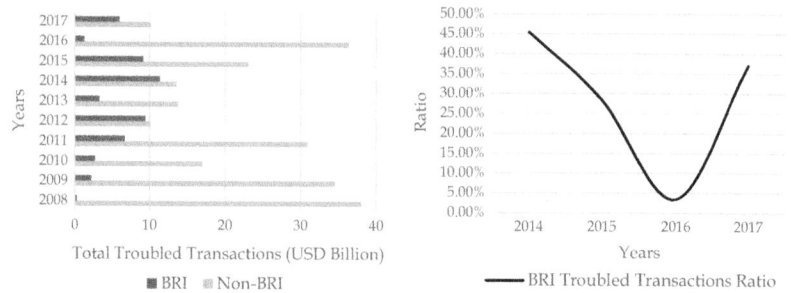

Fig. 2.13 Comparison of BRI and non-BRI countries' troubled transactions (*Data Source* The China Global Investment Tracker)

Indeed, the opposite trend seems to be making headlines, with cases of 'troubled' transactions. Figure 2.13 shows that troubled transactions fell for three consecutive years post-BRI but rose in 2017, mainly because troubled transactions in non-BRI countries fell, while it rose in BRI economies. There are many instances where BRI projects have stalled or been delayed or even cancelled outright. For example, the East Coast Rail Link project in Malaysia that was being built by China Communications Construction Co. Ltd., and started in 2017 was cancelled by the new Malaysian government in 2018.

The third politico-economic challenge concerns integration in the face of administrative and trade constraints. As highlighted in the above sections, successful connectivity and integration are sources of economic prosperity, as they nurture trade and other forms of economic cooperation (Yu 2017). Still, as discussed in Sect. 2.2, connectivity is a far cry from the levels it needs to be and this is mainly due to 'thick' borders, in that cross-border trade and investment are highly impeded by trade barriers and burdensome customs procedures (Konings 2018; Ruta 2018). Integration among BRI economies is likely to stall if the cost of doing business across borders persists.

Moreover, financial markets also face impediments to integration. As we documented in Sect. 2.2, the BRI average for financial market development is below the global average. As such, this is likely to pose a challenge to cross-border portfolio and direct investments in BRI countries. The lack of financial market development and integration is likely to prevent the RMB's internationalisation (Kroeber 2016, p. 146). Scholars argue that weak domestic financial markets, capital controls, exchange rate controls, and interest rate controls all work against this internationalisation goal. Consequently, the RMB has a long way to go before becoming an international currency of credence (Aizenman 2015; Tekdal 2018).

The final challenge is the challenge of going beyond rhetoric and perception. It has been argued that understanding what BRI actually entails can be quite testing and has been noted for its lack of clarity (Yu 2018). This is because it is hard to pin down a definition for it. This difficulty arises for two reasons. First, the initiative was not created from a policy document and therefore is best seen as a mission statement, without a proper definition and lacking a list of member economies (Baker Mackenzie 2017). Secondly, BRI is more a proposal or initiative rather than a plan, strategy, or project. In fact, when first announced it was more as a 'suggestion'. Unlike, for instance, the Asian Infrastructure Investment Bank—a formalised organisation with a well-defined remit—BRI is more of a slogan (Shichor 2018).

As such, the challenge is that BRI is a vague concept subject to diverse interpretations and often dubbed 'hollow government rhetoric' (Yu 2017). In essence, 'close scrutiny of the official BRI document published in 2015 reveals it to be largely an effort to advertise the BRI initiative. It suggests the proposed achievements of the initiative at the economic and strategic level, rather than referring to any concrete methodology to achieve them. The document does not offer any time frame or deadline, and more importantly, does not suggest any business model to make the initiative work' (Yu 2018, p. 14). There is a need for structure to reduce this 'ambiguity'. Henceforth, Chinese policymakers will have to provide tangible answers to fill these policy gaps (Baker Mackenzie 2017; Shichor 2018; Yu 2018).

2.6 Discussion and Conclusion

With three key economic facets of BRI set out, namely, drivers, challenges, and impact, this chapter can now draw certain implications. The first is to propose an integrative framework where one could think of all these three elements together. Figure 2.14 depicts this synthesised framework.

It shows how BRI is part of 'going global' and that there are drivers behind this initiative. The initiative is having, and will continue to have, an

Fig. 2.14 Drivers-challenges-impact of BRI

economic impact, but both drivers and impact are moderated by politico-economic challenges. All these elements are linked, in that in order to better understand the economic impact, we need to better understand the drivers and challenges. For instance, how we think about and make decisions regarding BRI can pose challenges, and that can in turn moderate the impact of the choice made. To illustrate this, a key motivator behind BRI is the need for economic cooperation to foster trade, with one of the strategic goals being 'unimpeded' trade to enable trade facilitation. We have also seen administrative burden and barriers to trade as potential challenges. Yet, if they fall drastically through a trade facilitation scheme, this could promote bilateral trade.

A second implication is the need for a 'facilitator'. This could take the form of a specific policy or entity that can mitigate the challenges, thereby reinforcing the link between what drives BRI and delivering a positive outcome.[13] An entity that can be a key facilitator is the Asian Infrastructure Investment Bank (AIIB). The role of AIIB in the BRI cannot be underestimated. Together with other financiers, it has been called upon to play a crucial role to promote BRI. While the Silk Road Fund and various Chinese policy banks support Chinese companies' outward venturing, BRI economies have been supported by the AIIB and the New Development Bank (Baker Mackenzie 2017). Indeed, Yu (2017) contends that the AIIB 'aims to facilitate and accelerate infrastructure improvement in the region by providing capital loans and technical services' (p. 353). As such, the AIIB is spearheading BRI.

Turning to *business* implication, there is the question of how Chinese and international companies can better navigate the uncertain business

---

[13] This can also be seen as permeating push and pull factors, when thinking of drivers.

environment in the BRI region. They need to devise risk-mitigating strategies as part of the decision-making process as they venture abroad. This is because although BRI represents business opportunities, there is also a risk element associated with it. Therefore, companies could use both exports and FDI when engaging in business in BRI countries, while possibly seeking partner companies in BRI countries to better navigate a host country's business environment. For large contracting projects, this may require insuring such projects with Sinosure for Chinese contractors to pre-empt the 'curse' of megaprojects.

Two major policy implications can be drawn. The first is that given the various challenges 'integrating' BRI economies, we see the importance of a continued effort to open up, financial sector reform and cooperation, and technological improvement so as to promote economic cooperation and integration in both goods and financial markets (Hu et al. 2018). For example, infrastructure development under BRI needs to be complemented with trade policy reform to boost connectivity (Ruta 2018).

Secondly, the politico-economic challenges posed by 'risks and governance' require stable institutional governance, such that BRI countries 'need to improve good governance in a period of rapid transformation, adhere to the rule of law, provide better education for their people, improve the business environment, curb corruption, and enhance government management capacity' (Hu et al., p. 222).

It is clear that the BRI is multi-faceted and replete with interesting economic facts. Taking stock of what has happened, and is happening, is important as we evaluate how BRI has emerged, is emerging, and will emerge. It has been driven by several factors and has the potential to be impactful; however, as a key mode of Going Global 2.0, BRI faces politico-economic challenges. These challenges can impinge on what is shaping it and most importantly, on what economic outcome will result from it, both for China and other BRI-participating economies.

APPENDICES

See Tables 2.7, 2.8 and 2.9.

Table 2.7   Regional distribution of BRI countries

Regions	Number of countries	Number of BRI countries	Name of BRI countries
East Asia and Pacific	38	15	Brunei Darussalam, Cambodia, China, Indonesia, Korea, Lao PDR, Malaysia, Mongolia, Myanmar, New Zealand, Philippines, Singapore, Thailand, Timor-Leste, Vietnam
South Asia	8	8	Afghanistan, Bangladesh, Bhutan, India, Maldives, Nepal, Pakistan, Sri Lanka
Europe and Central Asia	58	28	Albania, Armenia, Azerbaijan, Belarus, Bosnia and Herzegovina, Bulgaria, Croatia, Czech, Republic, Estonia, Georgia, Hungary, Kazakhstan, Kyrgyz Republic, Latvia, Lithuania, Macedonia, Moldova, Montenegro, Poland, Romania, Russian Federation, Serbia, Slovak Republic, Slovenia, Tajikistan, Turkey, Turkmenistan, Ukraine

(continued)

Table 2.7 (continued)

Regions	Number of countries	Number of BRI countries	Name of BRI countries
Middle East and North Africa	21	16	Bahrain, Egypt, Iran, Iraq, Israel, Jordan, Kuwait, Lebanon, Morocco, Oman, Qatar, Saudi Arabia, Syrian Arab Republic, United Arab Emirates, Yemen, Palestine
Sub-Saharan Africa	48	3	Ethiopia, Madagascar, South Africa
Latin America and Caribbean	42	1	Panama
North America	3	0	

Notes Palestine is included according to the Chinese 71 BRI country classification
Sources The World Bank; www.yidaiyilu.gov.cn

Table 2.8 Number of countries on the basis of income

Income group	No. of countries	No. BRIs
High income	81	20
Upper middle income	56	23
Lower middle income	47	24
Low income	34	3
Total	218	70

Notes (1) The total number of BRI countries is 70 based on the World Bank classification 2017, because Palestine is not included, but in Chinese 71 BRI country classification, it is included. (2) low-income economies are defined as those with a GNI per capita, calculated using the World Bank Atlas method, of $995 or less in 2017; lower middle-income economies are those with a GNI per capita between $996 and $3895; upper middle-income economies are those with a GNI per capita between $3896 and $12,055; high-income economies are those with a GNI per capita of $12,056 or more
Sources The World Bank; www.yidaiyilu.gov.cn

Table 2.9 Top ten rankings across foreign economic cooperation

BRI countries	Exports	Imports	OFDI flows	OFDI stocks	Engineering projects turnover	Personnel abroad for engineering projects	Personnel abroad for labour services
Afghanistan							
Albania							
Arab Emirates	10						7
Armenia							
Azerbaijan							
Bahrain							
Bangladesh					9	9	
Belarus							
Bhutan							
Bosnia and Herzegovina							
Brunei							
Bulgaria							
Cambodia			9	10			10
Croatia							
Czech							
Egypt							
Estonia							
Ethiopia					5	7	
Georgia							
Hungary							
India	3						
Indonesia	8	8	4	3	4	5	
Iran							

BRI countries	Exports	Imports	OFDI flows	OFDI stocks	Engineering projects turnover	Personnel abroad for engineering projects	Personnel abroad for labour services
Iraq						6	
Israel							
Jordan							
Kazakhstan	1		2				
Korea		1		4		8	3
Kuwait				7			
Kyrgyzstan							
Lao			6	6	6	4	8
Latvia							
Lebanon							
Lithuania							
Macedonia							
Madagascar							
Malaysia	6	2	3		2	2	6
Maldives							
Moldova							
Mongolia							
Montenegro							
Morocco							
Myanmar				9			
Nepal							
New Zealand							
Oman				8			
Pakistan			10	8	1	3	

(continued)

Table 2.9 (continued)

BRI countries	Exports	Imports	OFDI flows	OFDI stocks	Engineering projects turnover	Personnel abroad for engineering projects	Personnel abroad for labour services
Palestine							
Panama							
Philippines	9	10					2
Poland							
Qatar							
Romania							
Russia	5	5	5	2			4
Saudi Arabia		7			3	1	5
Serbia			1	1	7		1
Singapore	4	6					
Slovak							
Slovenia							
South Africa		9		5			
Sri Lanka							
Syrian							
Tajikistan							
Thailand	7	4	7		8		
Timor-Leste							
Turkey							
Turkmenistan							
Ukraine							
Uzbekistan							
Vietnam	2	3	8		10	10	9
Yemen							

REFERENCES

Aizenman, J. (2015). Internationalization of the RMB, capital market openness and financial reforms in China. *Pacific Economic Review, 20*(3), 444–460.

Anwar, S. T. (2018, June 18–20). The Belt and Road Initiative: Assessing global grand strategies and a survey. In *12th China Goes Global Conference Proceedings*. Shanghai, China.

Baker Mackenzie. (2017). *Belt & Road: Opportunity & risk—The prospects and perils of building China's New Silk Road.* Chicago, IL: Baker Mackenzie and Silk Road Associates.

Baldwin, R. (2016). *The great convergence: Information technology and the new globalization.* Cambridge, MA: The Belknap Press of Harvard University Press.

Bastos, P. (2018). *Exposure of Belt and Road economies to China trade shocks* (World Bank Policy Research Working Paper No. 8503).

Bellabona, P., & Spiragelli, F. (2007). Moving from open door to go global: China goes on the world stage. *International Journal of Chinese Culture and Management, 1*(1), 93–107.

Boffa, M. (2018). *Trade linkages between the Belt and Road economies* (World Bank Policy Research Working Paper No. 8423).

Bramall, C. (2009). *Chinese economic development.* New York: Routledge.

Buckley, P. J., Clegg, L. J., Voss, H., Cross, A. R., Liu, X., & Zheng, P. (2018). A retrospective and agenda for future research on Chinese outward foreign direct investment. *Journal of International Business Studies, 49*(1), 4–23.

Cai, P. (2017). *Understanding China's Belt and Road Initiative.* Sydney, Australia: Lowy Institute.

Chaisse, J., & Matsushita, M. (2017). China's 'Belt and Road' Initiative: Mapping the world trade normative and strategic implications. *Journal of World Trade, 52*(1), 163–186.

Chan, K. W., Henderson, J. V., & Tsui, K. Y. (2008). Spatial dimensions of Chinese economic development. In L. Brandt & T. G. Rawski (Eds.), *China's great economic transformation.* Cambridge, UK: Cambridge University Press.

Cheng, L. K. (2016). Three questions on China's "Belt and Road Initiative". *China Economic Review, 40*(September), 309–313.

China Policy. (2017). *China going global: Between ambition and capacity.* Beijing: China Policy.

Du, J., & Zhang, Y. (2018). Does One Belt One Road initiative promote Chinese overseas direct investment? *China Economic Review, 47*(February), 189–205.

Flyvbjerg, B. (2011). Over budget, over time, over and over again: Managing major projects. In P. W. G. Morris, J. K. Pinto, & J. Söderlund (Eds.), *The Oxford handbook of project management*. Oxford: Oxford University Press.

Flyvbjerg, B. (2014). What you should know about megaprojects and why: An overview. *Project Management Journal, 45*(2), 6–19.

Flyvbjerg, B. (2017). Introduction: The iron law of megaproject management. In B. Flyvbjerg (Ed.), *The Oxford handbook of megaproject management*. Oxford: Oxford University Press.

Gao, M. H. (2018). Globalization 5.0 led by China: Powered by positive frames for BRI. In W. Zhang, I. Alon, & C. Lattemann (Eds.), *China's Belt Road and Initiative: Changing the rules of globalization*. New York: Palgrave Macmillan.

Hu, B., Pan, Q., & Wu, S. (2018). The overall development of the Belt and Road countries: Measurement, ranking, and assessment. In W. Zhang, I. Alon, & C. Lattemann (Eds.), *China's Belt Road and Initiative: Changing the rules of globalization*. New York: Palgrave Macmillan.

Huang, Y. (2016). Understanding China's Belt & Road Initiative: Motivation, framework and assessment. *China Economic Review, 40*(September), 314–321.

Hillman, J. E. (2018, January 25). *China's Belt and Road Initiative: Five years later*. US–China Economic and Security Review Commission.

Holland, T. (2016, August 6). Why China's 'One Belt, One Road' plan is doomed to fail. *South China Morning Post*.

Jetin, B. (2017). *"One Belt-One Road Initiative" and ASEAN connectivity: Synergy issues and potentialities* (Institute of Asian Studies Working Paper No. 30).

Konings, J. (2018, June). *Trade impacts of the Belt and Road Initiative*. ING Economic & Financial Analysis.

Kroeber, A. R. (2016). *China's economy: What everyone needs to know*. Oxford: Oxford University Press.

Kuo, L., & Kommenda, N. (2018, July 30). What is China's Belt and Road Initiative? *Cities of the New Silk Road, The Guardian*.

Lin, J. Y. (2012). *Demystifying the Chinese economy*. Cambridge, UK: Cambridge University Press.

Lin, J. Y., & Wang, Y. (2017). Development beyond aid: Utilizing comparative advantage in the Belt and Road Initiative to achieve win-win. *Journal of Infrastructure, Policy and Development, 1*(2), 149–167.

Lu, H., Rohr, C., Hafner, M., & Knack, A. (2018). *China Belt Road and Initiative*. Cambridge, UK: Rand Corporation Europe.

Lv, P., Guo, C., & Chen, X. (2018). How the Belt and Road Initiative affects China's outward FDI: Comparing Chinese independent firms and business group affiliates. In W. Zhang, I. Alon, & C. Lattemann (Eds.), *China's Belt Road and Initiative: Changing the rules of globalization*. New York: Palgrave Macmillan.

Naughton, B. (2018). *The Chinese economy* (2nd ed.). Cambridge, MA: MIT Press.

Ruta, M. (2018). *Three opportunities and three risks of the Belt and Road Initiative*. World Bank, The Trade Post.

Schwab, K., & Sala-i-Martín, X. (2017). *The global competitiveness report 2016–2017*. Geneva: World Economic Forum.

Shambaugh, D. (2013). *China goes global: The partial power*. Oxford: Oxford University Press.

Shichor, Y. (2018). China's Belt and Road Initiative revisited: Challenges and ways forward. *China Quarterly of International Strategic Studies, 4*(1), 39–53.

Tekdal, V. (2018). China's Belt and Road Initiative: At the crossroads of challenges and ambitions. *The Pacific Review, 31*(3), 373–390.

Wuttke, J. (2017). The dark side of China's economic rise. *Global Policy, 8*(4), 62–70.

Xiao, H., Cheng, J., & Wang, X. (2018). Does the Belt and Road Initiative promote sustainable development? Evidence from countries along the Belt and Road. *Sustainability, 10*, 1–18.

Yu, H. (2017). Motivation behind China's 'One Belt, One Road' initiatives and establishment of the Asian infrastructure investment bank. *Journal of Contemporary China, 26*(105), 353–368.

Yu, J. (2018). The Belt and Road Initiative: Domestic interests, bureaucratic politics and the EU-China relations. *Asia Europe Journal, 16*, 223–236.

Zhang, J. (2012). Zhu Rongji might be right: Understanding the mechanism of fast economic development in China. *World Economy, 35*(12), 1712–1732.

Zhang, J., & Wu, Z. (2018). Effects of trade facilitation measures on trade between China and countries along the Belt and Road Initiative. In W. Zhang, I. Alon, & C. Lattemann (Eds.), *China's Belt Road and Initiative: Changing the rules of globalization*. New York: Palgrave Macmillan.

Zhang, W., Alon, I., & Lattemann, C. (2018). *China's Belt Road and Initiative: Changing the rules of globalization*. New York: Palgrave Macmillan.

Zheng, S. (2017, June 12). All you need to know about China's 'Belt and Road Initiative': What is it, who's paying, who'll benefit and who might lose out. *South China Morning Post*.

Zhou, W., & Esteban, M. (2018). Beyond balancing: China's approach towards the Belt and Road Initiative. *Journal of Contemporary China, 27*(112), 487–501.

CHAPTER 3

New Research Direction of the Joint Sea-and-Land Transportation of the Ningbo Port Under the Belt and Road Initiative

Shuojiang Xu, Fangli Zeng and Hing Kai Chan

3.1 Introduction

Based on the development requirements of the 13th Five-Year Plan, the marine economy has been promoted as a national strategy. It is an important task for China's economic development to constantly expand the blue economic space, adhere to the land-sea overall planning and develop the marine economy in the long run. As the distribution centre of marine transportation, the port is an important pillar of the development of the marine economy. The complex industrial model of the port integrates transportation, warehousing, freight forwarding and information industries. The port is also an indispensable and important part of the marine

S. Xu (✉) · F. Zeng · H. K. Chan
Nottingham University Business School China, University of Nottingham Ningbo China, Ningbo, China
e-mail: shuojiang.xu@nottingham.edu.cn

H. K. Chan
e-mail: hingkai.chan@nottingham.edu.cn

© The Author(s) 2020
H. K. Chan et al. (eds.), *International Flows in the Belt and Road Initiative Context*, Palgrave Series in Asia and Pacific Studies,
https://doi.org/10.1007/978-981-15-3133-0_3

economy. Coastal ports are the leading force in the development of the marine economy. Under the background of the Belt and Road Initiative, the only way for Chinese ports to progress towards informatization, diversification and personalization is to realize interconnection, build the gateway of the sea-and-land transportation hub and establish the intelligent logistics system of sea-land transportation.

As a key node of the logistics chain, ports need to frequently exchange data with external entities. The continuous innovation of modern electronic information technology brings new challenges and opportunities for the development of port supply chains. These emerging electronic information technologies can promote the interconnection, intercommunication and interaction of information resources; reduce the redundant intermediate links in the supply chain; promote the organic links of multimodal transportation; and form a complete and convenient "online silk road". However, the real world is complex. First, there are various players involved in the process of multimodal transportation, for instance, shippers, consignees, carriers, forwarders and custom. Furthermore, players use different modes of inner-organizational systems and inter-organizational communication tools, these lead to the low communication efficiency (Harris et al. 2015; Mondragon et al. 2017). Inter-communication is considered as one of the main issues existed.

There are numerous systems and technologies employed in supply chain, like Electronic Data Interchange (EDI), Radio Frequency Identification (RFID), Geographic Information System (GIS) and other emerging technologies, e.g., blockchain, Internet of Things (IoT) and cloud computing. The benefits of these systems and technologies are well-documented in the literature (Tob-Ogu et al. 2018), such as increase of real-time visibility and data exchange efficiency. However, the adoption of different information systems and technologies, especially the emerging technologies, in maritime industry is relatively slow, comparing with other industries. Furthermore, research investigating the benefits and adoption behaviour of inter-organizational communication tools in multimodal transportation is still at its infancy stage. The aim of this chapter is twofold: (1) display both industrial and theoretical background of inter-organizational communication systems and technologies in maritime transportation and multimodal transportation; (2) provide new research directions towards inter-organizational information communication technologies in the context of sea-and-land transportation with the Belt and Road Initiative.

3.2   Strategic Role of Ningbo

Ningbo has been a strategic location for sea trade since Song Dynasty, it was one of the three main ports for Maritime Silk Road in history. After the release of the Belt and Road Initiative, it has become one of the pilot cities under the Belt and Road Initiative (Belt and Road Portal 2017). Ningbo locates in the middle part of China's coastline and is in the south wing of the Yangtze River Delta, with vast land and sea hinterland. This is a superior geographical location, and abundant marine and hinterland resources, making it a key city for linking the land and sea transportation.

In 2017, Ningbo was listed as a national standard city for the innovative development of a marine economy during the 13th Five-Year Plan period, which established its position as a key city of the marine strategy during the 13th Five-Year Plan period. At present, the Ningbo-Zhoushan Port has established shipping routes with more than 600 ports in more than 100 countries. According to the annual report released by the Ningbo-Zhoushan Port Group, the container throughput of Ningbo-Zhoushan Port reached 21.56 million standard containers in 2016, with a year-on-year growth of 4.5%. This made the Ningbo-Zhoushan Port first among the world's top ports. In addition, the Ningbo-Zhoushan Port has formed a highway, railway, aviation and river-sea combined transportation system that includes water transfer and another omni-directional vertical distribution network. Through river-sea combined transportation system, the Ningbo-Zhoushan Port connects the coastal ports with the inland cities along the river (e.g., Wuhan and Chongqing). Goods can be shipped directly from all over the world to these cities. The Ningbo-Zhoushan Port can also connect to the Yangtze River and the Beijing–Hangzhou grand canal.

In general, the Ningbo-Zhoushan Port covers most area of east China and the Yangtze River basin. The railway in the port area is directly connected to the front of the wharf and is connected with the national railway network through the Xiaoyong double-track line. It is also very convenient for inland provinces and cities to tranship their trade by railway to river-sea. The Ningbo-Zhoushan Port directs the economic hinterland of the Ningbo and Zhejiang provinces, is superior to natural conditions, has a developed industrial and agricultural production system and is one of the country's most prosperous regions; the Yingtan, Quzhou, Shangrao, Jinhua, Yiwu and Xiaoshan inland "anhydrous harbour" regions have been critical to Ningbo-Zhoushan Port hinterland development in that they provide important support to the development of resource construction of the logistics system. Thus, Ningbo is considered as a strategic location to conduct empirical research of sea-and-land transportation under the Belt and Road Initiative.

3.3   Freight Transportation Industry

In recent years, most domestic ports have made remarkable achievements in their informatization and intelligence construction. In Tianjin, for example, the integrated logistics information service platform system has realized the government, ports and logistics enterprise tripartite electronic data interchange, which has not only greatly improved the degree of digitalization of the port, but has also established a comprehensive "one-stop" information service window for shipping companies, agencies, Inspection and Quarantine Bureau, customs and so on. The video monitoring system of the Qingdao Port has fully covered the main production sites in the port. In addition, the supervision efficiency has been improved through the on-site data collection using GPS positioning, electronic tags, GPRS communication and other technologies. The Shenzhen Port has adopted the centralized dispatching system from the container terminal and provides automated, professional and intelligent services for customers through wireless data terminal, container positioning and remote login and inquiry.

In 2015, Shanghai launched a "single window" platform. There is a ship declaration business section in the platform, which integrates maritime affairs, customs, inspection and quarantine and frontier defence to implement the opening of the data interface to all business sectors. At present, 100% of the Shanghai ship declaration business occurs through the "single window".

Similarly, due to the deep integration of shipping resources and with the support of constantly innovative intelligent logistics information technology, shipping e-commerce services are rapidly expanding and showing a new trend of shipping landscape. There are few examples: (1) Onetouch: Alibaba has successively developed a foreign trade integrated service platforms (Onetouch); (2) COSCO: COSCO successively launched the OSCO E-commerce and COSCO Epanasia; (3) Sinotrans: Sinotrans has developed a website called Sinotrans booking; (4) eWTP: The Electronic World Trade Platform (eWTP), which was based on the Belt and Road Initiative, was launched in Malaysia, becoming the first digital silk road e-road. To improve the efficiency and security of global trade; (5) Flexport: Flexport was the first foreign forwarder that moved the processes online. The aim of it is to reduce the paperwork in freight-forwarding, the services provided cover the processes of freight quoting, booking, realtime shipment tracking, customs compliance and so forth and (6) Open Platform: MSERSK and IBM announced the cooperation intention of a new platform using blockchain technology in 2018. It is aimed at allowing different stakeholders on the shipping chain to share information, which could increase the visibility of information and efficiency of work.

Overall, the development of information systems/platform in shipping chain puts different stakeholders and players from different countries on an electronic platform, effectively reduces the cost of all parties and improves efficiency and promotes the shipping logistics industry to upgrade from competition of price and scale to competition of service, experience and comprehensive ability.

The digitalization of shipping chain is still slow. Take the container booking process as an example. The process is still largely reliant on manual work. The booking process normally starts with a container using requirement from the shipper, the request will be transferred to a second-tier forwarder, then it will be passed to a first-tier forwarder and finally to the carrier which is always a shipping line. The booking request will be proceeded within the carrier. After that, the information of the booking, container and ship will be transferred back and forth till the container is loaded and ready to ship. van Oosterhout (2009) pointed out that 40 different organizations might be involved, and hundreds of documents are exchanged when dealing with one container. Different types of inter-organizational systems and technologies are used within these players only during this booking process, such as EDI, INTTRA, CargoSmart, E-mail, telephone, instant chatting tools like Skype and QQ. There are also visual forwarders which move the dashboard online, such as Onetouch and Flexport. It is believed that the efficiency of the booking process could be improved upon via an integrated and unified information platform. Nevertheless, the traditional approaches, like EDI, INTTRA, emails, telephones and others are still the main communication methods between organizations. Some of emerging products fail in the market while some are still struggling. In general, the adoption of new information systems and technologies are still slow. Sea-land transportation is more complicated, due to the fact that more players with different inter-organizational systems and more activities in various geographic locations are involved.

3.4   MULTIMODAL TRANSPORTATION

Multimodal transportation is the transportation of goods involving two or more modes, such as sea, road, rail and air. In general, there is a multimodal transportation operator (MTO) managing the whole chain (UN 1980). It could happen within one country or across different countries. The aim of multimodal transportation is to deliver the goods more efficiently with lower cost. Harris et al. (2015) claimed that multimodal transportation has become the main method in international transportation process as it enables all transportation modes into one continuous system to reach operational efficiency and cost-effective delivery of goods. International multimodal transportation occurs mainly by land-sea or sea-land transportation, such as in the far East, Europe and other regions. Sea-land transportation here refers to a combination of international transportation modes. The most obvious benefits of sea-land transportation are: operational efficiency, cost and environmental sustainability (Harris et al. 2015). Currently, sea-land transportation is primarily organized and operated by international shipping companies, such as companies with a shipping conference (Maersk of Denmark) or companies without a shipping conference (China Ocean Shipping (Group) Company and Evergreen Marine Corp.). This form of organization, with shipping companies as the main body, issues the combined transportation bill of lading and conducts a combined transportation business with inland transportation departments at both ends of the route, competing with the land bridge transportation. Land bridge transportation consists of a transcontinental railway (road) transportation system to transport containers, connecting the two ends of the continent with the ocean freight transportation mode. Very simply put, the two ends of the transportation chain are by sea, and the middle is by land. The continents connect the oceans to form a combined sea-land transportation, and the continents play the role of "bridge" so that they are called a "land bridge". In the land and sea combined transportation system, the continental transportation segment is known as "the land bridge transportation". In summary, sea-land transportation is highly consistent with the "One Belt and One Road" strategy. Maritime transportation is completed by the "maritime silk road", while continental transportation is completed by the "silk road economic belt". The research of Yu and Ye (2015) analysed the competitiveness and countermeasures of the container sea-rail combined transportation of the Ningbo-Zhoushan Port, which is in the hinterland of the Yangtze river economic belt. By analysing the time cost and economic cost of sea and rail transportation between the Ningbo-Zhoushan Port and other ports, the advantageous hinterland of the Ningbo-Zhoushan Port was demonstrated, and valuable suggestions were put forward for how the Ningbo-Zhoushan Port could improve the competitiveness of hinterland market. The guideline mentioned the need to build an IoT system for sea-rail transportation and emphasized the importance of integrating information across departments and regions.

Due to the complex nature of maritime industry, the management of sea-land transportation is challenging. There are numerous players involved, such as shippers, consignees, sea carriers, road and rail carriers, different tiers of freight forwarders, customs from multiple countries, port operators and so forth (Marchet et al. 2012). Furthermore, the operation systems differ from each player (Mondragon et al. 2017). These lead to higher request on timely data exchange and information visibility. Appropriate information communication systems would help to solve the difficulties on a large scale.

3.5   INFORMATION COMMUNICATION SYSTEMS IN MULTIMODAL TRANSPORTATION

Researchers have identified the benefits that information communication systems and technologies could bring, such as (1) reducing operating time at inter-modal terminal; (2) improving inter-modal infrastructures in terminal; (3) improving efficiency during the transhipment points; (4) decreasing the costs; and (5) improving customer satisfaction (Harris et al. 2015). Information communication technologies have become a way to gain the competitiveness of carriers and service providers on the shipping chain.

Research on information systems have started since last century and literature exists across multiple discipline, such as marketing, information systems and management. A large body of studies have focused on the benefits of information systems or information technologies (Roh et al. 2009). Researchers from management and information system (IS) disciplines have investigated the factors that affect the intention to adopt and adoption from different perspectives. For instance, Venkatesh et al. (2003) proposed the Unified Theory of Acceptance and Use of Technology to analyse the adoption behaviour of enterprises as individuals. Ke et al. (2009) examined the influence of intermediary and non-intermediary forces on the adoption of a digital supply chain management system. Adoption does not surely lead to better performance or other estimated results. Some groups have faced disappointing failures after adopting and implementing an innovative system (Roh et al. 2009). Furthermore, the diffusion of an innovation is a longitudinal process (Rogers 1995). Zhu et al. (2006) proposed a three-stage model that includes evaluation, adoption and implementation, which divided the diffusion of innovation into different stages based on the status.

To the best of our knowledge, very limited number of studies investigate the adoption of information communication systems in the context of sea-land transportation. Relevant studies address the topic in different ways. Ngai et al. (2008) tested the factors influencing the adoption of logistics information systems in the context of Hong Kong and found that perceived benefits or firm size does not significantly impact the adoption decision, which are inconsistent with prior studies (Reyes et al. 2016; Tu 2018). Instead, perceived barriers like resource shortage is found to play essential role.

Researchers use different methods exploring the adoption of information systems in sea-land transportation. Qualitative approaches, especially case studies, are widely employed in the research investigating the adoption in logistic and freight industry. Harris et al. (2015) selected 33 EU framework programme projects to explore the factors that affect the slow adoption of information and communication technologies (ICTs) in freight transportation. Three types of barriers to ICT adoption are identified: (1) user-related barriers, such as enterprise size and financial constraints; (2) technology-related barriers, like the compatibility and interoperability of systems; and (3) policy-related barriers, e.g., lack of policies. Mondragon et al. (2017) also used a multiple-case study research to identify the key elements that impact the adoption of ICT in a multimodal transportation context. The results show that both government legislation and dominant organizations running ports are greatly affected by the ICT adoption-related policies. The impact of policy is also identified in other studies (Osabutey et al. 2014). Researchers also investigated the adoption of emerging technologies in the context of maritime industry in recent years. Yang (2019) conducted a survey of blockchain applications and future improvements, aiming to evaluate the effects on use intention. Multiple dimensions are found to positively related to adoption intention, which are digitalization and paperless, standardization, platform development, customs clearance and management.

Due to the fact that multiple players are involved in the freight industry, the focus of prior studies differ, some test the adoption behaviours of carriers (Wang 2000) due to the fact that many of the information systems are provided by the carriers, while some pay attention to shippers (Lu et al. 2007). However, forwarders also play essential role in the shipping chain, as a large number of shippers book the container via forwarders. Thus, Hsu et al. (2009) argued that forwarder should be included while examining the adoption of information systems in freight transportation. Zeng et al. (2019) investigated the adoption of electronic container booking system at a chain level, which consists of shipper, consignee, carrier and two tiers of forwarders (first tier forwarder and second tier forwarder).

Maritime logistics is one of the main types of transportation, thus, the adoption of information systems and technologies would affect the whole supply chain management and logistics (Mondragon et al. 2017). Innovation diffusion models are widely used to investigate the adoption of information systems from various aspects in existing studies of supply chain management. Technology Acceptance Model (TAM) (Davis 1989), Innovation Diffusion Theory (IDT) (Roger 1995), Technology Organization Environment (TOE) Framework (Tornatzky and Fleischer 1990) and the Unified Theory of Acceptance and Use of Technology (UTAUT) Framework (Venkatesh et al. 2003) are considered to be the most effective models and theories. TAM and UTAUT are mainly employed to examine the diffusion at an individual level, while IDT and TOE are frequently used to investigate at organizational level (Oliveira and Martins 2011). Many studies explore the adoption of information systems at an individual level, for instance, from the perspective of employees (Brandon-Jones and Kauppi 2018) and managers (Tingling and Parent 2002). Only a few empirical studies attempt to examine the adoption of information systems or technologies at organizational level (Autry et al. 2010). Nevertheless, there are researchers identifying TAM as an appropriate model for the study of supply chain technologies at organizational level (Autry et al. 2010; Cheng and Yeh 2011). Furthermore, researchers like Wei et al. (2015) combined TOE, IDT, TAM and institution theory to examine the assimilation of RFID technologies within Chinese enterprises.

3.6   Research Opportunities

The Belt and Road Initiative provides both opportunities and challenges, we suggest the following areas for further research towards the adoption of information systems and technologies for multimodal transportation:

- The research on the adoption of information systems and technologies in sea-and-land transportation could pay more attention on the effect of environmental context, for instance, the impact of policy and regulation in different countries, supply chain partners and the characteristics of industry. Harris et al. (2015) identified policy factors as one of the barriers of the adoption of ICT in multimodal transportation. Under the Belt and Road Initiative, the products would be transferred in different countries where the policies and regulations differ. These policies and regulations would have different requirements towards customs, cargo category, transportation mode, safety standards, which would in turn affect the adoption of information systems and technologies, like ICT. Mondragon et al. (2017) found that the influence of governmental legislation is the strongest towards the adoption of ICT. Empirical studies addressing the effect of the Belt and Road Initiative on the adoption of information systems and technologies in the context of sea-and-road transportation would contribute to both theory and practice.
- The influence of the dominant position of the leading enterprise on the adoption of information system and technology should be examined. Maritime transportation operates in an oligopolistic market structure (Sys 2009). Shipping lines and alliances command high degree of power in the industry. This type of power might influence governmental policies (Mondragon et al. 2017) or enforce other enterprises in the shipping chain to follow the strategies which are beneficial to shipping lines and alliances themselves. Few studies investigate the adoption of technological innovation on maritime transportation on this perspective.
- Different adoption models and theories could be employed in the adoption in sea-and-land transportation. Although adoption models and theories are often used in the literature of supply chain management and other disciplines, few studies have used adoption models and theories to study adoption factors in the field of multimodal transportation or land-sea transportation.

• Increasing emerging technologies enter the market and are employed in different industries like cloud computing, Internet of Things, Big Data, blockchain and so forth. Empirical research on sea-and-land transportation should work closely with practice and explore the potential opportunities and challenges under the Belt and Road Initiative.

Acknowledgements The authors acknowledge the financial support by Major Collaboration Programme 2017 funded by Ningbo Science and Technology Bureau (reference number: 2017D10032).

References

Autry, C. W., Grawe, S. J., Daugherty, P. J., & Rickey, R. G. (2010). The effects of technological turbulence and breadth on supply chain technology acceptance and adoption. *Journal of Operations Management, 28,* 522–536.

Belt and Road Portal. (2017). Available at: https://eng.yidaiyilu.gov.cn.

Brandon-Jones, A., & Kauppi, K. (2018). Examining the antecedents of the technology acceptance model within e-procurement. *International Journal of Operations and Production Management, 38*(1), 22–42.

Cheng, Y. H., & Yeh, Y. J. (2011). Exploring radio frequency identification technology's application in international distribution centers and adoption rate forecasting. *Technological Forecasting and Social Change, 78,* 661–673.

Davis, F. D. (1989). Perceived usefulness, perceived ease of use, and user acceptance of information technology. *MIS Quarterly, 13*(3), 319–340.

Flexport. Available at: https://www.flexport.com.

Harris, I., Wang, Y., & Wang, H. (2015). ICT in multimodal transport and technological trends: Unleashing potential for the future. *International Journal of Production Economics, 122,* 56–66.

Hsu, W. K. K., Huang, S. H. S., & Yu, H. F. (2009). Shipper behavior to use EC services in liner shipping. *International Journal of Production Economics, 122,* 56–66.

Ke, W., Liu, H., Wei, K. K., Gu, J., & Chen, H. (2009). How do mediated and non-mediated power affect electronic supply chain management system adoption? The mediating effects of trust and institutional pressure. *Decision Support Systems, 46,* 839–851.

Lu, C. S., Lai, K. H., & Cheng, T. C. E. (2007). Application of structural equation modeling to evaluate the intention of shippers to use Internet services in liner shipping. *European Journal of Operational Research, 180,* 845–867.

Marchet, G., Perotti, S., & Mangiaracina, R. (2012). Modelling the impacts of ICT adoption for inter-modal transportation industry. *International Journal of Physical Distribution and Logistics Management, 37*(2), 148–163.

Mondragon, A. E. C., Coronado, C. E., & Coronado, E. S. (2017). ICT adoption in multimodal transport sites: Investigating institutional-related influences in international seaports terminals. *Transportation Research Part A, 97,* 69–88.

Ngai, E. W. T., Lai, K. H., & Cheng, T. C. E. (2008). Logistics information systems: The Hong Kong experience. *International Journal of Production Economics, 113,* 223–234.

Oliveira, T., & Martins, M. F. (2011). Literature review of information technology adoption models at firm level. *The Electronic Journal Information System Evaluation, 14*(1), 110–121.

Osabutey, E. L., Williams, K., & Debrah, Y. A. (2014). The potential for technology and knowledge transfers between foreign and local firms: A study of the construction industry in Ghana. *Journal of World Business, 4*(49), 560–571.

Reyes, P. M., Li, S., & Visich, J. K. (2016). Determinants of RFID adoption stage and perceived benefits. *European Journal of Operational Research, 254,* 801–812.

Rogers, E. M. (1995). *Diffusion of innovations.* New York: Free Press.

Roh, J. J., Kunnathur, A., & Tarafdar, M. (2009). Classification of RFID adoption: An expected benefits approach. *Information & Management, 46,* 357–363.

Sys, C. (2009). Is the container liner shipping industry an oligopoly? *Transport Policy, 16,* 259–270.

Tingling, P., & Parent, M. (2002). Mimetic isomorphism and technology evaluation: Does imitation transcend judgement? *Journal of the Association for Information Systems, 3,* 113–143.

Tob-Ogu, A., Kumar, N., & Gullen, J. (2018). ICT adoption in road freight transport in Nigeria—A case study of the petroleum downstream sector. *Technological Forecasting and Social Change, 131,* 240–252.

Tornatzky, L. G., & Fleischer, M. (1990). *The processes of technological innovation.* Lexington, MA: Lexington Books.

Tu, M. (2018). An exploratory study of Internet of Things (IoT) adoption intention in logistics and supply chain management: A mixed research approach. *The International Journal of Logistics Management, 29*(1), 131–151.

UN. (1980). *The convention on international multimodal transport of goods.*

van Oosterhout, M. (2009). Organizations and flows in the network. In *Port inter-organizational information systems: Capabilities to service global supply chains.* Delft: Now Publishers.

Venkatesh, V., Morris, M. G., & Davis, G. B. (2003). User acceptance of information technology: Toward a unified view. *MIS Quarterly, 27*(3), 425–478.

Wang, H. G. (2000). The application of EC for shipping company. *Shipping and Trading Weekly*, pp. 66–70.

Wei, J., Lowry, P. B., & Seedorf, S. (2015). The assimilation of RFID technology by Chinese companies: A technology diffusion perspective. *Industry and Management, 52,* 628–642.

Yang, C. S. (2019). Maritime shipping digitalization: Blockchain-based technology applications, future improvements, and intention to use. *Transportation Research Part E, 131,* 108–117.

Yu, P., & Ye, Y. (2015). *Analysis and countermeasure research on container sea-rail combined transport competitiveness of Ningbo-Zhoushan port, hinterland of Yangtze river economic belt.* Special Zone Economy, 5.

Zeng, F., Chan, H. K., & Pawar, K. (2019). The effects of technological factors on the adoption of electronic booking system: In the context of liner container shipping industry. In *Proceeding of the 27th Annual Conference of the International Association of Maritime Economists*, Athens.

Zhu, K., Kraemer, K. L., & Xu, S. (2006). The process of innovation assimilation by firms in different countries: A technology diffusion perspective on e-business. *Management Science, 52*(10), 1557–1576.

CHAPTER 4

International Market Integration in the Context of the Belt and Road Initiative

Marina Glushenkova

4.1 Introduction

Since the late 1970s, China has considerably expanded its economic cooperation and integration with other countries. Market-oriented reforms, privatisation, and the admission of China in the World Trade Organization intensified international trade, leading China to the position of the largest trading power in the world. Existing studies show the significant positive effect of these efforts on China's involvement in the world market, but this process was hindered by the global financial crisis. In the aftermath of the recent crisis, the enforcement of international cooperation has become particularly important for the economy.

Under these circumstances, in 2013, Chinese President Xi Jinping announced the establishment of a new regional cooperation programme named the 'Belt and Road Initiative' (BRI). In March 2015, China's National Development and Reform Commission issued an action plan for

M. Glushenkova (✉)
Nottingham University Business School China, University of Nottingham Ningbo China, Ningbo, China
e-mail: marina.glushenkova@nottingham.edu.cn

75
H. K. Chan et al. (eds.), *International Flows in the Belt and Road Initiative Context*, Palgrave Series in Asia and Pacific Studies,
https://doi.org/10.1007/978-981-15-3133-0_4

the initiative. According to this document, the goals of the BRI include the promotion of free flow of production factors, the enhancement of efficient resource allocation, and the deepening of market integration. Geographically, the Belt and Road programme covers six land routes (China–Europe, China–Mongolia–Russia, China–Mediterranean Sea, China–Pakistan, Bangladesh–China–India–Burma, and China–South Asia) and two maritime paths (China–South Pacific and China–Europe). By August 2015, according to the report of the China International Trade Institute, 65 countries officially expressed their interest in the initiative by signing the BRI 'implementation and partnership agreement' with China.

The BRI is a unique economic cooperation project undertaken by the Chinese government as it covers a large number of diverse countries in terms of geography, size, economic development, culture, and political regimes. While there have been many initiatives to foster economic cooperation in Asia (e.g. among the Association of Southeast Asia Nations [ASEAN] members), minimal effort has been made to enhance economic cooperation and development programmes between three geographically distant regions: Asia, Africa, and Europe. Although there is still no well-defined action programme of cooperation (which causes a problem with evaluation of BRI's impact on regional development), some studies have already predicted potential positive outcomes of the initiative. For instance, Herrero and Xu (2016) estimated the trade effects of the BRI and showed that landlocked European countries could benefit from participation in the initiative via considerable expansion of trade associated with the improvement of transportation infrastructure under the BRI. Chung (2017) provided evidence that the BRI can promote the economic growth and domestic political stability in China and other partner countries. Villafuerte et al. (2016) focused on Asia and found that the BRI can bring large but uneven benefits to its members. Similarly, Zhai (2018) predicted considerable global welfare gains for the BRI member countries and a significant boost in global trade.

Motivated by the BRI cooperation and development programme, which can potentially have great impact on international trade and global market convergence, this chapter assesses the extent of market integration across the BRI partners. The data show that average price dispersion across the BRI partners fell by 11% between 1990 and 2000, indicating a price convergence process operating to some extent. While in the next decade, between 2000 and 2010, the fall in price dispersion was more than five times smaller, at only 2%, suggesting significant slowdown in the convergence pace between the BRI partners. Next, we analyse the behaviour of prices in the BRI countries from 1990 until 2010 to answer some important questions. How did the degree of integration among the potential BRI partners evolve over time before the launch of the initiative? Did the degree of integration vary across goods? How different were prices in China as compared to the BRI partners? What can explain price differences between China and the BRI partners? Finally, how can the BRI contribute to the process of China's international price integration?

Many studies have investigated the economic integration of China with other Asian countries (e.g. Dang and Yang 2017; Binner et al. 2011; Kim et al. 2005; Lin 2012; Nagayasu 2010), or with European markets (e.g. Ke et al. 2003; Wang and Zhou 2009; Wang 2016). However, the literature is silent about the evolution of price integration across the BRI partners, including Asian, African, and European countries. This chapter focuses on the international market integration of the BRI partners by examining changes in the micro-price levels across the partner countries. It documents the evolution of price integration in the BRI member countries, evaluates LOP deviations for China relative to the BRI partners, discusses factors determining these differences, and assesses potential effects of the BRI on global market integration.

This chapter is organised as follows. The next section discusses economic measures used to assess market integration. The third section presents the empirical analyses of the price convergence across BRI countries. The fourth section discusses prices in China relative to potential BRI partners and the importance of tradeability and non-traded input share in determining price differences in China. The fifth section outlines impacts of the BRI on business. The final section provides the conclusions.

4.2   Measuring Market Integration

Market integration is an important topic for both economists and policymakers, as it leads to faster technological progress and knowledge accumulation, effective use of comparative advantages, and expansion of market size, thereby enhancing the economic development of countries. To quantitatively measure market integration of countries, economists typically focus on two main indicators—price dispersion across countries and their deviations from the LOP.

The evolution of *price dispersion* across countries is indicative of the changes in the degree of market integration over time. When markets become more integrated, price dispersion is expected to fall, whereas, when markets diverge, price dispersion typically rises. The time series analysis also allows one to discern how convergence patterns evolve over time and potentially identify factors behind the breaks in the integration process. A standard approach applied in economic literature to measure convergence across a group of countries is known as 'sigma-convergence', which refers to a reduction in the dispersion of a variable across economies. To capture convergence of markets, the standard deviation of prices is used as a variable of interest. For the first part of the analysis presented in this chapter, relative prices p_{ijt} for good j in country i at time t are calculated as a ratio between the price of good j in country i at time t, P_{ijt}, and the average price of the good at time t in all countries (i.e. $p_{ijt} = P_{ijt} / \bar{P}_{ijt}$). Then, price dispersion across countries for each individual item j at time t is calculated as follows:

$$\sigma_{jt} = \sqrt{\frac{N \sum_{i=1}^{N} (p_{ijt})^2 - \left(\sum_{i=1}^{N} p_{ijt} \right)^2}{N^2(N-1)}}, \tag{4.1}$$

and an average value of this measure is taken for three types of items: tradeables, non-tradeables, and all items.

The second approach to measure the degree of market integration relies on *the Law of One Price*, which states that as a result of arbitrage, identical goods sold in different locations will have identical prices. This law relies on the idea of arbitrage opportunities, which asserts that once there is a difference between prices of an identical good in different locations, sellers will buy the product in a market with a low price and sell it in a market with a high price. This process of arbitrage will increase the demand for the product in the location where the product is cheaper, thereby increasing its price; while the price of the product in the location where it is more expensive will fall in response to greater supply. Eventually, the price difference will be eliminated and the price will be the same in the two markets due to the arbitrage. Thus, LOP deviations can indicate the degree of market integration across any two locations at a point in time. Mathematically, the LOP deviations for each good j at time t in country i can be defined as follows:

$$q_{ijt} = \ln(P_{ijt}) - \sum_{i=1}^{N} \ln(P_{ijt}) \Big/ N, \tag{4.2}$$

where P_{ijt} is the price[1] in dollar of the good j in country i at a specific time and N is the number of countries comprising the average relative to which country i is being compared. For the purpose of this chapter, N is considered to be comprised of all available BRI countries to obtain q_{ijt}^{BRI}, and in some cases it is restricted to be comprised of the regional groups such as Southeast Asia to obtain q_{ijt}^{SEA}, South Asia to obtain q_{ijt}^{SA}, Africa to obtain q_{ijt}^{AF} or Europe to obtain q_{ijt}^{EU}. Detailed description of countries forming each group is presented in Table 4.1.

4.3 Evolution of Market Integration Across the BRI Partners

4.3.1 Price Dispersion Across the BRI Partners

Next, the concept of 'sigma-convergence' is used to illustrate the historical evolution of price differences. Figure 4.1 shows price dispersion across the BRI partners between 1990 and 2010 for different types of goods. First, dispersion for tradeables (red line) is smaller than for non-tradeables (blue line) for all periods in line with the idea of arbitrage opportunities, which asserts that price differences between any two locations will be eliminated via the trade, and prices will eventually be the same in the two markets. Therefore, one would expect price differences to be arbitraged away faster for traded products as compared to non-traded ones, leading to lower persistence of price differences for the former.

---

[1] The price data utilised in this chapter are from the Economist Intelligence Unit (EIU). The description of the data could be found in Glushenkova et al. (2018). The Economist Intelligence Unit survey covers 140 cities in 90 countries, but availability of data varies across locations and over time. The city with the largest available set of data for each country is chosen in order to analyse price convergence at the country level. The study is limited to those countries expressed their interest in the Belt and Road Initiative. Moreover, only prices of items that are available in Beijing have been utilised for the possibility of countries' comparison with Chinese economy. The final sample covers 80 unique product items in 22 countries available annually from 1990 to 2010.

Table 4.1   Countries along the Belt and Road available in the sample

Geographic region	Country	City
East Asia	China	Beijing
Southeast Asia	Indonesia	Jakarta
	Malaysia	Kuala Lumpur
	Philippines	Manila
	Singapore	Singapore
	Thailand	Bangkok
Africa	Bahrain	Manama
	Egypt	Cairo
	Israel	Tel Aviv
	Jordan	Amman
	Saudi Arabia	Riyadh
	UAE	Abu dhabi
South Asia	Bangladesh	Dhaka
	India	New delhi
	Pakistan	Karachi
	Sri Lanka	Colombo
Europe	Czech Republic	Prague
	Greece	Athens
	Hungary	Budapest
	Poland	Warsaw
	Russia	Moscow
	Turkey	Istanbul

Fig. 4.1

Sigma-convergence of countries relative to the BRI average

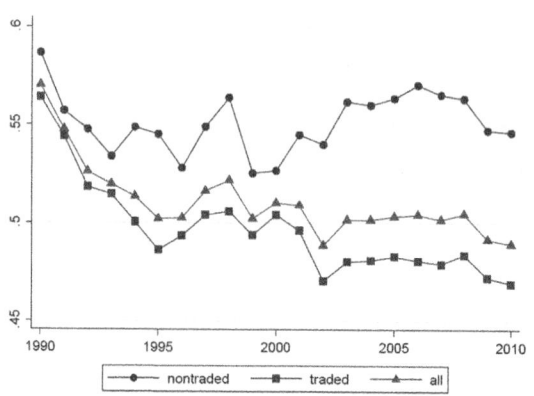

Second, for both types of goods, dispersion is seen falling until 1996; then, there is a temporary shock until the early 2000s, similar to the one found by Dang and Yang (2017), after which dispersion for tradeables stays almost constant, while dispersion for non-tradeables starts to increase. The changes in the late 1990s can be explained by the Asian financial crises that affected 20% of countries in the sample (such as China, Indonesia, Malaysia, Philippines, Singapore, and Thailand). Moreover, the divergence in the price of non-tradeables suggests that since 2000, the income gap between the BRI countries was significantly deepening.

Various statistical methods, such as unit root test, threshold autoregression (TAR), log t-test, and others can be used to quantify the significance of the price convergence. Following Dang and Yang (2017), this chapter performs the Phillips and Sul (2007) log t-test for the convergence of individual prices. The methodology employs the concept of 'relative' convergence, which means that two series share the same stochastic or deterministic trend elements in the long run, so that their ratio eventually converges to unity. Relative price convergence for each good j is defined as $P_{ijt+k} / P_{ljt+k} \to 1$, as $k \to \infty$ for any pair of countries $i \neq l$. Relative convergence is allied to standard σ-convergence definitions discussed above. The substantial evidence for the lack of overall convergence is documented after having applied the above test to each individual good. The log t-test reveals that only for 20% of goods (18 out of 84), there is evidence of a price convergence among the BRI partners; while for the majority of goods, the null of overall convergence can be rejected at the 5% significance level. Moreover, 17 out of 18 goods for which prices demonstrate convergent behaviour are traded goods, and only 1 item ('Electricity, monthly bill') is non-traded, which is consistent with existing arbitrage opportunities relevant for traded goods.

4.3.2   Deviations from the Law of One Price

Next, the degree of market integration among the potential BRI partners is measured using the second approach (i.e. LOP deviations). Figure 4.2a shows the empirical distributions of LOP deviations relative to the BRI average, q_{ijt}^{BRI}, for all goods and countries pooled together in 1990, 2000, and 2010. Each line represents the density function of LOP deviations (common currency prices compared to the cross-country mean), good-by-good, for a particular year. These densities support our previous

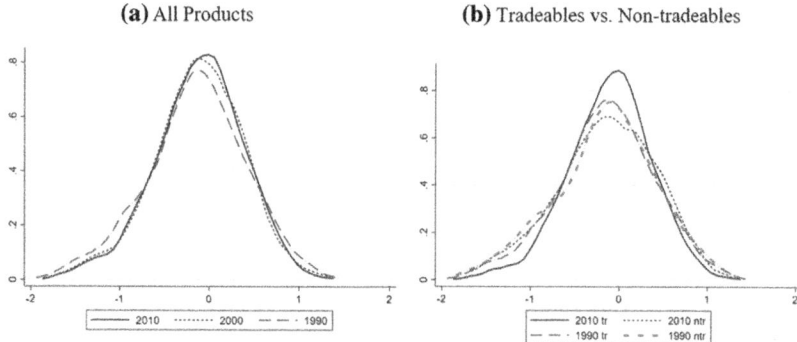

Fig. 4.2   Empirical distributions of LOP deviations for the BRI partners

findings that the degree of convergence has slightly increased over time between 1990 and 2010, while the process has stopped after 2000. One could see this as a motivation for the BRI—integration of markets requires development of countries' connectivity, stimulation of international trade, and cooperation, which are the main goals of China's BRI.

In addition to the visual evidence, the Epps–Singleton test for the null of equality of the empirical distribution functions been employed. The null hypothesis can be rejected at the 1% significance level when comparing LOP deviation distributions between 2010 (or 2000) and 1990 with p-value of 0.005 (0.002). This proves statistically that the LOP deviation distribution in 2010 (or 2000) is different than the empirical distribution for 1990. Instead, comparing empirical distributions between 2010 and 2000, the null of equality cannot be rejected at the 1% significance level with p-value of 0.701. Moreover, the average price dispersion across the BRI partners fell by 11% between 1990 and 2000 (from 0.564 to 0.503), indicating the price convergence process operating to some extent at the beginning of the period under study. While between 2000 and 2010, the fall in price dispersion was more than five times smaller, only 2% (from 0.503 to 0.493); this suggests significant slowdown in the rate of convergence between the BRI partners.

It is worthwhile to consider the driving forces behind the price convergence, specifically, whether convergence appears via the adjustment of national income levels that are reflected in the price of non-traded goods (services), or via the international trade channels mainly affecting the price of traded goods. To answer this question, it is necessary to distinguish between traded and non-traded goods and plot their separate distributions for 2010 and 1990. Figure 4.2b shows that dispersion for tradeables becomes lower over time as the density function for traded goods is more highly peaked in 2010 as compared with that of 1990 (with mean LOP dispersion values for tradeables in 1990 [0.555] greater than in 2010 [0.469]). Meanwhile, the dispersion for non-tradeables does not change significantly between 1990 and 2010,[2] suggesting that the price convergence in the BRI countries appears due to the fall in price dispersion for tradeables, for which the price arbitrage mechanism is more relevant.

Table 4.2 reports the LOP deviation averaged across goods j in each country i for selected time period t, $E(q_{ijt}^{BRI}|i,t)$, for goods that can be broadly categorised as traded versus non-traded. The average LOP deviations are informative about the fraction of goods that are cheaper (LOP deviations are negative) or more expensive (LOP deviations are positive) in a country, and the evolution of these price advantages (disadvantages) over time. Moreover, panel B of Table 4.2 presents income-adjusted LOP deviations, having removed the effect of income on price differences. Panel A of Table 4.2 shows that while non-tradeables in poorer countries like Bangladesh, India, Pakistan, China, Indonesia, Philippines, Egypt, and Thailand become cheaper between 1990 and 2010, and they become more expensive over time in wealthier countries like Russia, Malaysia, Turkey, Poland, Hungary, Greece, Czech Republic, Saudi Arabia, and Singapore, the picture is less clear for tradeables. Tradeables have actually become relatively cheaper over time in some of the wealthier countries like Malaysia, Turkey, and Saudi Arabia, while they have become more expensive in some of the poorer countries like India and Thailand by 2010. Finally, income adjustment has a large impact on the average LOP deviations, with prices in poorer countries becoming more expensive and prices in wealthier countries becoming cheaper after adjustment than before adjustment.

---

[2] Based on the Epps–Singleton test the null of equality of the LOP deviations distributions for non-tradeables between 2010 and 1990 cannot be rejected at the 1% significance level (with p-value of 0.381).

Table 4.2 Average across goods price deviations

| | | Panel A: Without income adjustment | | | | | | | | | |
| | | Non-traded goods | | | | | Traded goods | | | | |
Country	Inc. dev.	1990	1995	2000	2005	2010	1990	1995	2000	2005	2010
Bangladesh	−2.110	−0.465	−0.468	−0.432	−0.544	−0.622	−0.145	−0.251	−0.250	−0.499	−0.473
India	−1.883	−0.303	−0.782	−0.810	−0.658	−0.725	−0.641	−0.590	−0.534	−0.544	−0.539
Pakistan	−1.769	−0.411	−0.657	−0.716	−0.792	−0.807	−0.345	−0.376	−0.473	−0.609	−0.790
Sri Lanka	−1.273	−0.662	−0.407	−0.309	−0.496	−0.690	−0.254	−0.312	−0.294	−0.291	−0.134
China	−1.184	−0.014	0.037	0.245	−0.085	−0.063	0.277	0.370	0.505	0.258	0.082
Indonesia	−1.177	0.156	0.053	−0.331	−0.373	−0.234	−0.026	−0.008	−0.187	−0.331	−0.090
Philippines	−1.112	−0.375	−0.226	−0.619	−0.847	−0.720	−0.364	−0.216	−0.366	−0.545	−0.414
Egypt	−1.053	−0.108	−0.187	−0.041	−0.553	−0.233	0.251	−0.203	−0.045	−0.507	−0.324
Jordan	−0.610	−0.413	−0.366	−0.114	−0.171	−0.133	−0.207	−0.129	0.164	0.016	0.064
Thailand	−0.280	−0.102	0.144	−0.285	−0.320	−0.115	−0.233	−0.190	−0.292	−0.333	−0.128
Russia	0.062	0.137	0.625	0.379	0.470	0.483	0.199	0.230	0.064	0.279	0.281
Malaysia	0.287	−0.222	−0.166	−0.421	−0.310	−0.131	−0.158	−0.053	−0.253	−0.183	−0.259
Turkey	0.294	0.064	−0.380	−0.080	0.230	0.176	0.263	−0.131	−0.128	0.216	0.175
Poland	0.399	−0.690	−0.233	−0.032	0.086	−0.028	−0.657	−0.165	−0.225	0.100	−0.018
Hungary	0.645	−0.534	−0.648	−0.575	−0.053	−0.155	−0.504	−0.394	−0.567	−0.106	−0.108
Czech Republic	0.847	−0.967	−0.347	0.032	0.439	0.202	−0.831	−0.278	−0.406	0.117	0.115
Saudi Arabia	1.089	0.073	−0.065	0.069	−0.022	0.085	−0.133	−0.144	0.042	−0.135	−0.229
Bahrain	1.350	0.140	−0.060	−0.019	−0.189	−0.323	0.061	−0.044	0.113	−0.049	−0.193
Greece	1.549	0.009	0.162	−0.023	0.286	0.205	0.083	0.112	−0.117	0.178	0.090
Israel	1.748	0.507	0.365	0.452	0.221	0.336	0.231	0.205	0.363	0.118	0.160

Panel A: Without income adjustment

Country	Inc. dev.	Non-traded goods					Traded goods				
		1990	1995	2000	2005	2010	1990	1995	2000	2005	2010
Singapore	1.986	0.148	0.343	0.376	0.301	0.355	0.102	0.165	0.187	0.157	0.277
UAE	2.227	0.076	0.005	0.151	−0.057	−0.091	−0.203	−0.141	0.042	−0.023	−0.077

Panel B: After income adjustment

Country	Inc. dev.	Non-traded goods					Traded goods				
		1990	1995	2000	2005	2010	1990	1995	2000	2005	2010
Bangladesh	−2.110	0.303	0.388	0.374	0.336	0.268	0.410	0.364	0.331	0.134	0.167
India	−1.883	0.399	0.025	−0.031	0.099	−0.023	−0.133	−0.008	0.029	0.002	−0.031
Pakistan	−1.769	0.284	0.056	0.000	−0.038	−0.021	0.158	0.140	0.045	−0.065	−0.223
Sri Lanka	−1.273	−0.039	0.185	0.247	0.074	−0.228	0.198	0.119	0.112	0.124	0.205
China	−1.184	0.732	0.681	0.769	0.374	0.240	0.816	0.837	0.888	0.596	0.310
Indonesia	−1.177	0.703	0.527	0.261	0.194	0.194	0.373	0.340	0.244	0.083	0.226
Philippines	−1.112	0.106	0.237	−0.121	−0.263	−0.168	−0.011	0.124	−0.001	−0.120	−0.011
Egypt	−1.053	0.357	0.314	0.353	0.039	0.254	0.593	0.164	0.248	−0.076	0.033
Jordan	−0.610	−0.092	−0.010	0.231	0.214	0.240	0.033	0.136	0.422	0.302	0.342
Thailand	−0.280	0.135	0.285	−0.002	−0.025	0.154	−0.051	−0.076	−0.078	−0.110	0.076
Russia	0.062	0.100	0.786	0.703	0.566	0.508	0.188	0.359	0.306	0.362	0.314

(continued)

Table 4.2 (continued)

Country	Inc. dev.	Non-traded goods					Panel B: After income adjustment Traded goods				
		1990	1995	2000	2005	2010	1990	1995	2000	2005	2010
Malaysia	0.287	-0.142	-0.163	-0.367	-0.230	-0.052	-0.086	-0.035	-0.200	-0.112	-0.188
Turkey	0.294	0.100	-0.245	-0.047	0.220	0.201	0.303	-0.021	-0.090	0.224	0.208
Poland	0.399	-0.498	-0.177	-0.012	0.049	-0.057	-0.507	-0.110	-0.196	0.088	-0.023
Hungary	0.645	NA	-0.657	-0.566	-0.200	-0.196	NA	-0.385	-0.545	-0.194	-0.122
Czech Republic	0.847	-1.042	-0.439	-0.044	0.235	0.025	-0.869	-0.327	-0.444	-0.012	0.007
Saudi Arabia	1.089	-0.201	-0.248	-0.144	-0.236	-0.083	-0.310	-0.257	-0.091	-0.269	-0.331
Bahrain	1.350	-0.189	-0.342	-0.362	-0.490	-0.515	-0.155	-0.227	-0.112	-0.246	-0.312
Greece	1.549	-0.359	-0.193	-0.326	-0.090	-0.072	-0.160	-0.122	-0.314	-0.070	-0.089
Israel	1.748	0.049	-0.099	-0.033	-0.125	0.017	-0.075	-0.106	0.037	-0.109	-0.049
Singapore	1.986	-0.289	-0.226	-0.149	-0.167	-0.102	-0.190	-0.219	-0.166	-0.156	-0.028
UAE	2.227	-0.633	-0.588	-0.482	-0.616	-0.455	-0.685	-0.543	-0.387	-0.400	-0.317

4.3.3   Distributions of LOP Deviations for Individual Countries

Next, distributions of LOP deviations by country are considered to better understand the changes in the degree of integration for each individual economy. Figure 4.3 presents the density functions for each country available in the sample relative to the average price across all BRI countries. Each line shows an estimate of the density of good-by-good deviations from the LOP for 1990, 2000, and 2010.

As one can see in Fig. 4.3, there is a shift of the density function to the right for a number of wealthier countries such as the Czech Republic, Hungary, Poland, and Russia. This suggests that overall goods in these countries become relatively more expensive over time. This is also reflected in the mean LOP deviations presented in Table 4.2, where prices for both non-tradeable goods and tradeable ones become relatively more expensive between 1990 and 2010 in these countries.

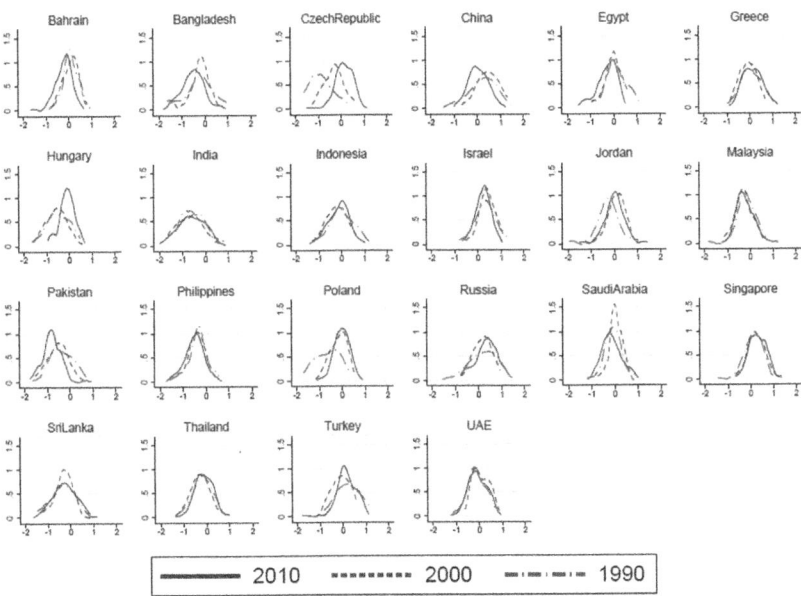

Fig. 4.3 Empirical distributions of LOP deviations for individual countries

For Bahrain, Bangladesh, China, Pakistan, and Saudi Arabia the density functions move in the opposite direction, to the left, suggesting that prices in these countries become relatively cheaper over time. As documented in Table 4.2, for most of these countries, except Saudi Arabia, this happens due to the downward adjustment of prices for both tradeables and non-tradeables over time. Finally, for a number of countries, such as Greece, India, Indonesia, Israel, Malaysia, Philippines, Singapore, Thailand, and the UAE, there are no visible changes in the position of the density functions. Furthermore, for the majority of countries, the density functions are not observed to become more highly peaked in the later periods as compared with 1990, reflecting no significant changes in the degree of integration of the BRI partners since 1990. This finding suggests the existence of barriers to price convergence across markets, which can be potentially overcome by the BRI. The development of regional connectivity along the BRI can lead to lower trade costs and the intensification of international trade, which is conducive to price convergence and can result in a higher level of market integration.

4.4   China and the Belt and Road Initiative

4.4.1   Changes in the Distribution of China's LOP Deviations Over Time

In what follows, the focus is on the price integration of China with other BRI members. The Chinese economy is of particular interest as China is the initiator of the Belt and Road Programme and a core country of the partnership. This section discusses the motivation and potential benefits for China from investment in the BRI.

In Fig. 4.4, the LOP deviations are presented for all goods and services in China relative to the BRI countries (q_{CHjt}^{BRI}), and also separately, relative to the partner countries located in Southeast Asia (q_{CHjt}^{SEA}), South Asia (q_{CHjt}^{SA}), Africa (q_{CHjt}^{AF}), and Europe (q_{CHjt}^{EU}). As shown in the first panel of Fig. 4.4, the distribution of LOP deviations for China relative to the BRI countries moves upwards to the left from 1990 to 2010. This is also evident from Table 4.3, where the mean dispersion of LOP deviations goes down from 0.605 in 1990 to 0.420 by 2010, and the mean LOP deviation falls from 0.200 in 1990 to 0.042 in 2010. This signals that prices in China did become relatively cheaper and more integrated with its BRI partners over time. However, the rest of the panels in Fig. 4.4 show that

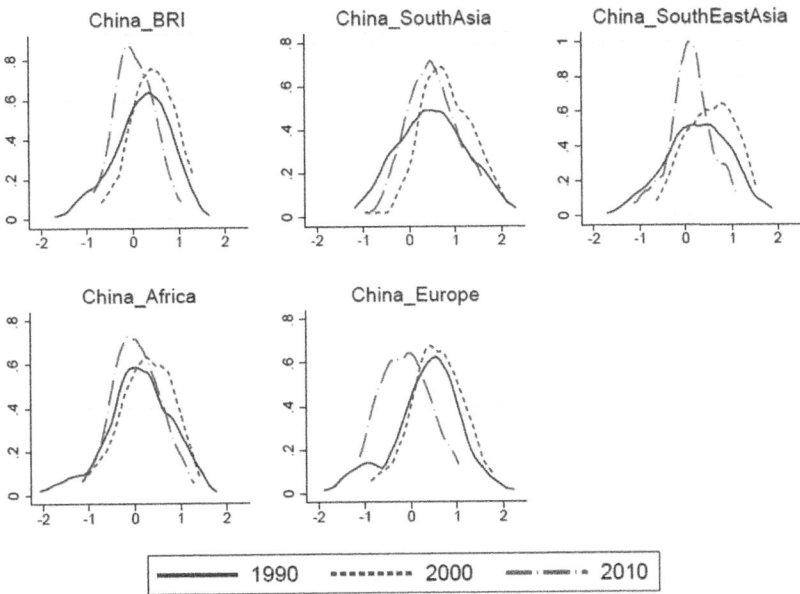

Fig. 4.4 Empirical distributions of Chinese LOP deviations

this happens mainly due to the intensified process of integration between China and Asia, while there is little evidence of China's integration with African and European markets.

In addition to the visual evidence, the Epps–Singleton (ES) test for the null of equality of the empirical distribution functions is considered. As shown in Table 4.3, the null hypothesis is rejected at the 5% significance level for the LOP deviations in China relative to the South Asian and Southeast Asian markets when distributions are compared over time. There is statistical evidence that the distributions of LOP deviations in China relative to Asian countries in 2010 and 2000 are different from the distributions of LOP deviations in 1990. Moreover, the LOP distributions for China relative to the average price in African countries are identical in 2010 (or 2000) and 1990 with a p-value of 0.185 (0.203). Similarly, the ES test reveals that the distribution of China's LOP deviations relative to its European partners was identical in 2000 and 1990 (with p-value of 0.177). However, this changed significantly between 2010 and 2000,

Table 4.3 Statistical characteristics of LOP deviation distributions

Panel A: Overall China's LOP deviations

	ES test			LOP dispersion			Mean LOP deviation		
	2010 vs 2000	2010 vs 1990	2000 vs 1990	1990	2000	2010	1990	2000	2010
China (BRI)	0.000	0.011	0.058	0.605	0.467	0.420	0.200	0.435	0.042
China (SA)	0.002	0.049	0.003	0.723	0.565	0.534	0.511	0.812	0.499
China (SEA)	0.000	0.003	0.016	0.674	0.521	0.464	0.249	0.544	0.093
China (Africa)	0.081	0.185	0.203	0.682	0.565	0.505	0.095	0.263	0.044
China (Europe)	0.000	0.004	0.117	0.717	0.560	0.532	0.333	0.568	-0.109

Panel B: LOP deviations for different types of goods

Traded vs Non-traded	ES test			LOP dispersion			Mean LOP deviation		
	2010	2000	1990	1990	2000	2010	1990	2000	2010
China (BRI) TR	0.718	0.231	0.080	0.606	0.430	0.448	0.277	0.505	0.079
China (BRI) NT				0.561	0.520	0.315	-0.014	0.245	-0.063
China (SA) TR	0.166	0.306	0.210	0.755	0.523	0.560	0.547	0.838	0.455
China (SA) NTR				0.631	0.676	0.446	0.410	0.743	0.620
China (SEA) TR	0.008	0.359	0.000	0.721	0.511	0.508	0.341	0.603	0.127
China (SEA) NTR				0.442	0.528	0.300	-0.008	0.383	0.000
China(Africa) TR	0.116	0.473	0.139	0.670	0.518	0.537	0.186	0.324	0.098
China (Africa) NTR				0.669	0.661	0.376	-0.157	0.097	-0.104
China (Europe) TR	0.504	0.005	0.088	0.681	0.528	0.530	0.402	0.687	-0.054
China (Europe) NTR				0.796	0.530	0.521	0.141	0.246	-0.260

such that the null that the distributions for China versus European partners in 2010 and 2000 (or 1990) are identical cannot be rejected at the 10% significance level, with a p-value of 0.000 (0.004) as reported in Table 4.3.

In Fig. 4.5, separate distributions for traded and non-traded goods are plotted for 2010 and 1990. These densities indicate that except for comparisons between China and its European partners, price dispersion is lower for non-tradeables as compared to tradeables, and that dispersion for both tradeables and non-tradeables becomes lower over time. This signals that the price convergence in the BRI countries, especially those located in Asia, is via income-related channels, rather than international trade. The results emphasise opportunities that the BRI can bring to all partners—investment in infrastructure development across the BRI partners can reduce trade costs, which is conducive to international trade and may trigger the process of market integration across countries.

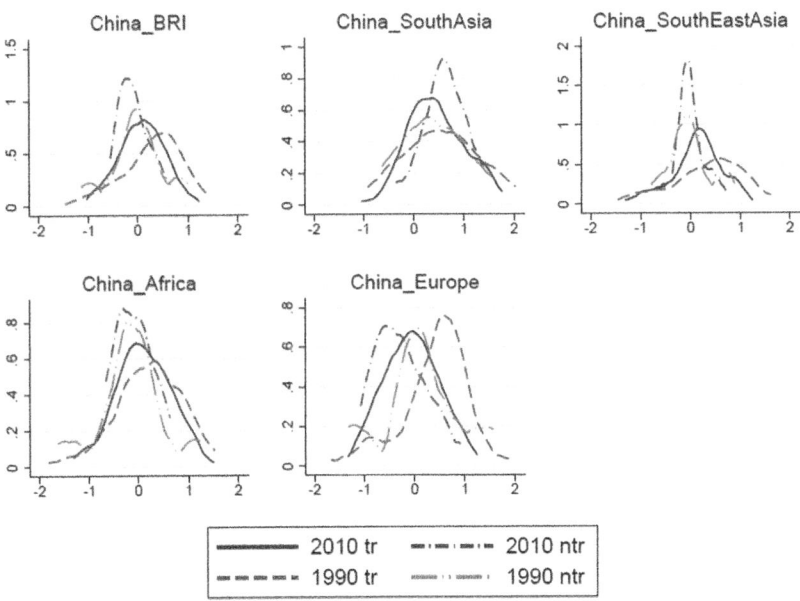

Fig. 4.5 Empirical distributions of China LOP deviations for tradeables (tr) and non-tradeables (nontr)

4.4.2   Explaining LOP Deviations in China Relative to the BRI Partners

After considering the evolution of price integration over time for different types of goods, we examine the factors that can explain the process of price convergence. In this subsection, we explore the determinants of absolute LOP deviations for China relative to its BRI partners using the basic retail price determination model proposed by Crucini, Telmer, and Zachariadis (2005) (CTZ).

The CTZ theory suggests that retail goods are produced by combining a traded input with a non-traded input, and therefore, LOP deviations are determined by the share and cost of the traded input used in the production of good j in country i at time t and the share and cost of the non-traded input required to produce the good. Thus, the LOP deviations could be explained by the traded and non-traded factor input shares and costs. Traded input is closely related to the cost of arbitrage as it captures the transportation cost of a good, while non-traded input costs are related to the productivity and wages in the country and are in line with the Balassa–Samuelson hypothesis. The hypothesis states that countries with high productivity growth experience increase in wages in both the tradeable and non-tradeable sectors of the economy, which leads to higher inflation rates and faster price convergence.

This subsection estimates the effect of tradeability and the share of non-traded inputs required for production of a good on absolute LOP deviations for China, $|q_{CH,ijt}|$ related to each BRI country i for individual good j at time t.[3] Following Glushenkova and Zachariadis (2014), tradeability measure is defined as imports $(M_{CH,ht})$ plus exports $(X_{CH,ht})$ of industry h in which good j belongs to over gross output $(Y_{CH,ht})$[4] in China in period t, $\gamma_{CH,ht} = \frac{X_{CH,ht} + M_{CH,ht}}{Y_{CH,ht}}$. The share of non-traded inputs required to produce goods in industry h in China at time t, $\alpha_{CH,ht}$ is calculated using national input–output tables from the China Industrial Productivity (CIP) Database Round 3.0 (2015). Using information on LOP deviations in China relative to the other twenty-one BRI partners

---

[3] The absolute LOP deviations for China related to each country i is defined as $|q_{CH,ijt}| = |\ln(P_{CHjt}) - \ln(P_{ijt})|$.

[4] Data on export, import, and gross output were obtained from the OECD STAN Trade in Value Added database for each industry for the period 1995–2010.

for 80 goods and service for the period 1995–2010 (23,968 observation in total) the following results have been obtained:

$$|q_{CH,ijt}| = \begin{array}{cccc} \beta_0 & +\beta_1 \gamma_{CH,ht} & +\beta_2 \alpha_{CH,ht} & +\varepsilon_{ijt} \\ 0.598 & -0.414 & 0.262 \\ (0.018) & (0.033) & (0.023) \end{array} \qquad (4.3)$$

Coefficients β_1 and β_2 capture the role of tradeable and non-tradeable inputs used to produce goods in industry h in determining LOP deviations, respectively. The estimated model includes country- and time-fixed effects as explanatory variables. Robust standard errors are reported in parentheses. Estimation results show that both coefficients β_1 and β_2 are statistically significant at the 1% level, and in line with the retail price determination model. Tradeability has a positive impact on reducing price differences; while a higher non-traded input cost is associated with the larger deviations from LOP. A negative sign of tradeability coefficient (β_1) suggests that greater price differences between China and its BRI partners can be attributed to the lower tradeability of goods due to high trade (or transportation) costs. At the same time, differences in wages and productivity of countries play important roles in explaining price differences across markets, with a higher non-traded input content share being associated with greater price differences between China and the BRI partners, as suggested by the magnitude of β_2 coefficient. Finally, the role of tradeability in lowering price dispersion between China and the BRI partners is found to be larger than the role of non-traded input cost. The impact of tradeability on China's LOP deviations equals to -0.414, while the estimated impact of non-traded input cost is 0.202. A relatively small role of non-traded inputs in explaining price dispersion between China and its partners could be associated with a certain degree of convergence in non-traded input costs, such as wages, for the BRI economies during the period under study.

The high importance of tradeability implies a key role for trade costs in determining price differences between China and the BRI economies. At the same time, the BRI countries, especially those located in Central Asia, are relatively expensive to trade with because of their geographic location, poor development of transportation modes, and low efficiency of logistics. Therefore, policies that encourage development of transportation networks and connectivity between countries could be conducive to trade integration and price convergence.

4.5   The Belt and Road Initiative and Business Environment

Next, we discuss how the BRI can promote market integration and what opportunities this programme creates for business. As was shown in previous sections, cross-border trade plays a key role in reducing price differences between countries and enhancing market integration. There are three key components of the Belt and Road Programme that directly affect trade, and consequently, market integration; namely, infrastructure development, financial integration, and political or institutional cooperation (see Fig. 4.6).

Infrastructure development is one of the core elements of the Belt and Road programme, which aims to improve connectivity of regions and enhance international trade. Currently, sea is the main transportation mode for the goods shipped from China to Central Europe, with an average transit time of about 30 days. An alternative solution for a faster delivery is air transport, which is obviously costlier for business. The improvement of transport infrastructure, for instance via expansion of the railways network, can benefit foreign trade companies, both in China and overseas. Successful implementation of the BRI can make trade between BRI economies easier, faster and, in some cases such as switching from air transport to rail, cheaper, which in turn allows business to gain easier access to new markets.

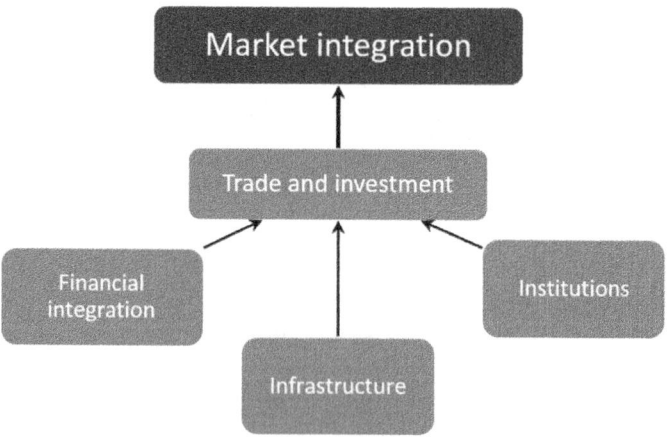

Fig. 4.6   Effect of the Belt and Road Initiative on market integration

Another important aspect of the BRI that triggers market integration and is sometimes considered as part of this process is *financial integration*. This implies a close linkage of financial markets in different economies. Financial integration enhances free movement of capital between countries and stimulates foreign direct investments. Various steps towards financial integration have been announced and carried out within the initiative, for instance, the development of new financial institutions (e.g. the Asian Infrastructure Investment Bank), promotion of cross-border economic cooperation zones, bond market development, and others. Implementation of the action plan proposed within BRI is expected to increase capital flows across borders, stimulate cross-border banking activity, simplify financial transactions across countries, and eliminate institutional barriers for further financial integration. Therefore, the BRI creates opportunities for development of financial institutions and their instruments, as well as stimulates demand for financial services.

Finally, *regulation and institutions* play important roles in market integration, and are of particular interest for the Belt and Road programme. According to the World Bank Doing Business data, some policy barriers, such as bureaucracy and complex customs procedures, are much higher in the BRI countries as compared to other regions. For instance, it takes around 50 days to comply with import regulations from Central and Western Asia, which is five times longer than in G7 countries. In this context, the BRI must explore opportunities for joint policy coordination, cross-border cooperation among tax and custom authorities, information exchange, and mutual recognition of regulations. It should be mentioned that China has already made prominent steps in this direction by signing free trade agreements with ASEAN and Eurasian Economic Union, reducing import tariffs on a wide variety of products, and signing over 100 double tax agreements worldwide. The customs tax free, tax reductions, and preferential tax rates create favourable conditions for foreign investors to access markets along the Belt and Road and stimulate international trade.

Successful implementation of the BRI with regard to the three main aspects discussed above could reduce barriers to international trade and capital movement, and therefore, create new opportunities for businesses. Participation in the BRI can bring significant benefits to the partner countries by stimulating financial integration, improving connectivity of regions, removing institutional barriers, and enhancing market integration.

4.6   Conclusions

This chapter assessed the extent of market integration across potential BRI partners, and provided new insights into the importance of the BRI for global market convergence and businesses. Two measures of international market integration such as cross-country price dispersion and deviations from the LOP have been discussed and used for the analysis.

Historical data show that price dispersion for tradeable goods was smaller than for non-tradeable ones for all periods between 1990 and 2010, consistent with the idea of existing arbitrage opportunities relevant for tradeable goods. However, the convergence test does not provide statistical evidence for the existence of overall price convergence across the BRI partners for the majority of goods. Densities of LOP deviations indicate that the degree of price integration has increased over time between 1990 and 2000, while the process of price convergence has stopped after 2000. Similarly, at the individual country level analysis no significant changes in the distributions of LOP deviations have been observed for the majority of the BRI partners, implying no considerable changes in the integration process between 2000 and 2010. In these circumstances, the BRI, which aims to increase connectivity of regions, develop transportation network between countries, and remove barriers to international market integration, can enhance the global market convergence process and be beneficial for all prospective members of the initiative.

In considering integration of China with other BRI members, it was noted that prices in China became relatively cheaper and more integrated with that of the BRI partners located in Asia, while gaps in prices between China and other regions, such as Africa and Europe, continue to widen. Regression analysis shows that price differences between China and the BRI countries can be explained by the share of non-traded inputs into production, and by tradeability of goods. The high importance of tradeability implies a key role for trade costs in determining price differences between China and the BRI countries. Taking into consideration relatively high costs of trade with most BRI countries, the Belt and Road Program opens opportunities for partner countries to catch up with each other via the development of transportation network and enhancement of trade cooperation along the 'Belt and Road'.

Finally, this chapter discussed the impacts of the BRI on business and showed that the programme's successful implementation could reduce barriers to international trade, improve connectivity of regions, stimulate cross-border capital movement, and therefore, create new opportunities for businesses.

REFERENCES

Binner, J., Chen, S.-H., Lai, K.-H., Mullineux, A., & Swofford, J. L. (2011). Do the ASEAN countries and Taiwan form a common currency area? *Journal of International Money and Finance, 30*(7), 1429–1435.

Chung, C. (2017). What are the strategic and economic implications for South Asia of China's maritime Silk Road initiative? *The Pacific Review, 31*, 1–18.

Crucini, M. J., Telmer, C. I., & Zachariadis, M. (2005). Understanding European real exchange rates. *American Economic Review, 95*(3), 724–738.

Dang, V., & Yang, Y. (2017). Assessing market integration in ASEAN with retail price data. *Pacific Economic Review, 22*(4), 510–532.

Glushenkova, M., Kourtellos, A., & Zachariadis, M. (2018). Barriers to price convergence. *Journal of Applied Econometrics, 33*(7), 1081–1097.

Glushenkova, M., & Zahcariadis, M. (2014). Law-of-one-price deviations before and after the Euro: The case of Cyprus. *Cyprus Economic Policy Review, 8*(2), 61–85.

Herrero, A., & Xu, J. (2016). *China's Belt and Road initiative: Can Europe expect trade gains?* (Bruegel Working Paper Series, Issue 5).

Ke, B., Wan, G., & Wu, L. (2003). *China's agriculture after WTO accession: Policy adjustment, trade development and market integration.* China Agricultural University Press, 51–73.

Kim, H., Oh, K. Y., & Jeong, C. W. (2005). Panel cointegration results on international capital mobility in Asian economies. *Journal of International Money and Finance, 24*, 71–82.

Lin, C.-H. (2012). The comovement between exchange rates and stock prices in the Asian emerging markets. *International Review of Economics and Finance, 22*, 161–172.

Nagayasu, J. (2010). Macroeconomic interdependence in East Asia. *Japan and the World Economy, 22*(4), 219–227.

Phillips, P. C. B., & Sul, D. (2007). Transition modeling and econometric convergence tests. *Econometrica, 75*, 1771–1855.

Villafuerte, J., Corong, E., & Zhuang, J. (2016). *The one belt, one road initiative: Impact on trade and growth.* Presented at the 19th Annual Conference on Global Economic Analysis, Washington, DC, USA.

Wang, R., & Zhou, S. (2009). Analyzing dynamic relationship between domestic and international cotton market price: Based on VECM model. *Journal of International Trade, 2*, 11–17.

Wang, Y. (2016). Price co-integration on agricultural products of China's high dependence on imports between domestic and international market: 2001–2013. *Journal of Industrial and Intelligent Information, 4*(2), 147–150.

Zhai, F. (2018). China's Belt and Road Initiative: A preliminary quantitative assessment. *Journal of Asian Economics, 55*(C), 84–92.

CHAPTER 5

Innovative Talent Development in Chinese Universities Under the Belt and Road Initiative

Li Cui, Jing Dai, Zhimei Lei, Jia Jia Lim and Zhiyu Sun

5.1 Introduction

The Belt and Road Initiative (BRI) is a macro strategy proposed by the leaders of the Chinese government under the current complex international political and economic environment. It is a concept of transnational strategic cooperation with the mission to gain mutual benefit, achieve a win-win situation for trade-cooperative parties, and to inherit and promote the ancient Silk Road. All parties in the society have responded

L. Cui · Z. Sun
School of Business, Dalian University of Technology, Panjin, China

L. Cui
China Business Executives Academy, Dalian, China

J. Dai (✉) · J. J. Lim
Nottingham University Business School China, University of Nottingham Ningbo China, Ningbo, China
e-mail: jing.dai@nottingham.edu.cn

Z. Lei
College of Mechanical Engineering, Chongqing University, Chongqing, China

© The Author(s) 2020   99
H. K. Chan et al. (eds.), *International Flows in the Belt and Road Initiative Context*, Palgrave Series in Asia and Pacific Studies,
https://doi.org/10.1007/978-981-15-3133-0_5

positively to this initiative. For instance, the Chinese government has held many relevant summits, meetings, and conferences, such as the 'Belt and Road' summit in Beijing, which led to the realisation of multifaceted cooperation between China and other countries along the 'Belt and Road'. Meanwhile, enterprises continue to innovate, not only to reduce costs, but also to support sustainable development. Meanwhile, colleges and universities remain committed to the cultivation of innovative talents, as demonstrated by the China Association of Higher Education and the Pakistan Association of Higher Education jointly holding the first China–Pakistan Academic Forum to discuss common problems faced by higher education in the implementation of the BRI.

The progress of the BRI requires not only infrastructure development and trade cooperation between countries, but also support for the cultivation of innovative talents. Outstanding talents are an important asset to firms; they are material resources to promote businesses and ultimately contribute to economic development. This is in line with BRI's goals. To cultivate innovative talents in the new era, it is challenging for colleges and universities to invest abundant manpower and material resources. It is an important responsibility and mission for China's colleges and universities to constantly improve the level of international education, to promote inclusive education, and to cultivate high-quality innovative talents that can adapt and enhance BRI processes, thereby meeting the strategic needs of the 'Belt and Road'. How do universities, as the cradle for cultivating talents, respond to the BRI? What patterns of training do they follow? What are the differences among the training programmes of different universities? Only by answering these questions can firms better understand the characteristics of talents, so as to select those that are suitable for their own business. However, there are few existing studies exploring these issues; specifically, a scientific research system is lacking.

Therefore, this study adopts qualitative research as the main research method to explore the measures adopted by different types of colleges and universities in talent cultivation under the background of the 'Belt and Road', as well as the deficiencies of these measures. Some suggestions for innovative talent cultivation are provided through comparisons of different education patterns.

This paper is organised as follows. Section 5.2 provides the literature review. Section 5.3 discusses the proposed methods and research procedures. Section 5.4 presents the analysis of three representative universities.

Finally, Sect. 5.5 provides the conclusion, research limitations, and suggestions for future studies.

5.2 LITERATURE REVIEW

This section provides the background of the BRI and innovative talent development. The linkage between the BRI and innovative talent development is also addressed in this section.

5.2.1 The Belt and Road Initiative

In September 2013, Chinese President Xi Jinping proposed the vision of jointly building the Silk Road Economic Belt during a speech at Nazarbayev University in Kazakhstan. In October of the same year, he proposed the strategic conception of the '21st Century Maritime Silk Road' on his visit to the Association of Southeast Asian Nations (ASEAN). These two ideas are jointly known as 'One Belt and One Road' initiative (Huang 2016). As soon as the Belt and Road Strategic Initiative was put forward, it has attracted huge attentions and positive responses from international communities. The BRI, which is a top-level national strategy, is designed to make full use of existing multilateral mechanisms between China and relevant countries, with the help of existing and effective regional cooperation platforms. It is expected to actively develop economic partnerships with countries along the 'Belt and Road', leading to the establishment of a community with shared interests, destiny, as well as responsibility that is characterised by mutual political trust, economic integration, and cultural tolerance (Cheng 2016). The proposal of the BRI is in line with the world's trend of multi-polarisation, economic globalisation, cultural diversity, and social informatisation. The BRI is beneficial to the expansion and deepening of China's intent of opening up, to the strengthening of mutually advantageous cooperation with Asia, Europe, Africa, and other countries worldwide, and to the progress and development of the world's economy and culture. It also reflects the rise of China's power and the requirements for the growth of its outbound investment, laying a foundation for maintaining and consolidating the relations between China and countries along the 'Belt and Road' (Sheu and Kundu 2018; Liu and Dunford 2016).

So far, research on the BRI has mainly focused on infrastructure construction, ports, cultural diversity, international relations, regional development, and other aspects. Many scholars have realised that the development of the 'Belt and Road' would bring new opportunities for regional development. For instance, Tan (2015) proposed promoting Zigong culture, which are related to industry, ecology, innovation, and well-being in the Sichuan province, to encourage the cultural and economic development of Southwest China. In addition, because the implementation of the BRI is carried out under the network of multi-country interests, it could be restricted by culture and system in the process of promoting trade facilitation (Liu et al. 2018). Huang (2016) discussed the coordination among different political systems and beliefs in Asia, Europe, and other regions and countries covered by the 'Belt and Road'. Shrestha (2017) insisted that the BRI may help improve transportation infrastructure and provide access to multiple transit points. For instance, Nepal, with its strategic geographic location, is able to become a land bridge between the world's two largest economies, China and India, as well as a gateway for China to enter South Asia. Han et al. (2018) found that trade integration has a positive impact on the countries, especially in the low- and middle-income countries. Moreover, some scholars also studied the issue of trade transport efficiency, as well as the corresponding countermeasures and suggestions (Li et al. 2018; Zeng et al. 2018).

5.2.2   Innovative Talent Development

In the twenty-first century, the competition of talents is of utmost importance in the competition between countries. The education field, being the foundation upon which innovative talents are cultivated, assumes responsibility for scientific research and innovative knowledge, especially in colleges and universities. Therefore, colleges and universities, the main source of talent, need to pay more attention to the strategy for training innovative talents. Zhuravlyova and Zhuravlyov (2015) believe that the educational environment in universities fosters knowledge assimilation and dissemination, prepares individuals to apply acquired skills, and provides an environment for the development of academic elites. Yachina (2015) revealed how university education is changing and evolving in modern society. Shutenko and Shutenko (2015) discussed that, in order to understand the driving force behind innovative practices in universities, it is necessary to deepen our understanding of established cultural norms. Under the background of the BRI, education research has become increasingly important. Improvements in the quality of teaching and innovation of education are complementary to the realisation of 'unimpeded trade'. This would support the BRI by way of cultivating international talents, and promoting talent flow and innovation sharing.

Studies by various scholars on the cultivation of innovative talents from universities vary. Some scholars focused on the course mode of universities, wherein curriculum innovation is an important way to cultivate innovative talents (Xiao 2012; Mateescu et al. 2015). Others emphasised the importance of carrying out activities and research projects in universities to cultivate innovative talents. For instance, Zhang et al. (2014) insisted that universities should organise more innovative activities, such as inviting internal and external experts to present academic reports related to some emerging topics, organising technical seminars, and encouraging students to publish papers. Other scholars suggested that one of the urgent needs of higher education is the internationalisation of research projects (Sava and Danciu 2015). They also pointed out that strengthening cooperation between industries and universities will benefit the cultivation of innovative talents. Kosogova and Araslanova (2015) suggested that if the interaction between higher education and the industry is initiated, then it is necessary to consider the experience of higher education in the Soviet Union to enhance the interaction between education and industry and give full play to the positive role of innovation projects. Stăiculescu et al. (2015) pointed out that schools have a duty to develop cooperation with enterprises to actively meet the needs of the society, professionals, and students since cooperation can bring many benefits to universities and employers.

With the ongoing development of the BRI, China's cooperation and exchanges with countries along the 'Belt and Road' continue to deepen, bringing huge development for China and even the world's economy and culture. At the same time, the need for talents to serve the BRI is increasingly urgent. It is apparent that the BRI brings not only development opportunities for the deepening reform of China's higher education, but also new challenges for the cultivation of innovative talents. In the study of talent cultivation, scholars in China mainly focus on the following aspects: (1) analysis of the education status of countries and regions that are covered by 'One Belt and One Road', (2) international exchanges and cooperation among colleges and universities, and (3) research on the development strategies of higher education (Xin and Ni 2016; Huang et al. 2015; Gao and Ma 2016). However, a majority of the studies focus on teaching languages and the internationalisation campaign, while the study of basic education activities is less considered. In addition, there is a lack of analysis on the nature of universities (such as Sino-foreign cooperative universities, local comprehensive universities, and others), as well as recommendations according to their characteristics. Therefore, this study combines grounded theory and interviews to explore the cultivation patterns of innovative talents that are practiced in different types of colleges or universities, under the background of the BRI.

5.3   METHODOLOGY

5.3.1   Research Methodology

Grounded theory is an important qualitative research method. It seeks theory from data itself through systematically collecting and analysing data. This strategy does not only deduce verifiable hypotheses from existing theories but also advocates the establishment and development of theories in data research (Brodsky 1968). Therefore, this study investigates the important aspects of innovative talent cultivation by open coding, axial coding, and selective coding in grounded theory, then designs questionnaires according to these aspects and explores the talent cultivation modes of different types of colleges and universities. After searching relevant literature, this study takes 83 articles on talent cultivation as the analysis sample. This sample covers different countries and regions, as well as different types of universities, such as key universities, local universities, and Sino-foreign joint universities, consistent with the research questions of this study. In addition, we believe that the 83 articles provide sufficient content as basis for this study.

5.3.2   Aspects of Innovative Talent Development

In this study, Nvivo11 software is used to organise and code the text of samples. The aspects related to innovative talent development are extracted. The main procedures are as follows.

1. Open coding: to extract concepts and categories

Open coding refers to the conceptual labelling of any data that can be coded in the original data. Specifically, according to certain principles, large amounts of data are narrowed step by step. Concepts and domains are used to correctly reflect the content of the data. Subsequently, the data and abstracted concepts are broken up, crushed, and re-synthesised through continuous comparison. In the initial stage of data analysis, this study used software to code the article (sentence by sentence, line by line), conceptual coding, and category extraction. Finally, we obtained 115 concepts and 21 categories.

2. Spindle coding: to extract the main categories

Spindle coding is the reanalysis and clustering of open coding information. That is, based on the open coding, genera, attributes, and dimensions are formed. Meanwhile, we need to develop and test the relationships between genera (Miles et al. 1994). Thus, this study extracted 5 main categories from 21 categories.

3. Selective coding

In the axial coding stage, with the constant broadening of the main category, the relationships between categories gradually appear. Through selective coding, the core categories are systematically linked with other categories to verify the relationships among them. Through in-depth analysis of 115 concepts, 21 categories and 5 main categories, two typical relationship structures are drawn, with the interactive comparison of the original materials. The first structure is to improve the school reform through curriculum, books, forums, research projects, and employment guidance; the second structure is to improve the talent cultivation mode through cooperation among the governments, schools, and enterprises. Based on the above typical relational structures, we identify the core category of 'collaborative cultivation inside and outside school'.

4. Determination of the aspects of innovative talent development

According to the results of the analysis, we can conclude that on the issue of talent cultivation, universities at home and abroad have paid more attention to the curriculum, conferences, scientific research projects, career guidance, and cooperation with governments, enterprises, schools, and other aspects, which are further classified into five aspects, as shown in Table 5.1.

Table 5.1 Aspects of innovative talent development and coding

Aspects	Open coding	Example for statement of the original sentence (Initial concept)
Curriculum, book	Curriculum mode improvement	I propose changes to the model, and discuss implications for teaching argumentation, developing EAP and course design
	Curriculum evaluation and control	These curricular innovations are followed by the monitoring and evaluation of the new curriculum
	Curriculum development	This paper reports on a project study that provided input into curriculum development through the use of a pedagogy of multiliteracies
	Curriculum system construction	The more effective teaching innovations in the nursing education system are in great demand
	Book selection	University libraries in Pakistan spend a large portion of their funds on buying books and these are still the most important part of libraries' collections. Selection policies and practices play fundamental role in developing a strong book collection
	Book management	Recommender systems are important tools in library websites that assists the user to find the appropriate books

Aspects	Open coding	Example for statement of the original sentence (Initial concept)
Conference, forum	Conference which benefits to improve ability	A successful workshop is that from which trainees have grasped the majority of the knowledge and skills imparted to them, with a positive progression
		The workshop described in this article was designed to develop and enhance the capacity of academic staff-in-leadership-role for the University
	Conferences which benefits to curriculum learning	Educators and students have embraced different ways to apply agile practices during their courses through lectures, games, projects, workshops and more for effective theoretical and practical learning
	Forums which benefits to broaden the horizons	The role of epistemic parts in the forums is displayed through encouraging further interaction, bonding, and attracting eligible dialogue partners
	Forums which benefits to communication	Web forums serve as communication hubs for people who work together to solve particular problems

(continued)

Table 5.1 (continued)

Aspects	Open coding	Example for statement of the original sentence (Initial concept)
Research project	Project development	Our findings and recommendations will help educators and students better coordinate and apply agile practices on industry-based projects in university contexts
		Collaborative university-industry R&D initiatives are usually organised as programs with a set of related projects associated
	Project training	In teachers also hired a line of engineering and technical personnel and rich practical experience of professional scholars as part-time teachers to the school, enterprise engineer experience, has the rich project experience, through the enterprise post demand and real project in our school is suitable for consolidating the student training project, led by enterprise engineers work with all items in the characteristic and demand which will accelerate and enhance the professionalisation process of students

Aspects	Open coding	Example for statement of the original sentence (Initial concept)
Careers guidance	Analysis of employment problem	Students are poorly informed about job opportunities, their expectations for the future are not connected with their own knowledge and abilities, they do not have a coherent career plan and encounter major barriers in the career decision process
	Analysis of employment opportunities	In the next few decades, a large number of enterprises in China will go out and extend from western provinces to Central and Western Asian countries. While promoting the economic development of relevant regions, they will also promote the employment of College students
	Employment training program development	Career intervention programs have also been shown to have a positive impact on achievement and study skills, motivation, school completion, career awareness, and career skills among low achievers
	Employment guidance curriculum setting	A Finnish study found that intensive guidance courses were more effective than subsidised employment

(continued)

Table 5.1 (continued)

Aspects	Open coding	Example for statement of the original sentence (Initial concept)
	Significance of employment guidance	This increases the importance of career guidance in helping to manage the transitions between education and working life and the transitions from one level of education to another
Cooperation with government, schools, and enterprises	Resource sharing	In this respect, the Higher Education-Business and Community Indicators (HE-BCI) for contract research, consultancy, equipment and facilities, regeneration and IP income, together with indicators for non-credit-bearing courses and KTP income inform about developments and performances
		Partners from different domains work together in collaborative partnership using each other's resources to come up with innovative solutions
	Co-constructing network platform	A growing number of intermediary organisations, such as Technology Transfer Offices (TTOs), University Incubators (UIs), and Collaborative Research Centers (CRCs) have been established to mitigate such barriers

Aspects	Open coding	Example for statement of the original sentence (Initial concept)
	Government support	The government plays a key role by funding universities and creating a research environment that meets the policy requirements of industry today
	Cooperative teaching activities	Through in-depth discussion and cooperation with enterprises in recent years, the design and implementation of school-based characteristic training courses, including personal engineering practice ability development plan, advanced workshops for scientific thinking training, advanced projects for engineering innovation training, etc.

5.4   Case Study

In this study, we first selected Dalian and Ningbo cities to conduct regional positioning studies, and analysed the differences between the two cities' regional positioning under the BRI. Then, we selected three universities with different characteristics from the two cities, the University of Nottingham Ningbo China (UNNC), Ningbo University (NU), and Dalian University of Technology (DUT). The different regions and backgrounds of the three universities have resulted in different characteristics of their innovative-talent training. Furthermore, we designed an open-ended interview questionnaire that comprehensively considers the BRI and the five extracted aspects. Finally, we interviewed teachers and other relevant people in universities as arranged in advance. The analysis framework is shown in Fig. 5.1.

5.4.1   Regional Analysis

As a national-level strategy to strengthen China's opening up and achieve mutually beneficial cooperation under the 'new normal' economy, the BRI has a major impact on the spirit of openness, especially for the cities from coastal areas. Dalian, as a core and important northeast coastal city in China with a strategic location, enjoys a natural competitive advantage to seize opportunities and generate new advantages of regional development through the BRI. First, Dalian, with superior customs clearance capability, has benefited from economic and foreign trade cooperation. Second, Dalian is a T-junction point, bridging Northeast China with Japan, South

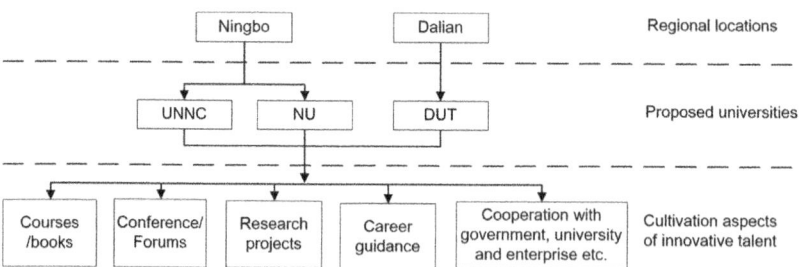

Fig. 5.1   Analysis framework of innovative talent development

Korea, Russia's Far East, and Southeast Asia. It is an important conflu-ence and transit centre for resources, capital, and technology exchanges in those regions. Driven by the BRI, Dalian actively promotes regional cooperation according to BRI guidelines. For example, the establishment of the logistics information network service between China, Japan, and Korea has reduced logistics costs. Meanwhile, the Dalian Port has become a vital node of the BRI. As the pioneer among Liaoning coastal port, Dalian Port has become the 'bridgehead' of the Northeast. This port, with its strategic locational advantages, could continue to strengthen the integration of regional economic development, opening up, the 'Belt and Road' construction, and world trade. Moreover, Dalian Port has out-standing operational performance. Notwithstanding Dalian Port is the nearest international port from Pacific Ocean, it has accumulated more than 90% of the import and export of foreign trade goods from the Northeast. Moreover, there are over 100 international and domestic ship-ping routes, covering more than 300 ports and regions worldwide. Over-all, Dalian Port is equipped with the basic conditions to establish a logis-tics channel for sea-rail intermodal transportation.

As a leading city for foreign economic and trade cooperation, Ningbo is connected with the BRI by building a port economic circle, and by setting up a bridge for trade with Central and Eastern Europe. Ningbo has four major positions in the BRI. First, Ningbo is a hub city connect-ing the 'China Silk Road Economic Belt' and the '21st Century Maritime Silk Road'. It represents a T-shape intersection as formed by the Yangtze River Golden Waterway and the North–South Sea Transportation Chan-nel. It has the geographic advantages of connecting the East and the West that radiate China's northern and southern areas. Second, Ningbo is the pivot point of the '21st Century Maritime Silk Road'. Ningbo Port, as one of China's four international deep-water hub ports and the ocean international trunk line transportation, has become an important infras-tructure between China and the national ports along the '21st Century Maritime Silk Road'. Meanwhile, Ningbo is also among the nine cities in China jointly declared as World Maritime Heritage of the 'Maritime Silk Road'; hence, it plays a supporting role in the construction of the '21st Century Maritime Silk Road'. Third, Ningbo is a leading city for eco-nomic and trade cooperation and cultural exchanges. Ningbo is one of the first batches of 14 Open Coastal Cities in China, and the eighth city with a total import and export volume exceeding 100 billion US dollars. Ningbo has a long history of frequent cultural cooperation with countries engaged in the BRI. For example, the Ningbo International Port Culture Festival was held in Ningbo in 2014. Fourth, Ningbo is one of the first five pilot cities that gained approval for cross-border trade e-commerce in China, where commodity exchange in East China is mainly carried out.

Under the BRI, with the respective natural and humanistic advantages of Dalian and Ningbo, these cities develop in accordance with the initiative by utilising their unique characteristics. The different development models of the two cities under the BRI have also influenced the talent development patterns of higher education schools in these cities. The analysis of talent development patterns of three distinctive higher education institutions are discussed in the next section.

5.4.2   Comparative Analysis of Innovative Talent Training Patterns of Universities

This study selects three different types of universities to conduct a comparative analysis of innovative talent development patterns. The first is the UNNC (located at Ningbo City), which is the first Chinese-foreign cooperative university approved by the Ministry of Education. It was founded by the University of Nottingham UK and Zhejiang Wanli College. The second type of university is exemplified by the NU from Ningbo city. NU is an emerging comprehensive local university that has developed along with the Chinese economic reform. The third type of university is represented by the DUT, located in Dalian City. It is a key vice-ministerial-level national university administered directly under the supervision of the central authorities and the Ministry of Education. It is one of the 'Four Major Engineering Colleges' in China and one of the national 'Double-First-Class' universities. These three distinctive universities are deemed to have different talent development patterns. Inspired by the BRI, this study analyses the differences in the innovative-talent-development patterns among these three universities and provides suggestions for innovative talent training in higher education schools. Through interviews with teachers from three universities, this study explores the five aspects of innovative-talent-development patterns of these three universities, involving undergraduate, postgraduate, and international students under the BRI. Based on the survey results for the three schools, the innovative-talent-development pattern of each school is summarised below.

1. The University of Nottingham Ningbo China

(1) Providing international training for Chinese students

The UNNC is a global campus that has attracted international students worldwide. The diversity of students promotes cultural exchanges through education. The university is a benchmark for Chinese-foreign cooperative education in China; it provides international training for Chinese students by providing a completely English-based teaching environment to strengthen the students' language skills and actively promote the communication between domestic and foreign students. Moreover, the university employs a strong faculty team made up of over 50 nationalities. The diverse group of talents from different parts of the world has enabled the university to compete in terms of providing international training and promoting students' ability towards internalisation.

(2) Strengthening the international cooperation with countries along the 'Belt and Road'

The UNNC has constantly established joint education programmes with a number of international schools to form an international exchange network. For example, the UNNC fully adopted the education system from the University of Nottingham UK to strengthen the internationalisation level of the school. Meanwhile, the university actively participates in the International Forum of the BRI to promote several cultural exchange activities. For example, on June 2017, the Nottingham University Business School (NUBS) China was invited to attend the 'Second China-CEEC Business School Summit' and the 'Belt and Road Countries Forum on International Business Education', to explore topics such as multinational and interregional talent exchange development mechanisms with the objective to contribute to the cultivation of international business talents. The new 'Alliance of Silk Road Business Schools' was officially launched during this forum. NUBS China is an important founding member.

(3) Encouraging international students to study and work in China

The UNNC encourages international students to study and work in China. International students at the UNNC take advantage of their language proficiency to participate in university-level projects that contribute to the BRI. For example, The Confucius Institute at the university attracts a large number of international students to visit and study at the university. It provides international students a platform to further understand the charm of the Chinese culture. The university also engages in partnerships with local universities in China, for instance, the establishment of exchange programmes for international students to promote their exchange and study in Chinese universities. Moreover, the university works closely with local enterprises as a source of internship opportunities for international students. Top-quality international students worldwide choose to stay at Ningbo after they finish their study at The UNNC; the talent pool has guaranteed human resources necessary for the BRI.

(4) Carrying out relevant academic research on the Belt and Road Initiative

The UNNC has set up the Institute of Asia and Pacific Studies (IAPS), with BRI in the priority research projects. The IAPS constantly holds symposiums and invites domestic and foreign experts to discuss academic research in fields related to the BRI, aiming to provide a platform for research projects related to the BRI for future potential cooperation. For example, in June 2017, the IAPS at the UNNC organised a seminar on 'Opportunities and Challenges of the Belt and Road Initiative'. It invited experts and scholars from the United Kingdom, Hong Kong, SAR, and domestic universities to explore the impact of the BRI on shipping, culture, innovative talents, and other fields to promote the development of the BRI.

2. Ningbo University

(1) Strengthening international student exchange

Under the BRI, NU attracts a large number of international students for further study and encourages local students to study or join exchange programmes in foreign universities. The university has set up a special scholarship to encourage international students to participate in the university's exchange programmes. The university strengthens cooperation with countries along the belt and road countries, including universities in Eastern European countries. Moreover, the university strengthens cooperative education with other countries (for instance, in the programmes called 2+2 with South Korea, and 2+2 with Russia), the mission being to encourage undergraduate students to join exchange programmes, study in partner schools, and improve their ability towards internationalisation. The participation of international students has improved the internationalisation level of Ningbo cities. For example, international students voluntarily spend their time tutoring to communicate with local students, eventually improving Ningbo's basic education facilities. Through foreign exchanges programmes, local university students are further encouraged to pursue higher education in countries along the BRI.

(2) Strengthening the employment potential of students

NU also pays great attention to students' employment prospects. NU strengthens cooperation with relevant government departments in establishing technical courses such as transportation and shipping. This provides motivation for students in relevant academic majors to acquire professional skills and motivates the school to focus on developing these academic majors. NU has held many innovation activities to cultivate students' practical ability and innovative capacity, improve the overall quality of students, and support the strategic development of the BRI and the local economic development. For example, NU held a business competition to promote the enthusiasm of undergraduates and international students, which also provided guidance for students' employment.

(3) Strengthening international cooperation

NU has held many cultural exchange activities, such as food festivals, singing, and dancing to facilitate cross-cultural understanding between various countries in order to broaden students' horizons and enhance their knowledge. Meanwhile, inter-campus visits encourage the interaction between higher education personnel to share educational resources and promote multicultural exchanges. Collaboration between several universities from Poland and other countries, and the NU for academic exchanges has promoted resource-sharing in the trade and economic major, and provided a platform for cultivating innovative talents with an international perspective.

3. Dalian University of Technology

(1) Focusing on the education of the Belt and Road Initiative

DUT highly appreciates activities relevant to the BRI and has engaged actively in the construction of the BRI. Lecturers from the DUT exchange knowledge related to the 'Belt and Road' with students during lectures, including the Belt and Road International Summit Forum and other related meetings, with the objective of encouraging students to pay attention to relevant activities of the initiative and to enhance students' sense of responsibility through consciousness of BRI-related events. In line with the Belt and Road Forum for International Cooperation held in Beijing, the book titled 'The Belt and Road of Cultural Economics', published by the DUT Press, has been translated into three languages, namely, English, Russian, and Arabic. Authoritative knowledge about the BRI is thus effectively disseminated internationally. This is of great significance to the policy formulation, theoretical research, consensus propaganda, and personnel training proposed by the BRI and also promotes China's external image. Meanwhile, for a practical contribution to the BRI, the DUT participates in professional-skills training. In the campus, lecturers deliver professional-skills training to students, promote the practical use of knowledge, and encourage students to participate in the construction of the 'Belt and Road'. Outside the campus, the DUT participates in the training of talents for the 'Belt and Road'. For example, the university continues to hold training classes for Xinjiang managerial staff. Through academics and life experiences at the university, the students benefit from a systematic form of university education, and also play active roles in promoting enterprise-university cooperation between Xinjiang and the DUT. More importantly, the university harmonises the economic and social development of Xinjiang with the university's 'scientific and technological' specialty and transports high-quality scientific and technological resources for Xinjiang's special industries. This rare interaction mechanism between training and scientific and technological exchanges of 'going out, leading back' has enabled the DUT to make greater contributions to the economic and social development of Xinjiang and the implementation of the BRI.

(2) Strengthening international cooperation among countries along the 'Belt and Road'

International cooperation motivates the DUT to participate in international exchanges and to strengthen the university in general. The DUT improves cooperation between universities in countries that are a part of the initiative by introducing talents and encouraging students from the DUT to step outside Dalian to understand the cultural environment of other countries and promote academic-exchange activities. For example, the DUT and the Belarusian State University conduct mutual visits to strengthen cultural exchanges between universities, improve the overall quality of students, and attract students from Belarus for further studies at the DUT. This helps to enhance internationalisation and diversification of cultures. To further strengthen national cooperation, the DUT actively cooperates with government departments by providing governmental guarantees. For example, the DUT strengthens cooperation with the Dalian Municipal Government through its commitment to study relevant national policies, continuously absorb new information with the mission to strengthen school competitiveness, and cultivate innovative talents.

(3) Encouraging international students to study and work in China

With close cooperation between the DUT and the countries along the BRI, more international students choose to study at the DUT. International students are able to learn the Chinese culture by exploring China's national conditions from the perspective of the BRI. Moreover, the DUT also cooperates with several international schools. Through these collaborations, the participants are able to better understand foreign innovative-talent-development patterns and learn how to disseminate this knowledge to the university. Moreover, these collaborations also help spread the culture of the DUT to foreign countries. This cultural exchange is expected to attract more international students to study at the university, further promoting cultural exchanges and personnel training, and encouraging international students to work in relevant fields in China, thereby accelerating the process of internationalisation.

(4) Promoting relevant academic research of the Belt and Road Initiative

The DUT has established the Belt and Road Higher Education Research Centre, which is currently committed to the language translation of higher education policies and regulations of countries engaged in the initiative. It facilitates the understanding of the educational environment and cultural background of the countries along the initiative and promotes talent for cultural exchange activities. Meanwhile, the 'Big-Data-based Belt and Road Cultural Co-construction and Sharing Project' declared by the DUT Press obtained RMB 7 million of financial support from the Ministry of Finance. This project is expected to take advantage of advanced digital publishing technology to integrate multi-country books, essays, multimedia, and other resources related to the 'Belt and Road' cultural research. It covers education, tourism, technology exchanges, and other fields in four languages: Chinese, English, Russian, and Arabic. This project strives to create a platform for cultural exchange for countries along the initiative and promote people-to-people exchanges for mutual cultural understanding. Multiple forums and lectures related to the 'Belt and Road' are held by the university to disseminate the activities of the 'Belt and Road' and promote multicultural exchanges.

5.5   Conclusion

Talent is the key for a successful implementation of the BRI, as well as an important resource for corporate business development. With the rapid growth of China's economy and society, local colleges and universities need to emphasise the development of innovative talents to adhere to the guidelines of the BRI. This study selected three universities: the UNNC, the NU, and the DUT to explore distinctive innovative-talent-development patterns designed to develop high-quality innovative talents that could help adapt and improve the BRI implementation process. Content analysis method was used to identify the aspects of innovative-talent development. Subsequently, open-ended questions were developed for interviewing experts. Finally, a comparative analysis of innovative-talent-training patterns was conducted.

The analytical results reveal that the innovative-talent-training patterns of the three universities have similarities and also differences. With regard to similarities, the three universities all focus on academic research of the BRI. The process of talent cultivation includes setting up research centres, expert reports, academic conferences, and others. These universities also pay significant attention to the students' employment, especially the international students. They provide varied and convenient ways to help students work in China, through employment guidance, information platform, practice base, and others. Meanwhile the differences among these three universities are as follows. First, with regard to course design, the UNNC provides English-based teaching as it has the support of foreign universities that enjoy the language advantage. Meanwhile, the NU and DUT, being Chinese universities, provide Belt-and-Road-related courses such as transportation and shipping. Second, the UNNC directly recruits local and foreign students, while the NU and the DUT implement student exchanges, including short-term and long-term exchange programmes.

In summary, different universities have different talent-training patterns in response to the BRI. This study contributes by providing references for the cultivation of innovative talents in Chinese universities, and we hereby make the following recommendations. It is advisable for universities to set up talent-training programmes in accordance with their own advantages. They need to combine their own sources and local advantages to develop distinctive talent. Students need to understand how different universities cultivate talents and decide according to their own interests and career plans. Firms need to grasp the capacity of students by understanding different talent-training patterns in different universities; only with this understanding can firms recruit the right talent for their business needs.

This study also has some limitations. We only considered three universities in two Chinese cities. Although the cities are located in the coastal areas and the universities have different characteristics, they are not representative of the vast number of universities in China. In future research, the proposed method in this study may be employed to investigate more representative universities.

REFERENCES

Brodsky, C. M. (1968). The discovery of grounded theory: Strategies for qualitative research—Psychosomatics. *Nursing Research, 17*(4), 377–380.

Cheng, L. K. (2016). Three questions on China's "Belt and Road Initiative". *China Economic Review, 40,* 309–313.

Gao, Y., & Ma, K. (2016). Study on talents demand and cultivation strategy under the "One Belt and One Road". *International Symposium on Business Cooperation & Development.* https://doi.org/10.2991/isbcd-16.2016.20.

Han, L., Han, B., Shi, X., Su, B., Lv, X., & Lei, X. (2018). Energy efficiency convergence across countries in the context of China' s Belt and Road Initiative. *Applied Energy, 213,* 112–122.

Huang, Y. (2016). Understanding China' s Belt & Road initiative: Motivation, framework and assessment. *China Economic Review, 40,* 314–321.

Huang, W. Z., Yu, L., & Zhang, S. (2015). Research on the novel information and communication technology talent training mode under the One Belt and One Road methodology. *International Conference on Education, Management and Information Technology.* https://doi.org/10.2991/icemit-15.2015.68.

Kosogova, A., & Araslanova, A. (2015). The role of the "human factor" in the context of strengthening interaction between higher education and industry in the USSR (the second half of the xx century). *Procedia—Social and Behavioral Sciences, 214,* 168–173.

Li, D., Zhao, L., Wang, C., Sun, W., & Xue, J. (2018). Selection of China' s imported grain distribution centers in the context of the Belt and Road Initiative. *Transportation Research Part E: Logistics and Transportation Review, 120,* 16–34.

Liu, A., Lu, C., & Wang, Z. (2018). The roles of cultural and institutional distance on international trade: Evidence from China's trade with the Belt and Road countries. *China Economic Review.* https://doi.org/10.1016/j.chieco.2018.10.001.

Liu, W., & Dunford, M. (2016). Inclusive globalization: Unpacking China's Belt and Road Initiative. *Area Development and Policy, 1*(3), 323–340.

Mateescu, B. N., Moraru, M., & Mărunțelu, L. C. (2015). Transdisciplinary education and human micro universe decipherment—The key to universal knowledge. *Procedia—Social and Behavioral Sciences, 180,* 389–394.

Miles, M. B., Huberman, A. M., Huberman, M. A., & Huberman, M. (1994). Qualitative data analysis: An expanded sourcebook. *Journal of Environmental Psychology, 14*(4), 336–337.

Sava, S., & Danciu, L. (2015). Students' perceptions while enrolling in transnational study programs. *Procedia—Social and Behavioral Sciences, 180,* 448–453.

Sheu, J. B., & Kundu, T. (2018). Forecasting time-varying logistics distribution flows in the One Belt-One Road strategic context. *Transportation Research Part E: Logistics and Transportation Review, 117,* 5–22.

Shrestha, M. B. (2017). Cooperation on finance between China and Nepal: Belt and Road Initiatives and investment opportunities in Nepal. *Journal of Finance & Data Science, 3*(1–4), 31–37.

Shutenko, E., & Shutenko, A. (2015). Socio-cultural trends in the development of the higher school's innovative potential. *Procedia—Social and Behavioral Sciences, 214,* 332–337.

Stăiculescu, C., Richițeanu-Năstase, E. R., & Dobrea, R. C. (2015). The university and the business environment—Partnership for education. *Procedia—Social and Behavioral Sciences, 180,* 211–218.

Tan, X. (2015). Research on the cultural Zigong from the perspective of One Belt and One Road initiative. *Journal of Studies in Social Sciences, 13,* 125–134.

Xiao, Y. (2012). International trade professional curriculum system innovation and personnel training model exploration. *Physics Procedia, 33,* 1420–1425.

Xin, Y. Y., & Ni, H. (2016). International talents connect the Belt and Road Initiative: Roles, demands and strategies. *Journal of Higher Education Management, 10*(4), 79–84.

Yachina, N. (2015). The problems of university education in Russia. *Procedia—Social and Behavioral Sciences, 191,* 2541–2545.

Zeng, Q., Wang, G. W., Qu, C., & Li, K. X. (2018). Impact of the Carat Canal on the evolution of hub ports under China's Belt and Road Initiative. *Transportation Research Part E: Logistics and Transportation Review, 117,* 96–107.

Zhuravlyova, I., & Zhuravlyov, S. (2015). Humanistic sense of creativity in professional university education: The role of creativity in forming innovation model and modernization of university training. *Procedia—Social and Behavioral Sciences, 206,* 445–454.

Zhang, J. S., Xiong, H. Q., Zhang, X., & Zhang, X. L. (2014). Demand-oriented reform on cultivating mode of safety management students. *Procedia Engineering, 84,* 178–187.

PART II

Politics

Opportunities and Risks Along the New Silk Road: Perspectives and Perceptions on the Belt and Road Initiative (BRI) from the Xinjiang Uyghur Autonomous Region

David O'Brien and Christopher B. Primiano

The Xinjiang Uyghur Autonomous Region (XUAR) is one of the key areas of development for the BRI project. Long described as the Pivot of Asia (Lattimore 1950), Xinjiang is perhaps China's most sensitive region, comprising as it does a complex ethnic makeup, vast mineral resources, and bordering eight of its neighbours in often uneasy relation. The site of serious ethnic conflict and terrorist attacks in recent years, Xinjiang has seen a major increase in security monitoring and restrictions on movement since new Party Secretary Chen Quanguo 陈全国 moved there

D. O'Brien
Faculty of East Asian Studies, Ruhr University Bochum, Bochum, Germany
e-mail: David.OBrien@ruhr-uni-bochum.de

C. B. Primiano (✉)
KIMEP University, Almaty, Kazakhstan

© The Author(s) 2020
H. K. Chan et al. (eds.), *International Flows in the Belt and Road Initiative Context*, Palgrave Series in Asia and Pacific Studies,
https://doi.org/10.1007/978-981-15-3133-0_6

127

from his previous role as Party Secretary of Tibet in August 2016. Stefanie Kam (2016) writes, "As China seeks to enhance connectivity with the economies of western neighbors through (the BRI) to enhance its influence in the region, a key challenge will be…to manage the security concerns associated with an increase in interconnectivity across its borders". While championed by local governments as vital to developing Xinjiang, BRI is also highly controversial with some in the region, particularly among some in the Uyghur ethnic majority who see it as a means to further increase Han migration into the region and deeper assimilation with Inner China.

This chapter seeks to explore the seeming contradiction of Xinjiang being both a central conduit of the new Silk Road and China's most rigidly controlled and restricted region. It will examine attitudes towards the project from people who live or have lived there from both Han and Uyghur backgrounds. Significant restrictions on movement, hugely invasive surveillance, and a campaign to prevent, according to the Chinese government, the radicalization of Uyghurs that has seen upwards of a million people interned in prison camps (Zenz 2018; Byler 2018) has become the reality of life for the citizens of Xinjiang. In this huge region comparable in the size to Western Europe, fiercely contested narratives exist over the initiative which may have an impact on its development both within Xinjiang and across its borders. This chapter seeks to explore some of these different narratives and the tensions that surround them in a region that is vital to the success of the BRI project.

6.1   A Hardening of Approach in a Border Region

The August 2016 appointment of then Tibet Party Secretary Chen Quanguo to the possibly even more sensitive position of Xinjiang Party Secretary saw a significant hardening of approach by the Chinese government. Chen would set in place new highly restrictive policies on religious practice (Zhang et al. 2018), culminating in campaign that would see upwards of a million people interned without trial and a highly sophisticated, highly invasive system of surveillance put in place to monitor the population, especially the Uyghur population (Byler 2019). For Beijing, Xinjiang is both a land of enormous potential containing a large proportion of China's oil and gas, but also conflict and instability. It is a region where China perceives a direct threat to its authority arising from what it calls the "three evil forces" of terrorism, separatism, and religious extremism (Zhao 2017). Edward Schwark (2019) writes that "regardless of whether Beijing faces a genuine threat of terrorism in its western regions, the Party evidently sees the problem as serious enough to implement a costly and utterly inhumane policy of mass internment and brainwashing". In a recent article, Sean Roberts uses Foucault's theory of biopolitics to examine the situation in Xinjiang. For Foucault a defining characteristic of the nation state is to make all politics into biopolitics: the focus on individual bodies, or citizens, as either productive or unproductive, with unproductive bodies being viewed as dangerous, needing to be "banished, excluded, and repressed" (2018, p. 286). Roberts makes a convincing case that this is exactly what is happening in Xinjiang.

While the region has experienced rapid economic development, the XUAR has also witnessed numerous violent incidents—the most serious being the 2009 ethnic riots in Urumqi which left almost 200 people dead. Serious violence in 2014 also spread to "Inner China" with attacks in Beijing and Kunming causing serious concern and anxiety (Zhang et al. 2018). The attack on Kunming train station in which 33 people were killed and over 100 injured by knife-wielding Uyghur attackers caused particular shock across the nation as it was the first major terrorist attack to take place in "Inner China" (Neild 2014).

6.2   Location of Xinjiang and Context

Given that Xinjiang is the place where several of the BRI "economic corridors" start and it is from Xinjiang where Chinese trains reach Western Europe, it is a springboard for several of the BRI's main routes. Due to the monumental role that Xinjiang plays in determining the success of the BRI, having stability in Xinjiang is of utmost importance. This is a major challenge. Central Asia, which borders Xinjiang contains a number of politically unstable countries and regions. In addition, three of the countries that Xinjiang borders (India, Pakistan, and Russia) are nuclear powers.

A major element of the BRI is to develop the poorer regions of western China and follows on from a number of initiatives most notably the "Western Development Plan/Develop the West" (Xibu da kaifa 西部大开发) campaign that began in 1999. Since the 1990s, the CCP has sought to develop western China and make it look more like inner China by demolishing anything that is old (i.e. areas where Uyghurs have preserved their houses and buildings for a long time) and constructing new and modern facilities that are widespread throughout much of China. Uyghur dwellings have been demolished by the Chinese government in the quest to remove Uyghur culture, as it is distinctive from Han culture and serves as a threat. Such Uyghur culture should not, according to the Chinese government, be on display. Xinjiang should look like another place in China—not like someplace in Muslim Central Asia (Chin and Burge 2019). According to the logic of the Develop the West campaign, spending on infrastructure projects will solve problems in Xinjiang—and, according to that reasoning, Uyghurs ought to appreciate this (Primiano 2013, pp. 456–459).

Pantucci and Lain argue that addressing the uneven development in the western part of China is a central objective of the BRI (2016, p. 17). In keeping with decades of CCP thinking, the Chinese government espouses the view that economic development will result in a politically stable Xinjiang in which people (i.e. Uyghurs) are content (2016, p. 17). Since the end of the Cold War in the early 1990s, the Chinese government has sought to have Xinjiang connect westward with trade and infrastructure in the province (Clarke 2016, p. 565). In other words, for the past three decades the Chinese government has sought to capitalize on economic development in Central Asia (Garver 2005, p. 206). Specifically regarding the BRI, Clarke goes on to add that it "is an outgrowth of Beijing's decades-long agenda to integrate Xinjiang and utilize this region's unique geopolitical position to facilitate a China-centric Eurasian geo-economic system" (2016, p. 563). Due to both the political volatility of the Middle East and how Central Asia is closer to China in distance than the Middle East, in recent years China has sought to tap into Central Asia for resources with BRI and obtain oil and natural resources from places geographically closer to China.

6.3   Perception of Uyghurs as Lacking Modernity and Thus in Need of BRI Assistance

It is common for the Chinese media and the Chinese government to present Xinjiang as a place that is backward in terms of development. As such, the living conditions of Uyghurs in Xinjiang, according to the argument, need to be brought into the modern era. *The Global Times*, China's most vociferously nationalist newspaper, offers the view that "China is upping its efforts to tear down mud-and-brick makeshift houses and replace them with modern concrete apartments in slum areas of the northwestern city Urumqi" (*Global Times*, May 17, 2011). Stating that the living areas of Uyghurs are "slum areas" and consisting of "mud-and-brick makeshift houses" presents the view that these are not modern people; instead, they are a primitive people. *The Global Times* article asserted that the "slum areas" in which approximately 250,000 Uyghurs live "are considered the breeding ground for the resentment which underpinned the deadly [July 5, 2009] riots that rocked the city [of Urumqi]". This view assumes that the 2009 riot was caused by the ostensibly poor economic conditions of the Uyghurs. After all, the CCP has often stated that grievances in Xinjiang are due to poverty and lack of development. This is the Chinese government's universal claim: poverty is the root cause of all things that it views as bad. In other words, tackle poverty, and all problems will be solved. Following that thinking, the Chinese government claims that the BRI, with its focus on infrastructure, will serve to alleviate tensions in other countries as well. In short, according to the CCP, the BRI is a win-win in which all involved will benefit (see "Visions and Actions" 2015).

The discontent among Uyghurs in Xinjiang goes beyond economic development. Many Uyghurs feel that their culture and language are threatened. In the southern city of Hotan posters appeared in 2018 telling Uyghurs not to grow a beard or wear the hijab. For some Uyghur men, having such a beard is essential to their sense of identity. Likewise, for some Uyghur women, wearing a hijab is also central to their sense of identity. Those attending mosque must sign their names before entering and there are surveillance cameras inside. Given that the Chinese government views Uyghurs who practice Islam as posing a threat to China, signing one's name before entering mosque is providing the Chinese government with an opportunity to question the loyalty of such individuals to China. On the streets of numerous cities in Xinjiang there are metal detectors for Uyghurs, and Uyghurs are asked to show their identification card and have their cell phone inspected (Buckley, September 8, 2018). Additionally massive Han migration from elsewhere in China to the province has resulted in Uyghurs feeling their culture is being diluted. In 1949, the Han population in Xinjiang comprised approximately six per cent of the province's total. With railroad construction, the Han population increased significantly. By 2000, Han Chinese comprised 40% of the population in Xinjiang. Infrastructure projects have played a major role in the changing demographics of Xinjiang.

6.4   2009 Crisis of Authority

The riots which erupted in Urumqi on a hot summer evening in early July 2009 were the worst outbreak of social unrest in China since the Tiananmen Square protests in 1989 (O'Brien 2015). They would have wide-ranging repercussions for local and national government that are still being felt, and brought the issue of political legitimacy in China's border regions to international attention. Beijing anticipated trouble in the highly sensitive year of 2009 sending 80,000 troops and People's Armed Police (PAP) officers to Tibet and Xinjiang ahead of the 60th anniversary of the founding of the People's Republic of China, the 50th anniversary of the failed Tibetan Insurrection in 1959 and the 20th anniversary of the 1989 student protest in Beijing (Lam 2009). Yet it seems despite the security presence, local and national leadership were taken completely by surprise by the riots and left reeling as they struggled to regain control of the streets in the days that followed (O'Brien 2015). According to official figures the riots which broke out in a number of areas in the city of 2.3 million people, left 197 people dead and over 1700 injured (Ansfield and Wong 2009).

Months later in a further crisis for CCP authority on September 3, 2009, a large and angry crowd of Han protestors gathered in front of government buildings in People's Square in the centre of Urumqi demanding the government improve security in the city and across the region. In an attempt to calm the situation the then Xinjiang Party Secretary Wang Lequan 王乐泉 appeared on the balcony and through a megaphone told those gathered below that the government was working hard to improve things. As he attempted to speak, however, he was shouted down by the crowd, some of whom pelted him with plastic bottles (O'Brien 2015). The significance of such a senior official being attacked by an angry crowd cannot be overstated. For Wang, a member of the central Politburo and who had at that stage been XUAR Party Secretary for 15 years to be shouted down by a clearly furious Han crowd was a most serious development and demonstrated that the relationship between the authorities and the Han population of Xinjiang as "partners in stability" (Cliff 2010) is far from secure.

6.5 CURRENT SITUATION OF INTERNMENT CAMPS

The Chinese government has established hundreds of detention camps in Xinjiang since 2017 in which in excess of one million Uyghurs and other Muslim ethnic minorities are being detained without being charged or information on when they will be released. At these camps, detainees must attend lectures lauding the CCP and praise the CCP, with the objective being to have Uyghurs abandon their religion (Buckley, September 8, 2018). While the Chinese government and Chinese media claim that this action is preventing violence from Uyghurs against Han Chinese, one person who was detained at one of these camps and was interviewed by the *New York Times* had a very different view: "That was a place that will breed vengeful feelings", he told the *Times* (Buckley, September 8, 2018). According to another Uyghur man who said he was in such a camp, detainees had to listen to lectures in which they were told they should not support radical Islam, Uyghur independence, or anything that goes against the CCP. According to this former detainee the main points that camp officials emphasized in these lectures were that the CCP is great, Chinese culture is great, and Uyghurs are not an advanced culture (Buckley, September 8, 2018).

Some United Nations member states have attempted to raise the issue of these internment camps and the inhumane treatment that is directed at Uyghurs in Xinjiang. In December, the United Nations said it had received "credible reports" that 1.1 million Uyghurs, Kazakhs, and Hui were being held in the camps as asked to be given access (Kuo 2019). Also in late 2018, reports began to emerge that inmates of the internment camps were being subjected to forced labour. An *Associated Press* report tracked down shipments which had originated in a camp in southern Xinjiang ended with an American sportswear supplier (AP 2018). Initially denying that the camps existed, in late 2018 the Chinese government dramatically changed position to one where it celebrated the "achievements" of the camps. "Many trainees have said they were previously affected by extremist thought and had never participated in such kinds of arts and sports activities. Now they realize how colourful life can be", Xinjiang Governor Shohrat Zakir told journalists in an interview in October 2018 (Kuo 2018). Due to the power of China in international politics, as will be discussed below with the case of Greece (see Cumming-Bruce and Sengupta 2017), few governments are willing to criticize China on such a sensitive issue for the Chinese government, as such governments do not want China to cut it off from loans or political support. The result is the lack of action to end the internment camps in Xinjiang and the suffering of the Uyghurs. The almost complete absence of criticism from the Muslim world has been especially striking.

6.6   Migration, Language, and Identity

According to the 2010 *Census of China*, Uyghurs make up 45.84% of the population of Xinjiang, numbering 8,345,622 people. The Han make up 40.48% with 7,489,919. Next come the Kazakhs who number just over 1 million, followed by: Mongol; Dongxiang; Tajik; Xibe; Manchu; Tuja; Uzbek; Russian; Miao; Tibetan; Zhuang; Daur; Tatar; and Salar. During the 1990s, Xinjiang's Han population grew by 31.6%, mostly due to inward migration. This is twice the rate of the indigenous ethnic groups (up 15.9%), who supposedly benefit from more relaxed family planning policies compared to the rest of China (Howell and Fan 2011). As the official number of Han does not consider the large number of military and security personnel based in the region, the actual number of Han is likely to now number a majority.

In a very broad sense the Han in Xinjiang can be divided into three distinct groupings: early migrants, those that arrived in Xinjiang between the 1950s and 1970s; the sons, daughters, and grandchildren of these early migrants; and more recently arrived economic migrants who have been drawn to Xinjiang in large numbers from poorer surrounding provinces since the 2000s (O'Brien 2015). Large-scale Han in migration has seen the ethnic makeup of the province radically altered since the establishment of the People's Republic of China when Han numbered just over 6% of the population (Howell and Fan 2011).

Today the provincial capital, Urumqi, and most of Xinjiang's cities are increasingly identical in appearance to any city in inner China. The same department stores, mobile phone retailers, and fast food noodle joints that render Chinese cities so homogenous are present here on almost every street. Across Xinjiang, traditional Uyghur buildings have been demolished, bazaars closed, and much of what remains of its rich architectural heritage has been repackaged into sterile tourist destinations. The once famed Silk Road city of Kashgar has seen its old quarter almost entirely rebuilt in the past five years with Uyghur residents whose families had lived there for generations relocated to suburbs on the edge of the city in favour of stalls selling cheap tourist trinkets and coffee shops. It remains eerily empty, however, as the tourists who were expected, have failed to come due to concerns of safety and terrorist attack.

Åshild Kolås (2004) writes that official government narratives highlighting the perceived "backwardness" of minority nationalities have produced an effect of distinguishing each group according to specific ethnic markers, such as dress, arts and crafts, architecture, typical livelihoods, festivals, and religious practices; these markers become "stereotypes [which] are currently being commodified for the sake of tourism, through the making of ethnic arts and handicrafts products, the creation of staged ethnic tourist performances, marketed locally and in ethnic theme parks and tourist villages" (2004, p. 281). This commodification of ethnic cultures is also visible throughout China from airport departure lounges selling ethnic dolls, to the "ethnic restaurants" found in most major cities where (usually Han) girls in colourful "traditional costumes" wait on tables and sometimes sing and dance, to the markets of Lhasa where largely Hui and Han merchants sell every imaginable "authentic" Tibetan souvenirs. In twenty-first-century China to be ethnic is to be something simpler, from another time, something which can be experienced—at a price—as an antidote to the pressurized modern Han world of competition, pollution, and overcrowding (O'Brien and Brown 2019).

6.7   Language Equality and the Law

While all of China's ethnic minorities have a constitutional right to use and be taught in their own language, a string of new policies since 2000 have accelerated the shift to an all-Chinese education, culminating in March 2002 with the introduction of Chinese from the third year in primary schools and the decision to teach almost all courses at Xinjiang University and other higher-level institutions in Chinese. There are mixed views among minorities on these policies. On the one hand, many parents and students resent having to learn Chinese, while on the other hand they recognize that the ability to speak Chinese greatly increases the chance of receiving a better education and securing good employment (Becquelin 2004). The government is aiming to institute Mandarin Chinese as the main teaching language in all schools across the region. Apart from being a controversial and contentious policy, problems have also arisen in the implementation of this policy, not the least of which is the shortage of teachers in predominantly Uyghur areas who can speak Mandarin Chinese proficiently (Taynen 2006).

Historically the Uyghur played a vital role on the Silk Road as interpreters of language, culture, and customs. They were the traditional middlemen for much of the commerce in the region. Indeed they played such an important role linguistically that at the time of the Mongol conquest of the Uyghur, the Mongols who did not have a written language had the Uyghur alphabet adapted for Mongolian imperial use (Morgan 1982; cited in Smith 2019). It is a linguistic legacy that the Uyghurs are rightly proud of. Indeed, it was an Uyghur, the celebrated scholar and lexicographer Mahmud al Kashgari who composed the first comprehensive dictionary of Turkic languages, the *Dīwān Lughāt al-Turk* ("Compendium of the languages of the Turks") in 1072–74 (Yong and Ping 2008). Yet today the Uyghur language is increasingly sidelined by the authorities in Xinjiang.

Lawyer and political scientist Barry Sautman has written that "China's ethnic law reflects a tension found in many states between notions of redistributive justice that addresses a broad spectrum of minority concerns and a more narrow instrumental outlook" (Sautman 1999). Ethnic law in the People's Republic has two main aims: (1) reversing the traditional Chinese pattern of marginalization and subordination of non-Han peoples. In other words, minority rights schemes generally provide the same legal entitlements to minority persons as are received by majority persons such individual group rights are necessary to preserve minority ethnic identity and compensate for discrimination. And (2) constructing a minority elite whose loyalty is essential to political stability (ibid.).

While the degree which minority rights are implemented in China is contested, and this implementation varies throughout the country, there are in fact some 280 national and local laws and regulations that concern minority protection in marriage, elections, culture, inheritance, education, language, family planning, and other areas (Sautman 1999). The main sources of these laws are the 1982 Constitution and the 1984 Law on Regional Autonomy. In fact, the very first article of the Constitution states that "it is necessary to combat big-nation chauvinism, mainly Han chauvinism", while Article 4 proclaims the equality of nationalities and prohibits acts based on "great nation chauvinism" (*da minzu zhuyi* 大民族主义) and "local nationalism" (ibid., p. 290).

6.8   Voices from the Region

Tensions that exist around government suppression of opposition, migration, language, and culture as well as genuine fears of violence and terrorist attacks are at the core of much of the contestation that exists over the Belt and Road Initiative. In spite of the difficulties in carrying out empirical work in Xinjiang, scholars such as Gladney (1998), Rudelson (1997), Smith (2002), and Dautcher (2009) have nevertheless researched Uyghur identity while others have focused on issues of ethnicity, nationalism, and state-minority relations (Bovingdon 2010; Gladney 2004; Moneyhon 2003; Mackerras 2001). Tom Cliff (2016) has recently published important anthropological work on the Han identity and experience which helps fill an obvious gap in the literature. There has also been a focus on the economic situation in Xinjiang in the overall context of the Chinese economic reform and opening up and the increasing social and economic ties with its Central Asian neighbours (Clarke 2011; Howell and Fan 2011).

However, the ability of scholars to carry out such empirical work is becoming ever harder and more fraught with potential legal and ethical threats. For this chapter, the authors have spoken with a small number of Han and Uyghur who are in a position to speak relatively freely, for reasons of living outside of China or because of established connections that ensure trust and safety. Yet the reality for both Uyghur and Han living in Xinjiang is that talking to foreign researchers is extremely risky and could result in severe repercussions. Indeed, for Uyghurs living in Xinjiang today even having a foreigner's name among their WeChat contacts is grounds to be sent to the internment camps (personal correspondents).

Despite these challenges, this chapter seeks to provide some insight into the current reality through the voices of people who live there. One such voice is that of Mr. Wu, a 42-year-old local government official from one of Xinjiang's more prosperous cities, who remains positive that despite the tensions that are so evident, Xinjiang will benefit greatly from the initiative. Mr. Wu[1] provided the following view to us during an interview:

> This initiative is the priority of our government, both local and national, and it will help transform our Xinjiang. My parents came here in the 1950s as part of the campaign to open the West. They endured great hardship

---

[1] All names a pseudonyms.

along with many others. In those days, this was a very poor place, life was hard, there were no hospitals, no roads, everything was a hard struggle. Since then, great progress has been made but there is still much poverty. Many of the Uyghur people and also the Han are still very poor. If you go outside the cities the poverty is still very bad in Xinjiang. The terrorists exploit the poor people, promise that they will make it better but they won't. Only government investment in the region, big investment can solve the problems. It is all of our duty to develop the region and to safeguard it against attack from outside and inside and that it what this BRI Initiative is aiming to do. (Personal Interview)

Mr. Wu is in many ways the elite in Xinjiang, from a family who arrived here in the 1950s, the original settlers of the region after "liberation" who have scaled the social hierarchy to positions of power and influence. He belongs to the old Xinjiang people, *lao Xinjiang ren* (老新疆人), who often refer to themselves as the "local people" *bendiren* (本地人). This term *bendiren* is not however used to refer to the indigenous Uyghur but only ever to the decedents of Han migrants who arrived in the 1950s and 60s. As Tom Cliff (2016) has described, these third or fourth generation migrants have particularly strong connection networks *guanxi wang* (关系网), giving them an edge over more recent arrivals in terms of access to jobs. They are also more likely to identify Xinjiang as their home and less likely to see their presence as temporary, to be followed by a return to their home once they have earned some money.

More recent arrivals often express frustration with their lack of opportunities relative to *bendiren*. In their view, they have not had access to the advantages and connection networks that are vital in their view to the achievement of success. To have good connections, *guanxi* (关系), in this context is to have relationships with the right sort of person for the right situation. Often, the right sort of person is a government official who will require some sort of favour in return (Cliff 2016). Some of these more recent arrivals express a clear view that BRI will only really benefit those with the right connections, those who form part of the local network of *bendiren*.

Mr. Li, a 34-year-old property developer who moved to Xinjiang from Hunan eight years ago feels that BRI will benefit the region but the opportunities will not be equally divided.

This will bring a lot of money to the region. You can already see so many new things being built. There are huge opportunities. But the way things work here, it is very old fashioned. In Xinjiang, it's all about having the connections, and they (*bendiren*) control so much. They have been here for so long, their parents even grandparents too and they have managed to control so much. (Personal Interview)

6.9   The Uyghur Voice

For all of the reasons described above, Uyghur voices are growing silent. Either as a deliberate strategy to assimilate and crush dissent or as more benign policy that aims to modernize, the reality is in fact the Uyghur community increasingly has no say in how their homeland is being transformed, as they have been almost completely isolated and silenced. For the Uyghur voice, we have to turn to those living outside of China, but even those who live outside of China fear for their family members still living inside of China only speak on condition of anonymity. One 32-year-old Uyghur woman now living in Europe explains (Personal Interview).

> My heart and the hearts of all the Uyghurs are broken. We have been crushed and the world does not care. The world does not care because they want the Chinese money, the money from this BRI. It is immoral. (Personal Interview)

Another Uyghur man, living in America, expresses the following:

> When I was in school I was taught the Han were better than us, that they would help us to develop and to become like them and then things would be better. They don't want us to be like them, they don't want us to be there. They want it for themselves. (Personal Interview)

Since the Chinese government has essentially become a bank for many countries to obtain a loan from, this places China in a position of strength when dealing with such states. Developing countries are always in need of capital, but if such countries are accused of human rights violations or do not support neoliberal economic policies, such countries are not viewed favorably by the IMF or the World Bank. China has a different approach. Instead of prioritizing human rights or neoliberalism, China provides loans to such countries, which then go to Chinese state-owned enterprises (SOEs). As a result of developing countries taking such loans from China, these governments then do not criticize China on human rights abuses. This explains the silence of many developing countries—especially Muslim countries—regarding the human rights abuses that China is caring out on its Uyghur population, a position not limited to developing countries. The Greek government, after being shunned by the West, decided to look to China for loans, which China has provided. Due to taking such loans, the Greek government in June of 2017 used its veto power to prevent the EU from issuing a resolution critical of China's crackdown on civil society—not the Uyghurs (Cumming-Bruce and Sengupta 2017). This is not something unique to the Greek government; instead, governments around the world that are lacking capital are looking to China for such capital. In July 2019 Pakistan, Saudi Arabia, Russia, Nigeria, and North Korea along with 32 other countries came out in China's defence in the United Nations, after envoys from 22 nations sharply criticized Beijing over the Xinjiang camps (AFP 2019). Many of the countries backing China already have deep economic connections or gain to benefit from the BRI. As a result, China has leverage with such countries, for said countries know that they need to adhere to China's views in order to keep the flow of cash coming.

6.10   Conclusion and Implications

The Chinese government has stated that BRI is a win-win for all involved. As China provides loans to other countries, this will only increase China's power and make such countries more dependent upon China. Due to that, as the case of Greece and other countries demonstrate, such states do not criticize China regarding the human rights abuses of Uyghurs (Cumming-Bruce and Sengupta 2017). There has been some criticism of China regarding its treatment of Uyghurs, but that has come from Western states—not countries with a majority Muslim population. In terms of the BRI benefiting Uyghurs, it is difficult to make the case that it will do so. As pointed out, if Uyghurs are in contact with people from abroad, the Chinese government views them with suspicion and thus are subject to internment. If the Chinese government develops Xinjiang in terms of infrastructure on the one hand, and on the other brutally represses the Uyghur population, then that will only exacerbate tensions between Uyghurs and Han. This is a fundamental contradiction of the BRI in Xinjiang.

As argued in the chapter, resentment among Uyghurs will only continue with such draconian policies. As demonstrated in ample cases throughout history, an oppressed people will seek to end such oppression. Moreover, both freedom of movement and the government allowing room for private enterprise are essential for commerce. Because Xinjiang today is essentially a police state, this is not conducive to businesses and the movement of goods and people. Multinational companies and international actors who engage in commerce are concerned about political stability, and the way Xinjiang is being governed does not reassure foreign investors that such an investment will pay off.

The Chinese government calls the BRI "a bid to enhance regional connectivity and embrace a brighter future" (Xinhua 2015).[2] According to this official narrative it "aims to promote the orderly and free flow of economic factors, highly efficient allocation of resources and deep integration of markets by enhancing connectivity of Asian, European and African continents and their adjacent seas". Addressing a conference in 2015, Xi Jinping stated that "[t]he programs of development will be open and inclusive, not exclusive. They will be a real chorus comprising all countries along the routes, not a solo for China itself" (ibid.). In Xinjiang however, China is engaging in security and surveillance which can only be understood in terms of a social engineering project. James Leibold (2018) has written that the internment camps, which the Chinese government first denied before claiming they are harmless vocational training centres intended to improve Uyghur's language skills and employability, reveal a familiar logic. This logic has long defined the Chinese state's relationship with its public and is in Leibold's words a "paternalistic approach that pathologizes deviant thought and behaviour and then tries to forcefully transform them". In Xinjiang the Chinese government will accept no interference in or negative comment on this project. They will not subject themselves to any moral judgement on the imprisonment of hundreds of thousands of men and women without trial or process. In the official narrative BRI is open and inclusive, but within China itself to express any alternative view is immediate grounds for heavy punishment. Perhaps Xinjiang, long a bell-weather for the strength of central government control, where the old Chinese proverb, "the mountains are high and the emperor far away" *shan gao, huangdi yuan* (山高皇帝远) has always had

---

[2] Taken from State Council of China Website http://english.gov.cn/news/top_news/2015/03/28/content_281475079055789.htm.

a particular resonance, is an indicator of how little in the way of discussion or opposition it will accept directed towards its strategy internally or externally.

Few can deny that the CCP has brought great economic development to Xinjiang. What was once one of the poorest regions in China is now relatively prosperous, at least compared to other regions in western China, yet despite this Xinjiang is a region where CCP power is threatened and where it will use the full extent of its vast security system to enforce its will. BRI partners will be watching closely to see how things develop in a region the Chinese call their New Domain (the literal meaning of Xinjiang 新疆).

References

AFP. (2019, July 12). *37 countries defend China over Xinjiang in UN letter.* https://www.msn.com/en-us/news/world/37-countries-defend-china-over-xinjiang-in-un-letter/ar-AAEeKmQ. Accessed 20 July 2019.

AP. (2018, December 19). https://apnews.com/99016849cddb4b99a048b863b52c28cb.

Ansfield, J., & Wong, E. (2009, August 25). Chinese president visits volatile Xinjiang. *New York Times.* http://www.nytimes.com/2009/08/26/world/asia/26china.html?_r=1. Accessed 28 Dec 2018.

Becquelin, N. (2004). Staged development in Xinjiang. *The China Quarterly, 178,* 358–378.

Bovingdon, G. (2010). *The Uyghurs: Strangers in their own land.* New York: Columbia University Press.

Buckley, C. (2018, September 8). China is detaining Muslims in vast numbers. The goal: 'Transformation'. *New York Times.* https://www.nytimes.com/2018/09/08/world/asia/china-uighur-muslim-detention-camp.html. Accessed 4 Jan 2019.

Byler, D. (2018, September 24). China distances children from families to subdue Muslim west. *New York Times.* https://www.nytimes.com/aponline/2018/09/20/world/asia/ap-as-china-orphans-of-the-state-abridged.html?utm_source=UW%20News%20Subscribers&utm_campaign=82ea5b6dac-UW_Today&utm_medium=email&utm_term=0_0707cbc3f9-82ea5b6dac-308907373&login=email&auth=login-email. Accessed 28 Dec 2018.

Byler, D. (2019, April 11). China's hi-tech war on its Muslim minority. *The Guardian.* https://www.theguardian.com/news/2019/apr/11/china-hi-tech-war-on-muslim-minority-xinjiang-uighurs-surveillance-face-recognition. Accessed 16 Apr 2019.

Chin, J., & Burge, C. (2019, March 20). After mass detentions, China razes Muslim communities to build a loyal city. *Wall Street Journal.*

Clarke, M. (2011). *Xinjiang and China's rise in Central Asia 1949–2009: A history.* London: Routledge.

Clarke, M. (2016). 'One belt, one road' and China's emerging Afghanistan dilemma. *Australian Journal of International Affairs, 70*(5), 563–579.

Cliff, T. (2010, April). China's partnership of stability in Xinjiang. *East Asia Forum.* http://www.eastasiaforum.org/2010/04/23/chinas-partnership-of-stability-in-xinjiang. Accessed 29 Apr 2012.

Cliff, T. (2016). *Oil and water: Being Han in Xinjiang.* Chicago: University of Chicago Press.

Cumming-Bruce, N., & Sengupta, S. (2017, June 19). In Greece, China finds an ally against human rights criticism. *The New York Times.* https://www.nytimes.com/2017/06/19/world/europe/china-human-rights-greece-united-nations.html. Accessed 20 July 2019.

Dautcher, J. (2009). *Down a narrow road: Identity and masculinity in a Uyghur community in Xinjiang China.* Cambridge: Harvard University Press.

Garver, J. (2005). China's influence in Central and South Asia: Is it increasing? In D. Shambaugh (Ed.), *Power shift: China and Asia's new dynamics* (pp. 205–227). Berkeley and Los Angeles: University of California Press.

Gladney, D. C. (1998). *Ethnic identity in China: The making of a Muslim nationality.* Forth Worth: Harcourt Brace.

Gladney, D. C. (2004). The Chinese program of development and control 1798–2001. In S. Frederick Starr (Ed.), *Xinjiang: China's Muslim Borderland* (pp. 101–120). Armonk: M.E. Sharpe.

Global Times. (2011, May 17). Urumqi's sweeping slum makeover gathers steam. http://www.globaltimes.cn/content/655953.shtml. Accessed 4 Jan 2019.

Howell, A., & Cindy Fan, C. (2011). Migration and inequality in Xinjiang: A survey of Han and Uyghur migrants in Urumqi. *Eurasian Geography and Economics, 52*(1), 119–139.

Kam, S. (2016, July 4). Making China's 'one belt, one road' more Turkic. *The Diplomat.* https://thediplomat.com/2016/07/making-chinas-one-belt-one-road-more-turkic/. Accessed 11 Jan 2019.

Kolås, Å. (2004). Tourism and the making of place in Shangri-La. *Tourism and Geographies, 6*(3), 262–278.

Kuo, L. (2018, October 16). Internment camps make Uighurs' life more colourful, says Xinjiang governor. *The Guardian.* https://www.theguardian.com/world/2018/oct/16/internment-camps-make-uighurs-life-more-colourful-says-xinjiang-governor. Accessed 17 Jan 2019.

Kuo, L. (2019, January 11). 'If you enter a camp you never come out': Inside China's war on Islam. *The Guardian.* https://www.theguardian.com/world/

2019/jan/11/if-you-enter-a-camp-you-never-come-out-inside-chinas-war-on-islam. Accessed 14 Jan 2019.

Lam, W. (2009, July 9). Hu gets a black eye in Uurmchi. *Asia Sentinel.* http://www.asiasentinel.com/index.php?option=com_content&task=view& id=1963&Itemid=373. Accessed 13 Apr 2012.

Lattimore, O. (1950). *Pivot of Asia: Sinkiang and the inner Asian frontiers of China and Russia.* Boston: Little Brown.

Leibold, J. (2018, November 28). Mind control in China has a very long history. *New York Times.* https://www.nytimes.com/2018/11/28/opinion/china-reeducation-mind-control-xinjiang.html. Accessed 28 Dec 2018.

Mackerras, C. (2001). Xinjiang at the turn of the century: The causes of separatism. *Central Asian Survey, 20*(3), 289–303.

Moneyhon, M. (2003). China's great western development project in Xinjiang: Economic palliative, or political trojan horse? *Denver Journal of International Law and Policy, 31*(3), 491–523.

National Development and Reform Commission. (2015). *Visions and actions on jointly building Silk Road economic belt and 21st-century maritime Silk Road.* http://en.ndrc.gov.cn/newsrelease/201503/t20150330_669367.html. Accessed 4 Jan 2019.

Neild, B. (2014, March 2). Kunming train station attack: China horrified as mass stabbinga leave dozens dead. *The Guardian.* https://www.theguardian.com/world/2014/mar/02/china-mass-stabbings-yunnan-kunming-rail-station. Accessed 16 Jan 2019.

O'Brien, D. (2015). If there is harmony in the house there will be order in the nation: An exploration of the Han Chinese as political actors in Xinjiang. In A. Hayes & M. Clarke (Eds.), *Inside China's new frontier: Analysing space, place and power in China's North-West.* London: Routledge.

O'Brien, D., & Brown, M. S. (2019). Harmony and dancing on the new frontier: The idealisation and commodification of ethnic 'otherness' in Xinjiang. In C. Ludwig & Y.-W. Wang (Eds.), *Reclaiming identity and (re)materialising pasts: Approaches to heritage conservation in China.* Amsterdam: Amsterdam University Press.

Pantucci, R., & Lain, S. (2016). Domestic drivers for the Belt and Road initiative. *Whitehall Papers, 88*(1), 17–29.

Philips, T. (2017, February 20). China troops stage show of force in Xinjiang and vow to 'relentlessly beat separatists. *The Guardian.* https://www.theguardian.com/world/2017/feb/20/chinese-troops-stage-show-of-force-in-xinjiang-and-vow-to-relentlessly-beat-separatists. Accessed 28 Dec 2018.

Primiano, C. B. (2013). China under stress: The Xinjiang question. *International Politics, 50*(3), 455–473.

Roberts, S. R. (2018). The biopolitics of China's "war on terror" and the exclusion of the Uyghurs. *Critical Asian Studies, 50*(2), 232–258. https://doi.org/10.1080/14672715.2018.1454111.

Rudelson, J. J. (1997). *Oasis identities: Uyghur nationalism along China's silk road.* New York: Columbia University Press.

Sautman, B. (1999). Ethnic law and minority rights in China: Progress and constraints. *Law and Policy, 21*(3), 283–315.

Schwarck, E. (2019, January 11). The failure of China's security policy in Xinjiang. *RUSI Newsbrief.* https://rusi.org/publication/newsbrief/failure-chinas-security-policy-xinjiang. Accessed 14 Jan 2019.

Smith, J. F. (2002). Making culture matter: Symbolic spatial and social boundaries between Uyghurs and Han Chinese. *Asian Ethnicity, 3*(2), 153–174.

Smith, N. (2019). Why "accommodation" makes the most sense for China's long-term Xinjiang strategy. *Journal of Muslim Minority Affairs.* https://doi.org/10.1080/13602004.2019.1688517.

Taynen, J. (2006). Interpreters, arbiters or outsiders: The role of the *Min kao Han* in Xinjiang society. *Journal of Muslim Minority Affairs, 26*(1), 45–60.

Xinhua. (2015, March 28). *China unveils acton plan on Belt and Road initiative.* http://english.gov.cn/news/top_news/2015/03/28/content_281475079055789.htm. Accessed 28 Dec 2018.

Yong, H., & Ping, J. (2008). *Chinese lexicography: A history from 1046 BC to AD 1911.* Oxford: Oxford University Press.

Zenz, A. (2018). *New evidence for China's Xinjiang re-education campaign.* Jamestown Foundation. https://jamestown.org/program/evidence-for-chinas-political-re-education-campaign-in-xinjiang/. Accessed 28 Dec 2018.

Zhang, X., Brown, M., & O'Brien, D. (2018, September). 'No CCP, no new China': Discourses of pastoral power in the Xinjiang region of China. *China Quarterly, 235,* 784–803.

Zhao, L. (2017, June 19). Xi vows to fight 'three evil forces' of terrorism, separatism and extremism. *The Telegraph.* https://www.telegraph.co.uk/news/world/china-watch/politics/xi-fights-three-evil-forces-terrorism-separatism-extremism/. Accessed 11 Jan 2019.

CHAPTER 7

Players or Spectators? Central Asia's Role in BRI

Neil Collins

Central Asia was historically the venue for the 'Great Game' between the British and Russian empires (Meyer and Brysac 1999; Morrison 2014). It was then subsumed by the Soviet Union. In 1991, the collapse of that Union led to the creation of five independent republics. The new states have been keen to assert their autonomy and improve their economies. They all share the need to negotiate their independence in relation to the two large countries in their neighbourhood—China and Russia. The Belt and Road Initiative (BRI), announced in 2013 in the largest Central Asian state, Kazakhstan, by President Xi, in some cases challenged and in others complemented the strategies they have adopted to date.

On the face of it, the BRI appears to be the 'win-win' opportunity as China presents it. Enhanced infrastructure and new financing could transform the region economically with improved roads, rail routes, pipelines, industrial parks and special economic zones. The five Central Asian states—Kazakhstan, Kyrgyzstan, Tajikistan, Turkmenistan and

N. Collins (✉)
Nazarbayev University, Astana, Kazakhstan
e-mail: neil.collins@nu.edu.kz

© The Author(s) 2020
H. K. Chan et al. (eds.), *International Flows in the Belt and Road Initiative Context*, Palgrave Series in Asia and Pacific Studies,
https://doi.org/10.1007/978-981-15-3133-0_7

147

Uzbekistan—are an essential geographical focus of the project. An alternative future, however, may be that the states of Central Asia simply provide the infrastructural basis through which the needs of Europe and China are addressed while they remain mere transit points.

This chapter will look at the dilemma facing Central Asian states to explore what strategies are available to maximise the benefits of the BRI. It will do this in the context of changing geopolitical and economic considerations. It will also seek to explain why projections about the success of the BRI would be more accurate if they disaggregated the idea of Central Asia. As Vakulchuk and Overland (2019, p. 116) suggest, "Central Asia, while a culturally and historically homogenous region, remains one of the least integrated regions in the world". Despite the formation of several trade, military and political blocs covering some of the republics, there is no regional organisation other than the Central Asian Nuclear-Weapon-Free Zone. Thus, China operates through bilateral agreements.

Although trade existed between Central Asia and China before the original Silk Road, it was during the Han Dynasty (207 B.C.–220 A.D.) that the concept took off. In an interesting parallel for today, from a Chinese point of view, it was the large trading surpluses enjoyed by the Han Dynasty that encouraged the initial development of the route. As well as an economic opportunity, Central Asia has historically also been a geostrategic concern, as its nomads raided and invaded the outskirts of the Han Dynasty's empire and later Tsarists and Bolsheviks posed a threat. Until the end of the Middle Ages, the new routes also facilitated Chinese military incursions into Central Asia, as well as trade.

The original Silk Road was constituted by the fusion of existing trade routes, but its scale was its innovative function. The first expansion of routes was from both the West and the South, but the symbolic height in the current narrative was the route from Xi'an to Rome. Necessarily, the goods exchanged were of sufficient value to absorb the high fixed costs of the 'road'. Thus, while silk, lacquerware, jade, etc., travelled west, Central Asian horses were much sought after in China. From Europe the Chinese imported garlic, castor oil and most frequently gold. At the same time commodities, people, philosophies, religions and culture were also exchanged.

The BRI is an ever-expanding project but the elements on which this chapter concentrates are:

- New Eurasia Land Bridge Economic Corridor: China, Kazakhstan, Russia, Poland and on to Rotterdam;
- Middle Corridor through China, Kazakhstan, Azerbaijan, Georgia and Turkey; and
- China–Central Asia–West Asia Economic Corridor: China, Kyrgyzstan, Uzbekistan, Iran, Turkey towards the Mediterranean Sea.

The exact routes of each are still somewhat vague but, according to Sági and Engelberth (2018, p. 22), "[t]he missing facts and specifics in the action plan do not indicate the signs of weaknesses but reflect the approach that the strategy must be flexibly executed since participants' goals might change in the future".

There are technical issues around the different gauges applied to railway tracks on the various points of the proposed routes, but these can be accommodated if the content of the trains is sufficiently valuable.[1] Passenger traffic, for example, may use trains capable of adjusting gauge. Similarly, dry dock facilities for transferring goods between systems are increasingly efficient. More critical, perhaps, is the competition between routes. The use of the Caspian Sea port of Aktau in Kazakhstan, for instance, would bypass Russia altogether. Once unloaded, containers would be shipped across the Caspian before continuing towards Europe through the Caucasus. Such a development would profoundly impact on the market for railway enterprises.

An essential consideration for Central Asian states is the extent to which the BRI simply facilitates rapid transit for goods between China and Europe as opposed to providing the basis for local businesses to develop. China is building more infrastructure in Central Asia than any other country or international agency, but the long-term question remains as to who will benefit and who will not. Frankopan (2018, p. 100) suggests that the economic case for the BRI is overstated: "Overland routes… are quicker than shipping by sea, but it's hard to see many goods to which the benefits of speed will be decisive".

---

[1] Central Asian countries and Russia use a 1520-millimetre gauge that differs from Europe and China.

He argues that sea-based transportation has and will retain a decisive economic advantage. Based on costing figures in Russia, Belarus and Kazakhstan, others have greater faith in the new railway network, suggesting that "[t]ariff rates for railway transportation on the New Silk Road are now highly competitive in relation to sea transportation... Taking into account the additional cost savings owing to a shorter delivery time, the railway can be an optimal solution for an even greater number of customers" (Van Leijen 2018a, n.p.).

The range of goods for which rail is financially justified will increase, it is argued, as return traffic volumes reach higher levels. Even at the present costings, the difference between land and sea transportation for a standard 40-foot container travelling from China to Europe is less than €875. Rail companies see even this gap diminishing, making the new land crossing competitive with shipping costs.

Much of the BRI-related funding is going to the oil, coal and gas sectors and is aimed primarily at harnessing the supply line of fossil fuels to the People's Republic of China (PRC), which raises important ethical questions about the development of renewable energy, an area in which China has been actively involved.

7.1   CHANGING GEOPOLITICS

With the collapse of the Soviet Union, Central Asia became the focus of renewed attention from world powers. It was as if the 'Great Game' had been given a modern form with several new players (Collins and Bekenova 2016). Each of the participants, though new to the game, was prepared to participate in it for the benefit of both internal and external audiences. The new regimes sought the recognition that came from engaging with China, Russia, the United States and the EU to legitimise themselves in the eyes of sceptical and divided domestic populations. The continued need to differentiate themselves for purposes of home consumption delimits the extent to which the five former Soviet republics can act in harmony. Added to these dynamics have been tensions over water resources, ageing Soviet-era infrastructure and tax and other impediments to cross-border trade.

a. Kazakhstan

As Marshall (2016, p. 15) points out:

Kazakhstan leans towards Russia diplomatically, and its large Russian-minority population is well integrated. Of the five, all but Tajikistan have joined Russia in the new Eurasian Economic Union [EEU][2]... which celebrated its first anniversary in January 2016... all five are in a military alliance with Russia called the Collective Security Treaty Organisation.

These formal alliances are, however, not the full story. As Ambrosio and Lange (2015, p. 537) assert, "Kazakhstan sits at the crossroads of Eurasia. Its foreign policy is heavily defined by geopolitics – the intersection of geography and international politics". Relations with Russia are particularly complex (Lewis 2018). Each of the new states relies on their northern neighbour to differing degrees but all see that their dependence on Russia needs to be reduced. For some, notably Kazakhstan, the presence of a substantial ethnic Russian population means that a delicate redefining of the relations between former constituent parts of the Soviet Union and its still powerful successor is a crucial task: "On several occasions, the Russian authorities have delivered harsh criticism of the treatment of Kazakhstan's Russian population... [As] the most powerful regional actor in this part of the world, Russia has considerable economic muscle to underpin its demands, since Kazakhstan is far more dependent on its trade with Russia than vice versa" (Kolsto 2018, n.p.).

As a counterpoint to Russia, renewed relationships with China were among the obvious options for several of the Central Asian states. The attraction of developing the China link is that a "key element in this process has been its promotion of a normative framework for interstate relations... which privileges the maintenance of 'stability' and non-interference in the 'internal affairs' of member states" (Clarke 2018, p. 34).

Nevertheless, traditional concerns relating to China's economic and military ambitions initially circumscribed any new arrangements. Even though the rhetoric has since changed, popular sentiment remains an issue

---

[2] The EEU consists of Russia, Kazakhstan, Belarus, Kyrgyzstan and Armenia. No customs are levied on goods travelling within the customs union. EEU members impose a standard external tariff on products entering the union.

in each of the Central Asian states regarding the PRC. As Burkhanova and Chen (2016, p. 2129) suggest, "the Central Asian populace does not look on Beijing's inroads into the region as favourably as do official discourses from Central Asian governments".

Public opinion survey evidence from the former Soviet republics is subject to some reservations (e.g. the openness of respondents) but the thrust of its findings are impressive. The result that only one in six Kazakh citizens sees China as a 'friendly country' is telling and much lower than the equivalent score for Russia (Bhavna 2018, p.101)

As with the post-1991 republics, the Chinese government's interests in Central Asia also have a domestic basis. Political stability, the Communist Party monopoly and national unity are top of its agenda. The BRI is, in part, about China's strategic goal of reducing its dependence on maritime routes the PRC deems potentially unreliable. But, as Indeo (2018, p. 136) suggests, it is also aimed at "the enhancement of a security buffer between Xinjiang… and Central Asia to preserve China's western provinces from instability and threats linked to Islamist terrorism".

Stable and predictable conditions on its borders are crucial, and the PRC has managed to resolve all the territorial issues that once caused tensions in the region. Similarly, though their rivalry is apparent:

As China is increasingly asserting its security, economic, and institutional interests in Central Asia… [i]ncreased mutual concern for continued regional stability has encouraged Beijing and Moscow to coordinate their policies across a wide range of issue areas. Stability allows them to focus attention and resources on each of their different geostrategic priorities. (Odgaard 2017, p. 41)

The remaining 'threat' in Central Asia, in Beijing's view, arises from religious extremists. China suggests that the cause of 'East Turkestan independence', promoted on the basis of transnational Islamic militancy, is a substantial threat to its territorial integrity. As will be discussed below, part of the PRC's response has been repressive and ethnically based, but there has also been the attempt to counter separatism with economic development. In part, the BRI is related to this policy: a more prosperous Xinjiang will be less susceptible to separatism. Similarly, Odgaard (2017, p. 45) suggests there is "serious destabilization in one or more Central Asian states… where deteriorating socio-economic welfare combined with rising militant Islamism poses a threat to unity and security in Kyrgyzstan,

Uzbekistan, and Tajikistan". Thus, prosperity would serve the interest of China's neighbours and reduce the potential for overspill.

For Kazakhstan's political elite, the fact that the BRI will pass through its territory, whichever options are eventually activated, provides an opportunity to leverage the country's strategic position for economic returns: "In Kazakhstan's propaganda, the idea of being a bridge from east to west is a consistent theme, so the symbolism of the Chinese initiative is powerful" (Ambrosio and Lange 2015, p. 538).

The government is determined to reduce Kazakhstan's dependence on natural resources such as oil. Ideally, a diversified Kazakh economy, rather than just additional infrastructure and transit fees, would be the result of greater engagement with China on its signature project. The dangers are, however, developing too great a dependence on China both politically and economically. The Kazakhstan political class are all too aware of the risks of losing popular support. As a result, there is a pattern of "elite manoeuvring between the lure of Chinese investments and appeasing popular anxieties about China's growing influence" (Dave and Kobayashi 2018, p. 267).

A vital boundary case dilemma for the government of Kazakhstan involves the situation in Xinjiang. There are many similarities between the two areas both culturally and geographically. Kazakhstan used to be at the margins of the USSR and Xinjiang was incorporated into China under the Han dynasty. Importantly though, while Kazakhstan is now an independent state, Xinjiang remains part of China. Its Uyghur inhabitants are coming under immense pressure from the Chinese authorities to measure up to Beijing's accepted definition of loyal citizens. As part of the campaign to 'stabilise' Xinjiang and counter a potential terrorist threat, many Uyghurs are subject to incarceration in so-called 're-education centres'. For the Kazakh government, the situation in Xinjiang represents a potential dilemma as many of its citizens are Uyghurs, especially in areas near the Chinese frontier, and there is a substantial Kazakh population in Xinjiang. The publicity surrounding divided families, contentious extraditions and the treatment of some Muslims holding dual citizenship have generated public sympathy for the Uyghurs, but the Kazakh establishment has held firm with the letter and spirit of its commitment to China.

The Shanghai Cooperation Organisation (SCO), initially the 'Shanghai Five',[3] was set up in 1997 to counter 'national separatism, religious extremism and international terrorism'. As President Nazarbayev of Kazhakstan was reported to suggest, "the most significant achievement of the 'Shanghai Five' summit is to have successfully solved the problems left during the era of the former Soviet Union, such as border issues as well as political and military tensions" (*People's Daily* 2001, n.p.).

The SCO reaffirmed its commitment to resisting 'separatist groups' from any other member state. This undertaking was later codified at a meeting chaired by President Nazarbayev. The SCO member states will:

- prevent any attempts on their territories to prepare and commit acts of terror, including those aimed against the interests of other countries;
- not provide asylum for individuals, accused or suspected of conducting terrorist, separatist and extremist activity; and,
- extradite such individuals at respective requests on the part of another SCO member state in strict accordance with the current legislation of the member states (*China Daily* 2005).

The SCO declaration has been at the core of the relationship between the PRC and Kazakhstan despite signs of public discontent, not only over the issues surrounding Uyghurs, but also over fears of Chinese land purchases and liberalised visa regulations.

b. Uzbekistan

If Kazakhstan's attitude towards China has shown some ambivalence, that of Uzbekistan has been much more straightforwardly cooperative.

Since independence, Uzbekistan has strived to balance Russian regional ambition and military power, China's rising socioeconomic presence and uncertainties regarding the U.S. government sustaining a high-profile presence in Central Asia... Uzbekistan has refrained from joining Moscow-led

---

[3] Includes Kazakhstan, Kyrgyzstan, Tajikistan, Russia and China. Uzbekistan joined in 2001, followed by India and Pakistan in 2017.

institutions, while enthusiastically pursuing opportunities within the framework of Beijing's Silk Road initiatives. (Starr and Cornell 2018, p. 59)

This approach is particularly true of the post-Karimov regime, following the smooth succession of 2016. Uzbekistan is the most populous country in Central Asia and the only one that shares borders with all the others, as well as Afghanistan. The new regime has committed itself to both political and economic liberalisation and sees the BRI as a potential advantage. In its list of policy priorities, the government of President Shavkat Mirziyoyev highlighted "implementing a balanced and constructive foreign policy, creating a security belt around Uzbekistan, achieving stability, and maintaining friendly relations with its neighbouring countries" (Rakhimov 2017, n.p.).

More than half the population is under the age of 30, and at least 10% of the people have emigrated to find work abroad. Foreign direct investment levels are way behind those of Kazakhstan, so the offer of Chinese input is particularly attractive. Already, China has overtaken Russia as the largest exporter to Uzbekistan, and the two countries have signed a 'comprehensive strategic partnership'. Uzbekistan has also kept the EEU at arm's length and is cautious about involvement with the Collective Security Treaty Organisation. Nevertheless, for Russia, Uzbekistan remains an important element in what it sees as its natural sphere of influence and the post-Karimov period has seen a noticeable increase in diplomatic links between the two countries. As with other Central Asian states, however, Uzbek authorities have had to deal with public misgivings about China by tightening migration controls and introducing strict limits on the number of Chinese workers in the country. However, "a major reason for Uzbekistan's 'rapprochement' strategy towards neighbours has been to take greater advantage of China's OBOR [i.e. BRI] initiative and maximise Uzbekistan's potential as a transport corridor and economic partner" (Starr and Cornell 2018, p. 62).

The BRI has already given rise to substantial investments in rail infrastructure linking Xinjiang to the populous Fergana Valley. Still, the Uzbek regime shows some caution in relation to the BRI.

c. Tajikistan

Tajikistan is the smallest and weakest Central Asian state, and more of its citizens live in exile than at home. After being granted independence in 1991, it endured a long and bitter civil war (1992–1997), the aftermath of which is still evident. As will be discussed below, Tajikistan is very vulnerable to business slowdowns in China and, particularly, economic conditions in Russia. To add to this problem, its security is literally threatened by the situation in neighbouring Afghanistan, and Russian troops are based near its capital city Dushanbe. The geopolitical situation could hardly be starker. Tajikistan, a vulnerable nation, and China, a major world power, share a 430-km border. Historically, dating back to the Silk Road, relations between Tajiks and Chinese have been predominantly mutually beneficial. In contrast, it has been Tajikistan's relations with other Central Asian republics that have been friction-full.

China invested $273 million in Tajikistan in 2015 – representing a 160 per cent increase over 2014 Chinese investment, and vastly outstripping other sources of foreign investment. The two countries are also deepening military cooperation [including]... new border checkpoints... to ensure stability [and] protecting... the [BRI]... of which Tajikistan lies on the southern border. (Long 2017, n.p.)

The regime in Tajikistan reflects the former Soviet attitude to social control even more than the other Central Asian republics. In 2018, for instance, it issued a 367-page official clothing guide for women (*Voices on Central Asia* 2018). The control exercised over its citizens is tight and reflects, in part, a suspicion of the Muslim faith and its possible links to Islamic militants. The Tajik government's concern with Islamic fundamentalism has as much to do with its relations with Russia as China. In April 2017, an attack in Saint Petersburg suggested a potential link between migrants from Tajikistan and terrorism. Later that year, police in the Russian Federation detained 250 Tajiks following an incident in a shopping centre in Moscow. Despite these incidents, relations with Russia appear to be positive overall, and Moscow continues to invest in mineral development projects in Tajikistan.

Like some of the other Central Asian countries, notably Kazakhstan, Tajikistan's official position is to have a multi-vectored foreign policy. In practice, this means taking an active part in as many international organisations as feasible and asserting the country's independence by maintaining relations with as broad a range of other states as possible. For Tajikistan, this involves its post-Soviet, Turkic and Islamic neighbours as well as Russia and China. It also means courting good relations with the EU and the United States. In the short term, its improving interactions with Uzbekistan, which have brought new cross-border contacts, may be the most influential both in practical terms and as a model for change to a less authoritarian regime.

As with the other republics, popular sentiment in relation to China is not favourable. Some of the negativity dates to border disputes. In recent decades, Tajikistan conceded mineral-rich territory in exchange for a partial debt write-off. Few Tajiks regarded the deal as fair, and the BRI has done little to alter public opinion despite elite enthusiasm for the project.

d. Kyrgyzstan

Kyrgyzstan is of less interest to China due to the small size of its market and its geographic location. Nonetheless, the Chinese presence in the country has had significant repercussions due to the economic projects promoted by Beijing (Vakulchuk and Overland 2019, p. 121).

As with Tajikistan, Kyrgyzstan may be tempted to accept China's 'win-win' promise in relation to the BRI and by the chance to decrease its security and economic reliance on Russia. It would also potentially improve the existing transportation infrastructure, which offers poor connection between the south and north of the country. The government must, however, cope with similar prospects of debt distress and popular dissent: "Unlike Western states, China is able to deliver financing quickly, without the lengthy process of detailed feasibility and socio-political and environmental effects of investments" (Dave and Kobayashi 2018, p. 271).

Nevertheless, the regime has to deal with disquiet at widespread poverty as well as ethnic divisions between north and south. Kyrgyz–Uzbek and Kyrgyz–Tajik interethnic animosity are particularly marked in parts of the state. In 2005 and 2010, these issues led to violence and regime change. China is also subject to negative public opinion: "After the announcement of BRI, the number of Chinese migrants... grew rapidly due to increased Chinese investment... [Kyrgyzstan] witnessed a rise in alarmist attitudes toward China and a surge in incidents against Chinese migrants... anti-Chinese sentiment has led to protests" (Garibov 2018, p. 143). In 2016, a suicide bomb attack reportedly carried out by the Turkestan Islamic Party targeted the Chinese Embassy in Bishkek.

The Kyrgyz political system has become more stable since the presidential election in October 2017 brought Sooronbay Zheenbekov to office, and a package of constitutional reforms followed.

Some of the projects in Kyrgyzstan, such as the China–Kyrgyzstan–Uzbekistan railway scheme which has been under discussion for 20 years, predate the BRI but have been stalled. The main benefit to Kyrgyzstan is that renewed infrastructural developments, both of rail and road, offer greater access to Afghanistan, Iran and Turkey, as well as China. Eventually, the BRI promises ready use of the ports of the Persian Gulf and the Pacific. Some of the barriers, however, are political, such as the previously strained relations between Kyrgyzstan and Uzbekistan. Also, while Kyrgyz policymakers want to link as many cities as possible, the Chinese want to privilege transit and minimise network expansion. The core issue is whether the gauge of any new track would be as China prefers—its own 1435-mm—or the Russian model—1520-mm. The latter would facilitate greater Kyrgyz integration, but the narrower Chinese model is compatible with Iran and Turkey, the other main participants on the projected southern route (Wu 2018). Some Russian commentators suggest that the gauge issue has more military implications: "they argue that narrow-gauge rail lines extended from China into Central Asia would allow Beijing to quickly dispatch its troops to the region in a potential future conflict with Moscow" (Sharip 2017, n.p.).

A more immediate risk is that of debt distress arising from BRI funding. According to a study by the Centre for Global Development, both Tajikistan and Kyrgyzstan already have unsustainable levels of sovereign debt (Hurley et al. 2018).

e. Turkmenistan

The territory that is now Turkmenistan was a vital part of the Old Silk Road. The present republic is, however, a poor and autocratic country with often difficult relations with its neighbours. Ironically, tensions with Russia and the former Soviet Central Asian republics have increased reliance on China. Its official non-aligned stance has been an asset that has been used to foster links with Beijing. As *Stratfor* (2017, n.p.) suggests, "[t]he expansion of the Central Asia-China pipeline will eventually enable Turkmenistan to export its natural gas to new markets, but in the meantime, it will be more reliant on China".

Turkmenistan's ambitions for the BRI include new electricity infrastructure and industrial zones. Currently, the pre-BRI 3666-km pipeline facilitating the export of gas is its major asset as it may allow some diversification of customers and frees Turkmenistan of its previous reliance on Russia. Significantly, the EU plans to start importing Turkmen gas in 2019. Political tensions with its neighbours remain, however, as signalled by the absence of the Turkmen leader from the summit of Central Asian heads of state in Astana in March 2018.

7.2   CHANGING ECONOMIES

The Central Asian economies are diverse in terms of size and strength, but for each the continued growth of the Chinese market is a significant factor. Between 1991 and 2016, the trade turnover between China and Central Asia grew exponentially, though this change was more marked in some states than others (Vakulchuk and Overland 2019).

a. Kazakhstan

> For China, Kazakhstan represents an important component of its New Silk Road project economically and, potentially, militarily. (Ambrosio and Lange 2015, p. 538)

For Kazakhstan, being a landlocked country has been a significant economic challenge. The BRI could potentially overcome this, with up to 80% of China's trade with Europe crossing Kazakh territory. Already, the dry port Khorgos has attracted significant investments from major PRC-owned companies. The facility in Kazakhstan is 49% owned by China. It has, in effect, halved the time it takes Chinese goods to reach Europe.

China's economic interests in Kazakhstan are substantial, and the volume of trade is steadily increasing. Chinese banks and investment companies have a growing presence in construction, agriculture and the processing industries. In relation to the extractive sector, Chinese companies control close to 25% of Kazakhstan's oil production and, together with gas exporters, have a major interest in its pipeline infrastructure.

China is increasingly significant but, for Kazakhstan, the BRI will also improve its steadily growing relationship with the EU, its major export partner with over 46% of the Kazakh export trade. The new infrastructure will address the European wish to have access to diverse energy resources, as well as Kazakhstan's ambition to diversify its energy routes.

Europe's approach to Central Asia generally reflects a naive wish for "a politically and economically stable and predictable space on its doorstep which observes European parliamentary standards and consists of organized and mutually cooperative states built on the EU model" (Laumulin 2000, n.p.).

But, as Nursultan Nazarbayev, Kazakhstan's president from 1991 to 2019, made clear, the country is guided by the principle of 'economy first and then politics'. The BRI offers more tangible benefits in this approach than political reform. Indeed, the EU seems to acknowledge this approach in terms of its relations with Kazakhstan: "the EU only promotes some elements of broad liberal democracy, in particular, puts less emphasis on political rights and horizontal accountability… it places more emphasis on state administrative capacity and less on socio-economic development" (Bossuyt and Kubicek 2015, p. 182).

For the EU, it is not Central Asia per se that is of primary importance but rather the Caspian states whose oil and gas resources are seen as necessary for maintaining European energy security. This outlook is reinforced by the unreliability of Russia in political terms. Thus, Kazakhstan, especially if the trans-Caspian route of the BRI is expanded, is the EU's most significant partner in the region. Further, as Kourmanova (2015, p. 7) suggests, "in Kazakhstan, the EU is increasingly perceived as a single actor in foreign policy, but this perception is still incipient: member states still have varying approaches and priorities".

The BRI may indeed divide the member states in terms of their support depending on the most favoured route, but Kazakhstan will almost certainly benefit whichever direction to Europe proves the most sustainable. The benefits will include diversifying its energy routes and decreasing its dependence on Russia, which imposes high transit tax rates: "the Kazakhstani government frequently manifested a relatively clear (if at times rhetorical) intention to commercialise its gas ties with the West… Astana's policy of ambiguity vis-à-vis the [Trans-Caspian Gas Pipeline]… constituted an indirect signal… strengthening its negotiating position in the Gazprom-dominated Eurasian gas market" (Anceschi 2014, p. 9).

In terms of economic reforms, the EU has called for easier modes of direct investment. As the World Bank investment indicators show, Kazakhstan has become a markedly more attractive place to do business. There are, however, risks associated with property rights and other intangible factors related to investment. It is for such reasons, for example, that the Astana International Financial Centre, a new project aimed to attract foreign money, has instituted a British-modelled Common Law system for arbitration, etc. According to the Transparency International Corruption Perceptions Index, Kazakhstan is 127th out of 180 countries and the 2016 GAN Business Anti-Corruption report maintains that corruption is the primary constraint for companies doing business there.

The economy is not sufficiently diversified. Despite its government's stated ambitions, Kazakhstan is still mostly dependent on the extractive sectors and has not attracted sufficient foreign investment. The programme for change, the 'Kazakhstan 2030 Strategy', has the stated aim of seeing the state as one of the world's 50 most competitive economies by 2030. The BRI offers the potential for Kazakhstan to improve its east-to-west connectivity radically, but economically north-to-south is also significant. In 2018, the train routes connecting the country to Uzbekistan, Turkmenistan, Tajikistan and Afghanistan were developed to drastically reduce turnover times and, as a result, exports of grain and flour increased exponentially (Van Leijen 2018b).

b. Uzbekistan

Uzbekistan is an attractive economic partner for China, as it has one of the most diversified economies in Central Asia. (Vakulchuk and Overland 2019, p. 126)

The Uzbek economy continues to strengthen in response to the more liberal regime of President Mirziyoyev. Nevertheless, it is, like Kazakhstan, very dependent on mining and hydrocarbons which represent a substantial share of exports. The country also has a high dependency on remittances from its diaspora community in Russia. More promisingly, Uzbekistan is the seventh largest uranium supplier in the world, and its output is increasing. China is its main market for this mineral so the BRI could be substantially beneficial. Nevertheless, despite its strategic position, along with some plans for the route, most foreign investors are likely to be wary of the high levels of state involvement in the economy, as well as the propensity for protectionism, together with poor utilities and transport infrastructure. This makes the PRC's interest particularly welcome to the regime.

> China's overall relationship with Uzbekistan has developed over the last two decades, which has contributed to a deeper and more mutually beneficial cooperation in energy... China has made major economic inroads into Uzbekistan where it has set up more than 380 ventures with Chinese investment and also the representative offices of 65 large Chinese companies. (Chen and Fazilov 2018, n.p.)

c. Tajikistan

Tajikistan's economy since independence has experienced market reforms, and the role of the state has diminished partly due to pressure from international donors. Nevertheless, it remains vulnerable to energy shortages, harsh climatic conditions and poor infrastructure. Despite attempts at industrialisation under the Soviet regime, Tajikistan remains heavily dependent on the agricultural sector with more than 50% of the labour force employed in it. The country's GDP is lower now than at the time of independence. Many people live below the poverty line and in the Human Development Index, Tajikistan is 129th of the 188 countries surveyed. Any slowdown in the level of remittances from Russia has a significant impact on the Tajik economy. Given these circumstances, Tajikistan is highly dependent on inward funding and, despite the World Bank's assessment of it as a place to do business, both China and Russia invest significantly in the country. In the latter case, the most notable area of activity is the construction of hydroelectric power plants. For China, the major investments have been in roads, especially the Dashan-Khujand-Chanak highway and the Sharshar tunnel. This action is primarily aimed at "facilitating China's access to the markets of Central Asia, also stimulating the export of Chinese goods to the region" (Vakulchuk and Overland 2019, p. 123). The balance of trade between the two countries is heavily in China's favour.

China is making no investment in railways in Tajikistan. Currently, exports to China are officially recorded as around 11%, roughly half the amounts sent to Turkey and Russia, but investment from the PRC is still significant for Tajikistan (Economist Intelligence Unit 2018, n.p.).

Tajikistan shares with eight other countries, according to the Centre for Global Development, possible debt problems as a participant in the BRI. Among the other potential risk nations is Kyrgyzstan. The difficulties of repayment may be cause for concern among Tajik policymakers, but they clearly feel that the returns on China's loans, in terms of economic development, will justify the risk. Currently, Tajikistan's main export partners are Kazakhstan, Turkey, Uzbekistan and Afghanistan, with aluminium, cotton fibre, precious metals and dried fruits the principal commodities. On the other hand, China is a significant source of imports (c. 19%) after Russia (c. 31%).

The BRI will bring much-needed investment to the country but will further rebalance the influence of Russia vis-à-vis China. For example, the planned China–Pakistan Economic Corridor (CPEC) goes through border regions in Tajikistan. If it is completed, it will facilitate Tajikistan's access to markets both north in China and south in the Indian subcontinent. Importantly, it will also reduce the country's dependence on Russia's military and security assistance.

d. Kyrgyzstan

Kyrgyzstan is an EEU member and, as a result, has less autonomy than Tajikistan in relation to Chinese investment. The Chinese continue to distinguish themselves by means of direct state-to-state contacts and they avoid cooperation with other donors present on the ground. They can rest assured that their economic expansion will continue undisturbed as long as no other relevant source of funding or form of development emerges in the region.

e. Turkmenistan

Turkmenistan's relations with its neighbours, most notably Russia and Iran, are fraught and, though it has the world's sixth largest reserves of natural gas, China is the only reliable customer. Thus, the completion of the Turkmenistan–Afghanistan–Pakistan–India Pipeline (TAPI) is critical as it will open up new market possibilities other than China. Its construction is supported by the Taliban but "[t]he TAPI gas pipeline construction project is fraught with security challenges, as well as Russian and Chinese interests to thwart progress on the project, but it is supported by the United States and India" (Barber 2018, p. 28). The suspension by Uzbekistan of a pipeline through its territory, however, restricts expansion even of the Chinese outlet.

The various routes to Europe and Southern Asia that the original Silk Road opened up in Central Asia were marked by cultural achievements of great significance. It is certain that the development of new infrastructure will expose artefacts and reminders of the cultures that flourished on the route. Some of these may challenge the authorised histories of the new republics by questioning the influence of nomadic lifestyles, dominant religions or ethnic identities. The process of discovery will also test the means by which heritage is preserved and presented. The BRI will also make parts of Central Asia more accessible and the tourism sector may well be the most obvious economic beneficiary in the short term (World Travel and Tourism Council 2018).

7.3   CONCLUSION

The BRI is a signature project for President Xi and may be both a vehicle for Chinese values and the PRC's alternative political model. It has reshaped China's global ambition and will herald a new type of great power relations. The most promising result of the BRI for any of the post-Soviet republics in Central Asia is to become more than a spectator facilitating the ambitions of others but taking little active part in the renewed game. To get the most from the BRI, individual states will need to engage actively to gain full economic benefits. For all of them, opening their economies to inward investment and facilitating domestic entrepreneurs are key objectives. Nevertheless, as with the original Silk Road, the enduring impact of the BRI may be found in the cultural ideas and philosophies it helps to propagate.

Each of the Central Asian republics is adjusting to independence and establishing itself as a new player in the political game. So far, they have experienced various degrees of autocratic rule. The Chinese and Europeans offer contrasting models of government and, as commercial activity and routine interaction increases, the individual post-Soviet republic may be influenced by them. The Chinese model of controlled governance may be seen as more attractive than the inherent emphasis on individualism and argument that seems central to the West's alternative.

The increased geopolitical significance of Central Asia will certainly trigger renewed cultural and scientific diplomacy in various forms. In

Europe, China is seeking to establish close relations with both individual member states and sub-EU groupings (such as the '16 + 1' group, made up of 11 EU member states and five Balkan countries). The European Commission is also trying to formulate a collective response to the BRI.

The development of the BRI in some parts of the globe has been interpreted as a threat to the sovereignty of individual countries disguised as economic assistance. Indeed, some of the port facilities, in particular, could readily serve a military purpose. As a result, some governments are keeping their distance from the project. None of the Central Asian republics is holding back cooperation on the basis of a threat to their independence. Indeed, the political elites have all embraced it even though their publics may harbour misgivings about China's intentions. The BRI is seen by all as an economic initiative and one that lessens their dependence on Russia.

Both Russia and China have strong geopolitical interests in Central Asia and, to an increasing extent, are accommodating each other's interests even if they eschew formal agreement. Their facilitating approach has increased since the Russian invasion of Crimea and China's trade disputes with the United States. Both seek an alternative to the values of the Western-dominated international system. Though their historical mistrust has not been entirely overcome, the new relationship between Russia and China represents an opportunity for Central Asia as a whole. This is a fortunate disposition for the republics in the region. Nevertheless, each of the post-1991 states has different and, to an extent, competing goals that reflect their size, location and level of development. To analyse them as a single group risks understating significant diversities of interest.

For China, several of the Central Asian republics represent troublesome neighbours whose regimes are less secure and whose territories represent security vulnerabilities. Turkmenistan's particularly authoritarian regime has distanced itself from Russia but, with China now a major trading partner, it may have simply swapped one dependency for another. Tajikistan has seen the PRC's role increase in terms of bilateral security and military cooperation and aid assistance. It has experienced economic expansion and important infrastructural development but may accumulate an unmanageable debt burden.

Kyrgyzstan shares a long border with China and security issues are to the fore with interethnic violence and potential terrorism prominent concerns. As in other Central Asian states, the political elite's welcoming of infrastructural investment is in contrast to the popular sentiment, which is often hostile to China. The most prominent problems for the country are unemployment, corruption and the lack of economic development. The BRI will do something to address these problems but the impact on Kyrgyzstan will be slight.

Post-Karimov Uzbekistan is a potentially weighty economic player. China's relations with the country are not primarily motivated by security concerns and the new Uzbek regime is keen to establish closer links. The country's current foreign policy is very much focussed on economic development and the BRI is seen as a major opportunity. As elsewhere, there may be popular resistance to an increased Chinese presence but, if the economy shows signs of improvement, the benefits will be widely welcomed. China has already markedly increased its trading links and, as with Kazakhstan, China's interest in Uzbekistan goes beyond just infrastructural development into joint economic and scientific ventures.

Kazakhstan is a critical partner for China and, to a significant extent, the BRI's success in the region will depend upon the stability and prosperity of the country. The PRC shares a common interest with Kazakhstan in improving the supply chain for oil and gas as well as securing an efficient supply line to Europe. The two countries are conscious of the need for secure borders and carefully managed relations with Russia. For Kazakhstan, the need to diversify its economy is also critical and the BRI fits well with its current Nurly Zhol infrastructural plans. Kazakhstan will be an influential player in the newly competitive geopolitical environment.

The Central Asian countries share a Soviet past and an over-reliance on extractive industries. They will all see in the BRI benefits in terms of access to markets that will counter their current landlocked isolation. Nevertheless, the extent of the benefit to each of China's partners is significantly different and the focus of Beijing's interest is not uniform. If some of the regimes simply respond to China's need for stable borders and national unity, they will have done enough. Others are destined to be central to the success of the project.

REFERENCES

Ambrosio, T., & Lange, W. A. (2015). Mapping Kazakhstan's geopolitical code: An analysis of Nazarbayev's presidential addresses, 1997–2014. *Eurasian Geography and Economics, 55*(1), 537–559.

Anceschi, L. (2014). The tyranny of pragmatism: EU-Kazakhstani relations. *Europe-Asia Studies, 66*(1), 1–24.

Barber, B. B. (2018). Far, yet so near: Normativity in Japan's diplomacy with the Central Asian republics. *Asian Affairs: An American Review, 45*(1), 18–39.

Bhavna, B. (2018). Silk Road Economic Belt: Effects of China's soft power diplomacy in Kazakhstan. In M. Laruelle (Ed.), *China's Belt and Road Initiative and its impact in Central Asia*. Washington, DC: The George Washington University.

Bossuyt, F., & Kubicek, P. (2015). Favouring leaders over laggards: Kazakhstan and Kyrgyzstan. In A. Wetzel & J. Orbie (Eds.), *The substance of EU democracy promotion: Concepts and cases* (pp. 177–192). London: Palgrave Macmillan.

Burkhanova, A., & Chen, Y. W. (2016). Kazakh perspective on China, the Chinese, and Chinese migration. *Ethnic and Racial Studies, 39*(12), 2129–2148.

Chen, X., & Fazilov, F. (2018). Re-centering Central Asia: China's "New Great Game" in the old Eurasian heartland. *Palgrave Communications, 4*(71). Retrieved from https://www.nature.com/articles/s41599-018-0125-5.

China Daily. (2005, July 5). Declaration of heads of member states of SCO, Astana. Retrieved from http://www.chinadaily.com.cn/china/2006-06/12/content_6020345.htm.

Clarke, M. (2018). China's war on 'terrorism': Confronting the dilemmas of the internal external security nexus. In M. Clarke (Ed.), *Terrorism and counter-terrorism in China: Domestic and foreign policy dimensions* (pp. 17–38). Oxford: Oxford University Press.

Collins, N., & Bekenova, K. (2016). Fuelling the New Great Game: Kazakhstan, energy policy and the EU. *Asia Europe Journal, 14*(1), 1–20.

Dave, B., & Kobayashi, Y. (2018). China's Silk Road Economic Belt initiative in Central Asia: Economic and security implications. *Asia Europe Journal, 16*(3), 267–281.

Economist Intelligence Unit. (2018). *Report for May 2018.* Retrieved from https://search-proquest-com.ucc.idm.oclc.org/docview/2131565184/fulltextPDF/3ED92886FB244883PQ/1?accountid=14504.

Frankopan, P. (2018). *The New Silk Roads: The present and future of the world.* London: Bloomsbury.

Garibov, A. (2018). Contemporary Chinese labor migration and its public perception in Kazakhstan and Kyrgyzstan. In M. Laurelle (Ed.), *China's Belt and Road Initiative and its impact in Central Asia* (pp. 143–152). Washington, DC: The George Washington University.

Hurley, J., Morris, S., & Portelance, G. (2018, March). *Examining the debt implications of the Belt and Road Initiative from a policy perspective* (Policy Paper 121). Washington, DC: Center for Global Development. Retrieved from https://www.cgdev.org/publication/examining-debt-implications-belt-and-road-initiative-policy-perspective.

Indeo, F. (2018). The impact of the Belt and Road Initiative on Central Asia: Building new relations in a reshaped geopolitical scenario. In W. Zhang, I. Alon, & C. Lattemann (Eds.), *China's Belt and Road Initiative: Changing the rules of globalization* (pp. 135–154). Cham, Switzerland: Springer.

Kolsto, P. (2018). *Political construction sites: Nation building in Russia and the post-Soviet states.* London: Routledge.

Kourmanova, A. (2015). National views: Kazakhstan. In S. Peyrouse (Ed.), *How does Central Asia view the EU?* (p. 7). Working Paper 18, EUCAM.

Laumulin, M. (2000). Kazakhstan and the West: Relations during the 1990s in retrospect. *Central Asia and the Caucasus.* Retrieved from http://www.ca-c.org/journal/2000/journal_eng/eng02_2000/05.laum.shtml.

Lewis, D. G. (2018). Geopolitical imaginaries in Russian foreign policy: The evolution of 'Greater Eurasia'. *Europe-Asia Studies, 70*(10), 1612–1637.

Long, K. (2017, May 23). Tajikistan takes up Chinese. *The Diplomat.* Retrieved from https://thediplomat.com/2017/05/tajikistan-takes-up-chinese/.

Marshall, T. (2016). *Prisoners of geography.* London: Elliott and Thompson.

Meyer, K., & Brysac, S. (1999). *Tournament of shadows: The Great Game and the race for empire in Central Asia.* New York: Basic Books.

Morrison, A. (2014). Introduction: Killing the Cotton Canard and getting rid of the Great Game: Rewriting the Russian conquest of Central Asia, 1814–1895. *Central Asian Survey, 33*(2), 131–142.

Odgaard, L. (2017). Beijing's quest for stability in its neighbourhood: China's relations with Russia in Central Asia. *Asian Security, 13*(1), 41–58.

People's Daily. (2001, November 6). *"Shanghai Five" enters new stage: Kazakh President.* Retrieved from http://german1.china.org.cn/english/FR/14392.htm.

Rakhimov, M. (2017, April 17). New priorities of Uzbekistan. *Journal of International Affairs.* Retrieved from https://jia.sipa.columbia.edu/online-articles/new-priorities-uzbekistan.

Sági, J., & Engelberth, I. (2018). The Belt and Road Initiative—A way forward to China's expansion. *Contemporary Chinese Political Economy and Strategic Relations: An International Journal, 4*(1), 9–37.

Sharip, F. (2017). Controversial railway project consolidates China's foothold in Central Asia. *Eurasia Daily Monitor, 14*(149). Retrieved from https://jamestown.org/program/controversial-railway-project-consolidates-chinas-foothold-central-asia/.

Starr, S. F., & Cornell, S. E. (2018). *Uzbekistan's new face*. Lanham, MD: Rowman & Littlefield.

Stratfor. (2017, June 14). *In Central Asia, China finds a crowded playing field*. Retrieved from https://worldview.stratfor.com/article/central-asia-china-finds-crowded-playing-field.

Vakulchuk, R., & Overland, I. (2019). China's Belt and Road Initiative through the lens of Central Asia. In F. M. Cheung & Y. Y. Hong (Eds.), *Regional connection under the Belt and Road Initiative: The prospects for economic and financial cooperation* (pp. 115–133). London: Routledge.

Van Leijen, M. (2018a, December 28). *Price of railway on New Silk Road closer to 'sea level'*. RailFreight.com. Retrieved from https://www.railfreight.com/beltandroad/2018/12/28/price-of-railway-on-new-silk-road-closer-to-sea-level/.

Van Leijen, M. (2018b, July 20). *New agriculture railway line Kazakhstan-Afghanistan*. RailFreight.com. Retrieved from https://www.railfreight.com/uncategorized/2018/07/20/new-agriculture-railway-line-kazakhstan-afghanstan/.

Voices on Central Asia. (2018, October 25). *Transforming post-Soviet Tajikistan: An interview with Hélène Thibault*. Retrieved from http://voicesoncentralasia.org/transforming-post-soviet-tajikistan-an-interview-with-helene-thibault/.

World Travel and Tourism Council. (2018). *Travel & tourism: Economic impact 2018 Central Asia*. Retrieved from https://www.wttc.org/-/media/files/reports/economic-impact-research/regions-2018/centralasia2018.pdf.

Wu, S. S. (2018, February 13). China's one-track mind in Kazakhstan. *Asia & the Pacific Policy Society*. Retrieved from https://www.policyforum.net/chinas-one-track-mind-kazakhstan/.

CHAPTER 8

China's Belt and Road Initiative and the South China Sea Disputes: Toward a New Mutual Deterrence Equilibrium

Rongxing Guo and Kaizhong Yang

8.1 Introduction

The 2010s was bound to be an uneasy decade for countries surrounding and in relation to the South China Sea. In 2010, China surpassed Japan as world's No. 2 economy; and there were reports that at its current rate

Supported by China National Science Foundation Project entitled "A Study of China's Industrial Agglomeration: Evolution and the Cultivation of New Driving Forces" (No. 71733001). An earlier version of this research was included in the "The Return of Geopolitics: An International Conference" (University of Arizona, April 4–5, 2016). In the present version, all mathematical formulas are removed so as to satisfy general readers.

R. Guo
Capital University of Economics and Business, Beijing, China

K. Yang (✉)
Chinese Academy of Social Sciences and Peking University, Beijing, China
e-mail: ykz@pku.edu.cn

© The Author(s) 2020
H. K. Chan et al. (eds.), *International Flows in the Belt and Road Initiative Context*, Palgrave Series in Asia and Pacific Studies,
https://doi.org/10.1007/978-981-15-3133-0_8

171

of growth, China would have replaced the United States as the world's top economy in about a decade. Indeed, this was good news for China, but bad news for the United States.

The US military and diplomatic "pivot," or "rebalance" toward Asia (also called the "Indo-Pacific Strategy" under the Trump administration) became a popular buzzword after Hillary Clinton, then US Secretary of State, authored "America's Pacific Century," in the *Foreign Policy* magazine in November 2011. Clinton's article emphasizes the importance of the Asia-Pacific, noting that nearly half of the world's population resides there, making its development vital to American economic and strategic interests. She believed that the US renewed political and military involvement in Asia is vital to the region's future:

> The region is eager for our leadership and our business – perhaps more than at any time in modern history. We are the only power with a network of strong alliances in the region, no territorial ambitions and a long record of providing for the common good... Our challenge now is to build a web of relationships across the Pacific that is as durable and as consistent with American interests and values as the web we have built across the Atlantic.[1]

Since 2013, China has made the "New Silk Road" policy, which connects China with Europe, a key part of China's international relations. On September 7, 2013, Chinese President Xi Jinping proposed to build a "Silk Road Economic Belt" during his speech at Kazakhstan. On October 3, of the same year, he proposed to build a "Twenty-first Century Maritime Silk Road" during his speech at Indonesia. China and Europe stand at either end of the New Silk Road. In each of his speeches, President Xi drew attention to the long connections between China and Europe from ancient times along both the land and the sea routes. By stressing the contribution that commercial relations make to cultural interaction and peaceful development, he pointed out:

> [C]ivilizations are equal, and such equality has made exchanges and mutual learning among civilizations possible. All human civilizations are equal in terms of value. They all have their respective strengths and shortcomings. There is no perfect civilization in the world. Nor is there a civilization that is devoid of any merit. No one civilization can be judged superior to another.[2]

[1] Cited from Clinton (2011).
[2] Cited from Xi (2014).

Since the end of World War II, many of the Asian economies have been the political or military allies of the United States. On the other hand, thanks to its open door policy from the late 1970s onward, China, in economic terms, has been increasingly integrated with the rest of the world (and with Asia in particular). Then, since the US "pivot" or "rebalance" to Asia (or the "Indo-Pacific Strategy") started in 2011 and China's "21st Century Maritime Silk Road" Initiative was proposed in 2013, what have happened in the field of the U.S.–China relations, especially concerning the issues relating to Asia? More specifically, with regard to the territorial disputes and other issues relating to the South China Sea, our analytical interests focus on the following: (i) What will induce a claimant state to give in or fight against China if China goes in? (ii) How will the United States choose between staying out, allying with the claimant state, and colluding with China?

In order to deal with the above issues, we will use an analytic narrative approach. Narrative matters because it is inherently concerned with causality recognizing that from the historical perspective specific events can yield a multiplicity of equilibria. But narrative alone is insufficient since many questions relate to events that did not take place (or have not yet taken place) or are concerned with the motivations behind why certain behavior or events have not occurred. This is arguably especially true when the accuracy or adequacy of the data and information on which the narrative are based is in question. Addressing these issues requires an appropriate model for linking what is observed (or observable) with what is not observed. More often than not, the combination of 'analytics' and 'narrative' can capture the conviction that data linked to theory is more powerful than either data or theory alone. A priori, the most relevant advantage of the analytic narrative method is that it allows us to model historical "one-off" processes and events that have unique characteristics. Likewise, the method renders some problems of empirical testing of hypotheses manageable (Bates et al. 1998, p. 10). Some political and cultural events pose insurmountable difficulties to traditional panel data or time series methods.

This paper is organized as follows. Section 8.2 presents a brief narrative of four typical cases—including the Scarborough Shoal standoff (April–June 2012), the HYSY 981 drilling rig crisis (May–July 2014), the US navigation incidents (2015–), and the long existing, though informal, scheme on shelving territorial disputes—all relating to the territorial disputes in the South China Sea. Most, if not all, of the events included in these cases were occurring in parallel with the implementation processes of both the US strategy toward Asia and China's BRI and, thus, are quite ideal for our analysis. Our interests focus on their geopolitical implications to all the stakeholders concerned.

In Sect. 8.3 a three-player, non-cooperative game is constructed for policymakers to handle the South China Sea disputes. Theoretically and analytically, conditions under which the strategy combination is a mutual deterrence (subgame perfect) equilibrium are examined. Using the three-player, non-cooperative game, we try to evaluate—qualitatively and, if necessary, quantitatively—the four cases mentioned in Sect. 8.2. Our analytical interest focuses on the political and economic incentives for all the players involved in the South China Sea disputes to reach (or move away from) a mutual deterrence (subgame perfect) equilibrium.

Finally, we conclude, with a few suggestions to policymakers.

8.2   Narrative[3]

On April 8, 2012, a Philippine Navy surveillance plane spotted eight Chinese fishing vessels docked at the waters around the Scarborough Shoal. Located at the southeast part of the South China Sea (also called the West Philippine Sea in the Philippines), the Scarborough Shoal (called "Huangyan Dao" in Chinese) is claimed by both China and the Philippines. The dispute arose when the Philippines sent its navy to search the Chinese fishing vessels operating in the disputed area. Chinese Maritime Surveillance Forces vessels subsequently arrived. A standoff has ensued, with the Philippines requesting a diplomatic resolution to the crisis but refusing to retreat. Bilateral relations have quickly deteriorated, with China introducing restrictions on imports of Philippine bananas and calling on tour groups to leave, dealing a severe blow to the Philippine economy. On May 11, Filipinos organized a protest near the Chinese Consulate in Manila against China's policies on the Scarborough Shoal. Though the protest in Beijing ended peacefully, the Hong Kong activists organized stronger protests on May 11, to reiterate China's claim over the Scarborough Shoal near the Philippine Consulate in Hong Kong.

---

[3] Unless stated otherwise, this section is written by authors based on Guo and Yang (2019), Xue (2015) and other, miscellaneous news clippings in the Chinese and English media.

After a months-long confrontation with each other, the Philippines withdrew their forces from the Shoal on June 5, hoping that a deal over its ownership could be reached. China, however, did not retreat and kept on maintaining its presence at the Shoal. By July 2012, China had erected a barrier to the entrance of the Shoal. Since the standoff, vessels belonging to the China Marine Surveillance and Fisheries Law Enforcement Command have been observed in the nearby disputed Shoal and they have been turning away Filipino vessels sailing to the area. In response, the Philippines stated that it would be preparing to resend vessels to the Shoal, in what has been described as a "cold standoff." In the following years, China has continued to maintain a presence within the Shoal, among heightened tensions regarded a new law which requires non-Chinese fishing boats to seek permission from China when in the South China Sea; however, Philippine fishing boats sometimes were still able to fish around the Shoal without Chinese interaction.

The Haiyang Shiyou (HYSY) 981 oil rig crisis refers to as the tensions between China and Vietnam arising from a Chinese state-owned company moving its oil platform to waters near the disputed Paracel Islands in the South China Sea, and the resulting Vietnamese efforts to prevent the platform from establishing a fixed position. The crisis is regarded as the most serious development in the territorial disputes between the two countries ever since the Johnson South Reef Skirmish in 1988.[4] On May 2, 2014, China National Offshore Oil Corporation (CNOOC) moved its HYSY 981 oil rig to a location 120 nautical miles east of Vietnam's Ly Son island and 180 nautical miles south of China's Hainan island, in which the last two nearest undisputed features generate a continental shelf. The location is also at the edge of hydrocarbon blocks 142 and 143 which were already created by Vietnam but had not been offered for exploitation to foreign oil companies, nor had been acknowledged by China.

Soon after the CNOOC moved its oil rig to south of Paracel Islands and established an exclusion zone around it, Vietnam vociferously protested the move as an infringement of its sovereignty. It sent 29 ships to attempt to disrupt the rig's placement and operations. The ships met

---

[4] The Skirmish was an altercation that took place on March 14, 1988 between Chinese and Vietnamese forces over who would annex the Johnson South Reef in the region of the Spratly Islands in the South China Sea—see Barnes (2016) for a more detailed analysis.

resistance from Chinese ships escorting the rig, and Vietnam stated that its ships were repeatedly rammed and sprayed with water resulting in 6 people being injured, while China stated that its ships were also rammed and it sprayed water in self-defense. Domestically, the tensions with China resulted in people protesting against Chinese actions. Starting from May 11, 2014, a series of unprecedented anti-China protests flared up across Vietnam. On May 13 and 14, these anti-Chinese protests in Vietnam escalated into unrests and riots in which many foreign businesses and Chinese workers were targeted, with four deaths and more 130 injuries. In addition, about 1000 businesses and factories, owned by foreign investors from China, Taiwan, Singapore, Japan, and South Korea, were subject to vandalism and looting due to the confusion by protesters who believed the establishments to be Chinese. Previously, on May 8, the VN-Index—Vietnam's benchmark stock index—had plunged by about 6% amid escalating tensions with China over disputed waters, marking the biggest drop since 2001. On July 15, 2014, China announced that the platform had completed its work and withdrew it fully one month earlier than originally announced.

On October 27, 2015, the USS Lassen, a guided-missile destroyer of the US Navy, sailed within 12 nautical miles of Subi and Mischief reefs in the Spratly archipelago. The region is widely considered as international waters but Beijing claims islands, reefs, and other features in large part of the South China Sea. Many nations including Vietnam, the Philippines, Taiwan, and Malaysia are entangled in the messy territorial claims in the region. The United States and China have been locked in a battle of words over the US challenge of China's territorial claims in the South China Sea by entering within 12 nautical miles of the Chinese islands built on top of reefs in the Spratly Islands. The dispute has gotten so heated that it's forced the United States into a difficult position: balancing the interests of allies in the region, such as the Philippines, with respect for China's legitimate claims and to avoid fraying ties to the fast-growing regional power.

Since 2014, China has extensively reclaimed several islets and atolls in the Spratlys, prompting the United States and other nations to intensify counter-measures. This has even led to confrontation between US forces and the Chinese navy. China's outposts in the middle of the ocean may not be as vulnerable as some thought. If war breaks out, China can declare that it makes no difference between an attack on these islands and an attack on its mainland. The artificial islands can serve as strong points of control, robust hubs of logistics, and effective bases of power projection in peacetime and in gray zones between war and peace. The runways and other facilities China built on the Subi and Mischief reefs have alarmed the United States and its partners in the region. Washington has repeatedly stated it does not recognize any Chinese claim of territorial waters around the reclamations built on previously submerged reefs.

The South China Sea, which encompasses a portion of the southwestern Pacific Ocean, stretches roughly from Singapore and the Strait of Malacca in the southwest, to the Strait of Taiwan (between Taiwan and mainland China) in the northeast. The area includes hundreds of small islands, rocks, and reefs, the majority of which are located within the Paracel and Spratly Island chains. Many of these islands are partially submerged islets, rocks, and reefs that are little more than shipping hazards not suitable for habitation. Even though most of these islets are not arable, do not support permanent crops, and have no meadows, pastures, or forests, the surrounding water areas are abundant in oil, natural gas, minerals, and seafood.[5] What is more important, more than half of the world's annual merchant fleet tonnage passes through the Straits of Malacca, Sunda, and Lombok, with the majority continuing on into the South China Sea.

At present, most of the islands and reefs in the South China Sea have been occupied by China, the Philippines, Vietnam, Taiwan, and Malaysia (see Table 8.1 for more details). China's rising energy demands, decreasing ability to meet demand growth with domestic energy sources, and continued reliance on oil have propelled China to look to alternative energy sources. Despite these territorial disputes and the uncertainty over the South China Sea, the above claimants have involved energy companies in exploration and exploitation in their respective claims. However, past cooperation arrangements, in the absence of a settlement of the maritime boundaries, have been based on a fragile equilibrium of powers.

8.3   Analyzing the Narrative as 3-Player Games

The "Silk Road Economic Belt" and the "21st Century Maritime Silk Road" (also known as the "One Belt One Road" or "Yidai Yilu" in Chinese) Initiative is a development strategy and framework that was

---

[5] For example, oil and natural gas reserves in the Spratly region are estimated at 17.7 billion tons (Guo 2005, p. 113). The Spratly reserves place it as the fourth largest reserve bed worldwide.

Table 8.1   Competing over the waters and islets at the South China Sea, by claimant

Claimant	South China Sea	Spratly islets	Paracel islets
Brunei	UNCLOS	1 (0)	None
China	All*	All (9)	All (all)
Indonesia	UNCLOS	None	None
Malaysia	UNCLOS	3 (3)	None
Philippines	UNCLOS	Significant number (8)	None
Taiwan (ROC)	All*	All (1)	All (0)
Thailand	Not available	None	None
Vietnam	Significant portion	Significant number (29)	All (0)

Notes (1) UNCLOS denotes "claims to areas of the ocean to be made using a 200 nm exclusive economic zone (EEZ) and/or the continental shelf principle"; (2) "*" excludes buffer zone along littoral states (calculations for buffer unknown); and (3) figures within parentheses are the numbers of islands that are actually occupied
Sources EIA (2008) and author's estimates

proposed by the President of the People's Republic of China in 2013. This Initiative focuses on connectivity and cooperation among China and the selected countries in Eurasia and at the seas. As a measure for China to countervail the US strategy of military and diplomatic "pivot" or "rebalance" toward Asia that was proposed by the Obama administration in late 2011 (which was renamed as the "Indo-Pacific Strategy" under the Trump administration in 2017) and to take a bigger role in global affairs, the Chinese Initiative is bound to evolve into, and to be decided by, a number of geopolitical games.

In this paper, we assume that a mutual deterrence (subgame perfect) equilibrium, in which claimant states don't challenge each other, exists if and only if the following conditions are satisfied: (1) that, if no state challenges, the amount of each state's expected economic benefit is larger than its investment in military strength; and (2) that the amount of each state's investment in military strength is larger than what is required to deter the other state from challenging for any investment in military strength that that state can make.

In order to present more rigorous analytical results, we try to simplify each case of the South China Sea disputes as a three-player game. Each of the players—China, another South China Sea claimant state, and the United States—could freely choose its decisions or strategies in relation to the territorial and maritime disputes at the South China Sea. Specifically, under a new situation in the South China Sea, China could choose either "Go in" or "Stay out." In response to China's "Go in" strategy, state x could choose either "Fight" or "Give in" while the United States could "Fight" side by side with state x against China, "Collude" with China, or even "Stay out" (see Fig. 8.1 for all the possible scenarios).

Let us return back to Sect. 8.2 and divide the events that have occurred in the South China Sea from 2010 to 2015 into four cases, as the following:

Case (i): The Scarborough Shoal standoff (April–June 2012)
Case (ii): The HYSY 981 drilling rig crisis (May–July 2014)
Case (iii): The US navigation incidents (2015–)
Case (iv): The long existing, though informal, scheme on shelving territorial disputes.

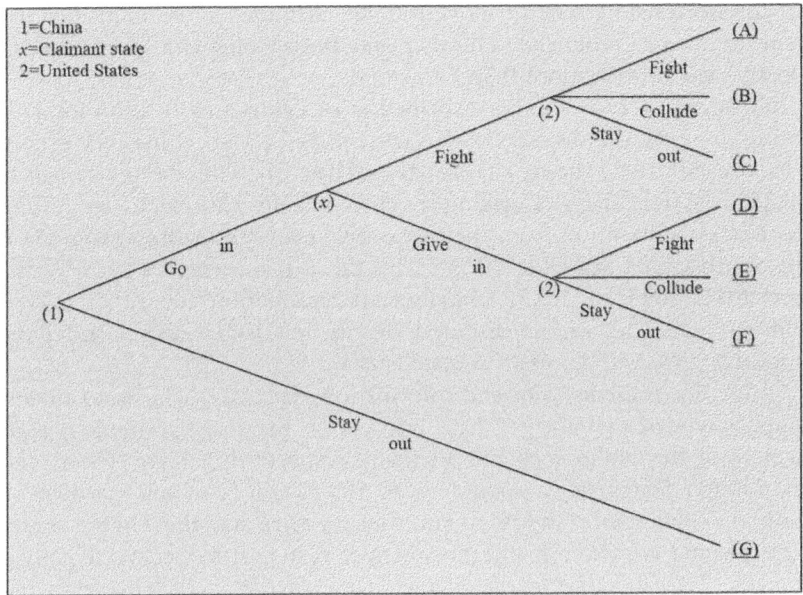

Fig. 8.1 A 3-player, non-cooperative game: a conceptual model (*Note* The payoffs to all the players in each of the outcomes [A, B, C, D, E, F, and G] are summarized in Guo 2018, p. 135)

The Scarborough Shoal standoff, which is labeled as Case (i), came to an end in June 2012, with the Philippines choosing to "give in" and the United States—a close strategic major ally of the Philippines—choosing to "stay out." As a result, China is thought to be the winner.

By way of contrast, it is difficult to define the winner(s) and loser(s) in Case (ii), that is, the HYSY 981 drilling rig crisis. And it is still more difficult to measure the payoffs to all the players involved in the crisis. In general, the case may be described as the one in which China chooses "go in," Vietnam responds with "fight," and the United States decide to "stay out" but it has more complicated effects than Case (i). Specifically, the following viewpoints are worth of noting: First, China won since it had erected its drilling rig for more than two months in the disputed waters and had effectively removed all the provocative actions taken by the Vietnamese side. Secondly, Vietnam won since it had not only won sympathy and moral support from most, if not all, of the US-led allies but it had also forced China to move the 981 drilling rig one month earlier than originally announced. Thirdly, while both China and Vietnam were losers, Vietnam lost more than China did.

However, there is another explanation of China's motivation for activating its territorial disputes with Vietnam. With a good mastery of Sun Tzu's (c. 500 BC) theory of *The Art of War*, the Chinese policymakers might have used the 981 drilling rig crisis as a diversion tactic to shifting the outside's attention from their expansive land reclamation program in the South China Sea (Xue 2015). This can explain why, for most of the time from 2014 to 2015, China's land reclamation and other related construction work in the disputed islands and land features had gone smoothly. (We will discuss this issue later on.)

Table 8.2 presents data and information that may help us to understand how Cases (i) and (ii) have impacts on the socioeconomic performances of the Philippines and Vietnam, respectively.[6] Here, China and the United States are supposed to be the major economic partners of both the Philippines and Vietnam. Since China and the United States were playing completely different roles, it is logical to believe that their

---

[6] It should be noted that there had been many other factors and events—both domestically and internationally—that could have influenced the Philippines' and Vietnam's foreign economic performances. The best way to estimating the influence of a specific factor or event is to develop a multivariable, econometric model by which to control for the remaining explanatory variables (domestic and international factors and events).

Table 8.2 Quantifying the impacts of the South China Sea disputes: Cases (i) and (ii)

Indicator		(i) Philippines, 2012	(ii) Vietnam, 2014
Annual GDP growth rate (%) change		3.10	0.60
Annual bilateral tourism growth rate (%) change[a]	From China	−25.60	−87.64
	To China	−0.40	5.13
	From USA	10.00	−5.30
	To USA	30.00	...
Annual bilateral import/export growth rate (%) change	From China	−18.1	−6.15
	To China	9.30	−1.75
	From USA	4.92	−0.11
	To USA	2.43	−9.81
Annual bilateral FDI growth rate (%) change	From China	−72.88	−608.75
	To China	37.19	...
	From USA	9.26	−5.78
	To USA	117.05	−145.00[b]

Notes (1) FDI = foreign direct investment, GDP = gross domestic product. (2) All figures are in percentage points. (3) Cases (i) and (ii)—specifically, the Scarborough Shoal standoff (April–June 2012) and the HYSY 981 drilling rig crisis (May–July 2014)—are supposed to have impacts on the Philippines' economic performances in 2012 and Vietnam's economic performances in 2014, respectively. (4) Each indicator's growth rate change, of the Philippines in 2012 and of Vietnam in 2014, is measured by its current year's annual growth rate (in %) minus its previous year's (in %). "..." denotes that data are not available. [a]Except for the US–Philippine figures, which are calculated based on the receipts and payments (in million US dollars), all the other figures are based on the number of visitors (in persons). [b]Since the FDI figures in 2013 and 2014 are negative, the FDI growth rate in 2014 is calculated as: −(|FDI in 2014| − |FDI in 2013|)÷|FDI in 2013|, where "|···|" denotes "absolute value of ···."
Source Calculated by author based on World Bank (2015), National Bureau of Statistics (2011, 2012, 2013, 2014), U.S. Census Bureau (2015), ITC (2015), BEA (2015a), GSO (2012, 2013, 2014), NTTO (2015), TCG (2015), VNAT (2015), and PSA (2015)

economic relations with the Philippines and Vietnam should also be differently influenced in 2012 and 2014, respectively. Specifically, for the Philippines, each indicator's growth rate change in 2012, in which the Scarborough Shoal Standoff occurred from April to June 2012, is measured by 2012s annual growth rate (in %) minus 2011s (in %); and for Vietnam, each indicator's growth rate change in 2014, in which the HYSY 981 drilling rig crisis occurred from May to July, is measured by 2014s annual growth rate (in %) minus 2013s (in %). It is reasonable to assume that, as for the year 2012, the effects of the Scarborough Shoal standoff on the Philippines' economic cooperation with China should be quantitatively negative and that, ceteris paribus, those on the United States should be quantitatively positive; and that, as for the year 2014, the effects of the HYSY 981 drilling rig crisis on Vietnam's economic cooperation with China should be quantitatively negative and that, ceteris paribus, those on the United States should be quantitatively positive.

The HYSY 981 drilling rig crisis (in which China chooses "go in," Vietnam responds with "fight," and the United States decide to "stay out") is more physically violent than the Scarborough Shoal standoff (in which China "goes in," the Philippines "gives in" and the United States "stays out"). This results in the following hypotheses: that the negative impacts on the China–Vietnam economic relations (in the former case) are greater than those on the China–Philippine economic relations (in the latter case); and that the positive impacts on the U.S.–Vietnam economic relations (in the former case) are greater than those on the U.S.–Philippine economic relations (in the latter case).

Even though most of the figures shown in Table 8.2 may be used to approve the above hypotheses, some impact coefficients on the Philippines (in 2012) and Vietnam (in 2014) include those that are endogenously determined and thus do not conform to our hypotheses. For example, with the reductions of Vietnam's foreign direct investment (FDI) from China (with the impact coefficient of −608.75%) and of its import from and export to China (with the impact coefficients of −6.15 and −1.75%, respectively), the HYSY 981 drilling rig crisis also had negative impacts on the Vietnamese trade with and the FDI from and to the United States. This phenomenon is quite unusual; but it does show that, compared with Case (i) in which China and the Philippines didn't resort any physical violence to each other, Case (ii) had, in most, if not all circumstances, more serious economic impacts on *all* the players and stakeholders concerned (see Table 8.2).

Indeed, it is a difficult task for us to explain why China and the United States have had so significantly different economic relations with their East Asian partners (including the Philippines and Vietnam) (shown in Table 8.3). Nevertheless, these differences have stemmed from, in addition to various domestic policies and international events, many other—geographical and cultural—factors. Specifically, the US geographical disadvantages, which are thought to have affected America's military supremacy in Asia, have also reduced the efficiency of the long-distance, trans-Pacific trade and economic cooperation. In 2004, using a gravity model of trade and the US and Chinese panel data, we found that, while geographical distance had become less important in foreign trade than

Table 8.3 Changes of trade dependence on China and the United States (2010–2014), by trade partner, %

Trade partner	China[a]			USA[a]		
	2010	2014	Change	2010	2014	Change
Australia	18.55	27.40	8.85	8.86	7.80	−1.06
Brunei	9.02	13.73	4.71	1.19	4.12	2.93
Cambodia	12.07	15.46	3.39	20.57	13.06	−7.50
China	–	–	–	15.36	13.73	−1.64
Hong Kong[b]	18.78	23.01	4.24	2.51	2.86	0.35
Indonesia	14.57	17.93	3.36	7.98	7.80	−0.18
Japan	20.34	20.73	0.39	12.37	13.33	0.97
Macau	34.84	29.99	−4.85	5.64	4.02	−1.62
Malaysia	20.44	23.03	2.59	11.01	9.82	−1.19
Philippines	25.25	34.29	9.04	13.97	14.34	0.38
Singapore[b]	10.10	12.36	2.25	5.58	4.81	−0.77
South Korea	23.23	26.45	3.22	9.84	10.38	0.54
Taiwan	27.65	33.74	6.08	11.77	11.44	−0.33
Thailand	14.07	15.94	1.87	8.42	8.55	0.13
USA	11.87	13.81	1.94	–	–	–
Vietnam	19.15	27.90	8.75	11.82	12.12	0.29

Notes [a]The bilateral trade of China includes re-exports and re-imports, while that of the United States does not. [b]For Hong Kong and Singapore, the total trade includes re-exports and re-imports
Source Calculated by author based on (1) WTO (2015) for data on each economy's total trade (merchandise exports and imports); (2) National Bureau of Statistics (2011) and ITC (2015) for data on China's bilateral trade in 2010 and 2014, respectively; and (3) U.S. Census Bureau (2015) for data on theUnited States' bilateral trade

cultural links since the end of the Cold War, it did reduce the US trade (especially export) with the rest of the world.[7] In addition, we also found that, although religious retardation on foreign trade was more significant in China than in the United States, religious dissimilarity would retard the US export more than that of China; and, by contrast, it would retard the Chinese import more than that of the United States (Guo 2004).

The US navigation incidents since October 2015, that is, Case (iii), largely stemmed from China's extensive reclamation in the Spratlys,

---

[7]For example, the estimated coefficient on the natural log of distance is −1.256, which is statistically significant at greater than the 1% confidence level, suggesting that, with a one percent increase of distance between the United States and its trade partners, there would be a 1.256% reduction of the US export (Guo 2004).

prompting the US and other nations to intensify counter-measures. The land reclamation activities have been conducted in eight areas, namely Mischief (Meiji in Chinese) reef, Johnson South (Chigua in Chinese) reef, Fiery Cross (Yongshu in Chinese) reef, Cuarteron (Huayang in Chinese) reef, Hughes (Dongmen in Chinese) reef, Gaven (Nanxun in Chinese) reef, Subi (Zhubi in Chinese) reef, and Eldad (Anda in Chinese) reef. In the artificial islands that are based in the Meiji, Chigua, and Yongshu reefs, airports, seaports, and various civil and military facilities have also been constructed. At present, it is unlikely for any other claimant states to substantially join in the United States' challenges to China's claims in the South China Sea. Why that?

China has been pursuing a double-track mechanism by which to deal with the territorial issues relating to the South China Sea. On the one hand, China claims the major portion of the South China Sea and all the islands, reefs, shoals, and rocks thereof. On the other hand, China is implementing a "shelving disputes" strategy and, in most, if not all circumstances, has not been showing any substantial harm to the states that China believes have "illegally" occupied its territories in the South China Sea.[8]

It must be noted that, no matter whatever happens in the remaining cases (outcomes), any other claimant state (represented by state x in Fig. 8.1), except China and the United States, will not obtain any positive payoffs for itself. The most likely result is that China would use its geographical advantages to win a medium-sized war against the United States, as long as the war is conducted near the Chinese mainland and far away from the US mainland. All this is also endorsed by the fact that China has been wielding more formidable conventional militaries brandishing weapons such as highly accurate anti-ship ballistic and cruise missiles, increasingly powerful anti-satellite missiles and jammers, and quieter and more lethal submarines, all handled by better trained and professionalized military personnel. However, the payoffs to both China and the United States will be further worse off, till both of which

---

[8] More details about China's official statements about the so-called double-track mechanism, see https://www.fmprc.gov.cn/mfa_eng/zxxx_662805/t1181523.shtml (accessed 2019-4-15).

become negative in a long-lasting war.[9] Of course, if either side—China and the United States—recognizes the pros and cons of the Sino-US confrontation, a large-scale war would not likely occur in the South China Sea. As a result, the United States–China collusion will be the optimum choice. In addition, even though most, if not all Southeast Asian economies would not welcome China as a dominative power over the South China Sea, they may not be the eventual beneficiaries in the large-scale Sino-US confrontation.

As a matter of fact, even if China is defeated in an unlikely war against the United States, other claimant states—the Philippines and Vietnam—would still not benefit from what the United States has promised, or, at the very least, they would not benefit as much as they would otherwise (see Table 8.3 for more empirical evidence that supports that the Philippines and Vietnam have had increasing economic interests in trading with China vis-à-vis the United States). Here, we suppose that, as the result of the disappearance of the China threat, the United States would no longer provide any *unnecessary* military aid to its allies near the South China Sea, or at least as much as what has been needed for the implementation of its "rebalancing" policy toward Asia. In fact, neither would the United States be too stupid to be involved in a long-lasting war that is neither of any certainty to win nor helpful for all the stakeholders concerned. Thanks to its "rebalancing" policy, the United States has now ranked as the leading supplier of defense aircraft for Asia-Pacific partners and allies.[10] As a result, it is almost certain that "game is going on" can always make the United States better-off than "game is over" can in Asia.

---

[9] In general, three scenarios of the Sino-US war may exist: (a) A short-lasting, small-scale war, which would end in favor of the United States (since the latter may be decades ahead of China in terms of military technology), but which would likely evolve into a longer, larger-sized war thereafter. (b) A medium-scale war, which would end in favor of China (since the latter has distinct geographical advantages over the United States), but which would likely evolve into an even longer, more costly, and larger-sized war thereafter. (c) A large-scale war, which would eventually end with the mutual destruction of both China and the United States (since both of them have the military capacities to destroy each other) (Source: based on the judgment of an anonymous PLA general).

[10] According to an Aviation Week Intelligence Network (AWIN) analysis, between 2009 and 2023, the United States would have sold about US$79.2 billion worth of defense aircraft and related equipment, including both development and production costs, to Australia, India, Indonesia, Japan, Malaysia, Pakistan, Singapore, South Korea, Taiwan, and Thailand (Fabey, November 26, 2013).

While the United States' political and military relations with most, if not all of the Southeast Asian nations have been enhanced, China's economic and trade relations with Southeast Asia have grown more rapidly than the United States have (see Table 8.3). For example, from 2010 to 2014, East Asia's dependence on trade with the United States, though having a much lower starting level than that with China, had still decreased (with a few exceptions in Brunei, Hong Kong, Japan, the Philippines, South Korea, and Vietnam). On the other hand, during the same period, East Asia's dependence on trade with China, though having a much higher starting level than that with the United States, had still increased steadily (with the only exception in Macau). Particularly noteworthy is that, from 2010 to 2014, Australia, the Philippines, South Korea, and Taiwan—all of which are the close allies of the United States— had significantly raised their shares of trade with China from 18.55, 25.25, 23.23, and 27.65% in 2010 to 27.40, 34.29, 26.45, and 33.74% in 2014, respectively. However, during the same period of time, their dependence on trade with the United States had only been slightly improved (in the cases of the Philippines and South Korea) or even worsened (in the cases of Australia and Taiwan).

It is interesting to note that the years from 2010 to 2014 had seen both the US "pivot" (or "rebalance") toward Asia and the Chinese "New Silk Road" initiative. However, during this period of time, when the trade dependence of many East Asian economies, including that of China, on the United States had *decreased*, the United States' dependence on the trade with China had *increased* from 11.87% in 2010 to 13.81% in 2014 (see Table 8.3).[11] Indeed, the U.S.–China economic relations from 2010 to 2014 are too complicated to be explained by the current geopolitical situation in East Asia and Pacific, neither can they be fully decided by the US "pivot" (or "rebalance") toward Asia or the Chinese "New Silk Road" initiative. And the multilateral relations between theUnited States, China, and their Asian partners—political, military, or economic— can never be understood by the so-called "all-or-none" thinking pattern. And, any worsening geopolitical situation in the South China Sea could evolve into a lose-lose game for all the players and stakeholders concerned. (The HYSY 981 drilling rig crisis, shown in Table 8.2, is one example.)

---

[11] In 2014, the US exports to China accounted for 7.1% of total US exports, and the US imports from China accounted for 16.9% of total US imports (BEA 2015b).

China's military build-up and any indications of employing its increasing power may drive a number of regional states to increase their own defense spending. While these countries (the Philippines, Vietnam, Malaysia, Singapore, or Brunei) are unable to compete with China's forces on a one-to-one basis, new acquisitions in submarines, anti-submarine helicopters, fighters, and advanced patrol vessels can raise the potential risk and costs of Chinese action. Nevertheless, after the China threat disappears, most, if not all of these nations will not invest as much as they did in purchasing American arms. Even worse, they may even not welcome any American presence at the South China Sea.[12] Therefore, the U.S.–China game should not be treated as a zero-sum game, which could easily evolve into a lose-lose game. Instead, the most feasible solution to the U.S.–China equation should be the one in which all players can find a new mutual deterrence equilibrium.

8.4 Concluding Remarks

Over the course of human history, boundary and territorial disputes have often stemmed from historical and cultural claims; they may have also resulted from fundamental geopolitical changes. In certain circumstances, boundary and territorial disputes may even evolve into a vicious circle of rivalry and competitions. Therefore, it seems unlikely that some, if not all, boundary and territorial disputes can be easily resolved. However, provocative actions, which are aimed at the seizing of part or all of the disputed territories or any benefits thereof, sometimes are very costly. When the costs of a provocative action exceed its benefits, the disputant parties may find that "shelving disputes strategy" is the most logical solution to cross-border conflicts.

Till present, the US strategy toward China has coupled engagement with balancing. The engagement, half of this strategy, has been geared toward enmeshing China in global trade and international institutions, discouraging it from challenging the status quo. The other half attempts

---

[12] This can be witnessed by the fact that, in December 1992, shortly after the end of the Cold War, then Philippine President Corazon Aquino issued a formal notice for the United States to withdraw from the Subic Bay naval base by the end of 1992. Another example is that, after the Permanent Court of Arbitration ruled in favor of the Philippines in the South China Sea Arbitration on July 12, 2016—a result that has been generally believed to be sported by the United States, the new Philippine administration began to fawn on China instead of the United States.

to maintain the balance of power, deter aggression, and mitigate any attempts of coercion (Friedberg 2012). The United States' focus on Asia may be appropriate for its Asian allies. Without such a move, many, if not all of its allies would think that there would have been a danger that China, with its hard-line, realist view of international relations, would conclude that an economically exhausted United States was losing its staying power in the Pacific (Rudd 2013). With the United States now fully investing in Asia, Washington and Beijing must create long-term cooperative strategies that accommodate each other's interests. Doing this would significantly reduce miscalculation and the likelihood of conflict.

At a moment when China and the United States were launching initiatives in Asia, their South China Sea policies created new sources of friction (or uneasiness) in Southeast Asia. Yet, despite promulgating tensions throughout the region, China could unilaterally define the region's trajectory, as, on the one hand, the ASEAN remains divided and uncertain of the way forward on the South China Sea and, on the other hand, the Chinese economy is decreasingly determined by external factors.[13] Ultimately, it is incumbent on international and regional partners, like the United States, to provide Southeast Asian states with strategic diversity in their diplomatic, economic, and security engagements, so that they have the confidence to resist coercive actions and help advance a rules-based order in the Asia-Pacific region.

China's activities in the South China Sea, on the one hand, and its huge, "Belt-and-Road Initiative"-related investment, on the other, will raise profound global and regional implications. During an earlier regional charm offensive, China entered in a landmark agreement with ASEAN to diffuse tensions and prevent a land grab for the disputed islands. Signed in 2002, the Declaration on the Conduct (DOC) of Parties in the South China Sea forbids the types of land reclamation and military build-up China is now undertaking.[14] To be clear, each country in Asia seeks a positive and stable relationship with China. China's economy and rising

---

[13] For example, China's foreign trade as percentage of GDP has decreased from as high as 66% in 2007 to 42% in 2014 (World Bank 2015). Obviously, if the above trend continues in the years to come, the Chinese leaders will become more self-determined in dealing with international affairs.

[14] See   http://www.southchinasea.com/documents/law/303-declaration-on-the-conduct-of-parties-in-the-south-china-sea.html (accessed 2019-4-15) for more details about the DOC.

middle class offers tremendous opportunities, China's US$40 billion financing programs, through the "21st Century Maritime Silk Road" Initiative, can help to drive regional infrastructure development and integration, and there are strong cultural and people-to-people connections. However, these elements are not enough to form the sorts of enduring relationships and alliances that a great power requires for international success—including a friendly periphery coupled with burden-sharing partners. Given the trust deficit with China, regional states are limiting areas of sensitive cooperation and seeking a strategic diversity in their engagement to serve as a potential hedge against unilateral Chinese actions.

History has revealed that smaller and relatively weaker states usually were marginalized or even became losers in various bilaterally- or multilaterally-based political games. In addition, the current situation in the South China Sea is not necessarily bound to evolve into a zero-sum game between the United States and China—the No. 1 and 2 economies of the world. Technically, the fuzziness of international laws concerning the territorial sea of artificial islands that are based on rocks, reefs, and other features in the South China Sea may enable China and the United States to negotiate for a win-win outcome for themselves.[15] At the very least, given that an active dispute cannot be resolved within a short period of time, delaying (i.e., shelving the dispute and doing nothing to compromise or escalate) is in many circumstances the least costly strategy for all policymakers to adopt. This policy has followed Mr. Deng Xiaoping's (1904–1997) famous remark when the Sino-Japanese Treaty of Peace and Friendship was signed in 1978:

> It is true that the two sides maintain different views on this [Diaoyu/Senkaku] question... It does not matter if this question is shelved for some time, say, ten years. Our generation is not wise enough to find common language on this question. Our next generation will certainly be wiser. They will certainly find a solution acceptable to all.[16]

---

[15] According to the United Nations Convention on the Law of Sea, "[a] low-tide elevation is a naturally formed area of land which is surrounded by and above water at low tide but submerged at high tide... Where a low-tide elevation is wholly situated at a distance exceeding the breadth of the territorial sea from the mainland or an island, it has no territorial sea of its own" (UNCLOS 1982, Article 13).

[16] Cited from Lo (1989, pp. 171–172).

The rationale for "shelving disputes" is based on an understanding that some or all participants will have to pay more additional costs than what they can benefit from finding an immediate solution to a territorial dispute. Claiming a piece of territory controlled or claimed by other state(s) always carries some price. By challenging another state's sovereignty, territorial claims foster uncertainty about the security of the most vital of national interests, territorial integrity, and mistrust about the intentions of the opposing state more broadly. Uncertainty and mistrust, in turn, "sustain poor and tense diplomatic relations that limit the willingness of states to engage in or deepen cooperation with each other, creating security, diplomatic, or economic opportunity costs for contesting land" (Fravel 2008, p. 16).

The main purpose of the dispute-shelving strategy is to shift attention from sovereignty dispute to more essential concerns which countries involved could try to tackle together, and which do not necessarily depend on a resolution of the sovereignty dispute. Regular meetings or workshops can be held, with participation of the officials and expert groups from the countries involved in the dispute. The idea is to build confidence, initiate cooperative projects, lay the foundation for joint management of shared resources, and ensure cross-border environmental protection. Sovereignty issues have been banned from the agenda at all meetings. Even though the term "shelving disputes" is defined here as a dispute-settlement strategy, it is only considered an approach to conflict *prevention* instead of conflict *resolution* (Guo 2012, p. 152). Nevertheless, in most circumstances it can be applied by policymakers and practitioners to reduce or delay existing tensions in disputed areas.

REFERENCES

Barnes, Mark. (2016). *The impact of the Johnson South Reef Skirmish on the South China Sea conflict*. Norderstedt: Grin Publishing.

Bates, R., Greif, A., Levi, M., Rosenthal, J.-L., & Weingast, B. (1998). *Analytic narratives*. Princeton, NJ: Princeton University Press.

BEA. (2015a). *Direct investment and activities of multinational enterprises: Philippines and Vietnam*. Bureau of Economic Analysis (BEA), Department of Commerce, Washington, DC. Available at http://bea.gov/international/factsheet/factsheet.cfm. Accessed 18 Dec 2015.

BEA. (2015b). *U.S. international trade in goods and services: China.* Bureau of Economic Analysis (BEA), Department of Commerce, Washington, DC. Available at https://www.bea.gov/international/factsheet/factsheet.cfm. Accessed 21 Dec 2015.

Clinton, H. (2011). America's Pacific century. *Foreign Policy, 90*(November), 56–63.

EIA. (2008). *South China Sea territorial issues.* U.S. Energy Information Agency (EIA), Washington DC. Available at www.eia.doe.gov/emeu/cabs/South_China_Sea/SouthChinaSeaTerritorialIssues.html. Accessed 14 Apr 2010.

Fabey, M. (2013, November 26). *U.S. leads international defense aircraft suppliers in Asia Pacific.* The Aviation Week Intelligence Network (AWIN), Arlington, VA. Available at http://aviationweek.com/defense/us-leads-defense-aircraft-suppliers-asia-pacific. Accessed 13 Dec 2015.

Fravel, M. T. (2008). *Strong borders, secure nation: Cooperation and confliction in China's territorial disputes.* Princeton, NJ: Princeton University Press.

Friedberg, A. (2012). Bucking Beijing: An alternative U.S. China policy. *Foreign Affairs, 91*(5, September–October), 48–58.

GSO. (2012, 2013, 2014). *Statistical yearbook of Vietnam* (3 vols.). Statistical Documentation and Service Centre, General Statistics Office of Vietnam (GSO), Ha Noi, Vietnam.

Guo, R. (2004). How culture influences foreign trade: Evidence from the U.S. and China. *The Journal of Socio-Economics, 33,* 785–812.

Guo, R. (2005). *Cross-border resource management: Theory and practice.* Amsterdam and Boston: Elsevier Science.

Guo, R. (2012). *Territorial disputes and conflict management: The art of avoiding war.* London and New York: Routledge.

Guo, R. (2018). *Cross-border resource management: 3E.* Amsterdam and Boston: Elsevier Science.

Guo, R., & Yang, S. (2019). The South China Sea disputes (in Chinese: "nanhai zhengyi"). *Economic Geography, 39*(10), 11–17.

ITC. (2015). *Trade map: Trade statistics for international business development.* Market Analysis and Research, International Trade Centre (ITC),Geneva, Switzerland.

Lo, C.-K. (1989). *China's policy toward territorial disputes: The case of the South China Sea Islands.* London: Routledge.

National Bureau of Statistics. (2011, 2012, 2013, 2014). *China Statistical Yearbooks* (4 vols.). Beijing: China Statistics Publishing House.

NTTO. (2015, October). *U.S. travel and tourism balance of trade: Philippines.* National Travel and Tourism Office (NTTO), U.S. Department of Commerce.

PSA. (2015). *Foreign investments—Previous releases.* Philippines Statistics Authority (PSA), Quezon City, The Philippines.

Rudd, K. (2013). Beyond the pivot: A new road map for U.S.-Chinese relations. *Foreign Affairs, 92*(2, March–April), 9–15.

Sun, T. (c. 500 BC) (Trans. by Griffith, S. B., 1963). *The art of war.* Oxford: Oxford University Press.

TCG. (2015). *China tourism.* Travel China Guide (TCG), Beijing. Available at http://www.travelchinaguide.com/tourism/. Accessed 22 Dec 2015.

Xi, J. (2014, March 27). *Speech by H.E. President Xi Jinping on civilization dialogue at UNESCO headquarters.* United Nations Education, Science and Culture Organization (UNESCO), Paris. Available at http://www.nishan.org.cn/eng/news/201405/t20140518_10277909.html. Accessed 5 Dec 2015.

Xue, L. (2015). *The construction of China's New Silk-Road initiative and the new situations in the South China Sea (in Chinese).* Institute of World Economics and Politics, Chinese Academy of Social Sciences (CASS), Beijing. Available at www.iwep.org.cn/upload/2015/03/d20150309154526102.pdf. Accessed 18 Oct 2015.

UNCLOS. (1982). *United Nations convention on the law of sea.* New York: United Nations.

U.S. Census Bureau. (2015). *Bilateral trade statistics.* Foreign Trade Division, U.S. Census Bureau, Washington, DC.

VNAT. (2015). *Tourism statistics.* Vietnam National Administration of Tourism (VNAT), Ha Noi, Vetnam. Available at http://vietnamtourism.gov.vn/english/index.php/items/8149. Accessed 22 Dec 2015.

World Bank. (2015). *World Bank indicators.* Washington, DC: The World Bank.

WTO. (2015). *Statistics database: Time series.* World Trade Organization (WTO): Geneva, Switzerland.

CHAPTER 9

The Making of the Finnish Polar Silk Road: Status in Spring 2019

Julie Yu-Wen Chen

9.1 Introduction

This chapter aims to use the empirical case of the making of the Polar Silk Road in Finland to problematize the current approach in understanding China's Belt and Road Initiative (BRI) and its influence. The existing approach often looks at China's economic, political, and diplomatic calculations in venturing into the BRI. As China's geopolitical interests are the starting point for analysis, existing studies often fall into the trap of assuming that if China has an interest and has the capital to invest, then it will somehow have a huge influence. The Finnish case will show that China has no way of exerting influence and making inroads into any state unless local gatekeepers open the door, provide narratives that can tap into locals' interests (mostly economic), and endeavor to link up their own development plan with the BRI.

J. Y.-W. Chen (✉)
Department of Cultures, University of Helsinki, Helsinki, Finland
e-mail: julie.chen@helsinki.fi

© The Author(s) 2020   193
H. K. Chan et al. (eds.), *International Flows in the Belt and Road
Initiative Context*, Palgrave Series in Asia and Pacific Studies,
https://doi.org/10.1007/978-981-15-3133-0_9

In Finland's case, entrepreneurs have attempted to take the lead in realizing BRI in Finland. The most publicly known project is the construction of the tunnel between Finland's Helsinki and Estonia's Tallinn, led by Peter Vesterbacka, the former Angry Bird founder. The Finnish case will support my argument for an alternative bottom-up approach to studying the BRI, proposing an examination of local actors' efforts in producing a localized understanding of the BRI, policy coordination, match of interest, and resonances of identities in potential BRI recipient states.

Before we commence the discussion of the Finnish case, let us have a look at the background of China's interest of having BRI projects in Nordic countries and the Arctic. In June 2017, China issued a document called "Vision for Maritime Cooperation under the Belt and Road Initiative" to synchronize development projects and plans along what China calls the "21st Century Maritime Silk Road" (China's National Development and Reform Commission and the State Oceanic Administration 2017). In this document, China envisioned a "blue economic passage... leading to Europe via the Arctic Ocean." In addition, China clearly expressed that it wanted to take part in Arctic affairs, ranging from conducting scientific research and encouraging the involvement of Chinese enterprises in the commercial use of Arctic routes and resources to participating in events organized by Arctic-related international organizations. This document paved the way for the release of China's first official Arctic policy several months later.

In January 2018, China presented its Arctic policy paper, which articulates and justifies Beijing's interests in Arctic affairs and describes its proposal for a "Polar Silk Road" as an extension of its BRI (China's State Council Information Office 2018; Tillman et al. 2018). These official moves are in contrast to China's many years of a low-profile stance on Arctic matters for fear of attracting international suspicion of its ambitions in the Arctic region. Previous studies have addressed China's interests in the Arctic (e.g., natural resources, shipping routes, participation in Arctic governance) (Huang et al. 2015; Peng and Wegge 2015). This article, however, aims to examine whether and how China's aspirations find resonance in Arctic states as Beijing becomes more vocal in Arctic affairs. It analyzes how such resonance enables China to take the idea of the Polar Silk Road beyond political rhetoric.

Finland is the focus of this study because it seems that Finland "might" be able to construct very concrete transportation lines with the support of Chinese funding and that these routes can be counted as an extension of the BRI, thus the so-called Polar Silk Road. I stressed the term "might" because the construction of transportation lines is still in its infancy as of early 2019. Only time will tell if they will be successful. The nature of this study is hence exploratory. I will present the current status and future plans for this construction and, most important of all, I will unpack how this construction can take place. Who is making the Polar Silk Road happen?

Before delving into the Finnish experience, I intend to first present some thoughts on the nature of the BRI that I believe are vital to understanding how it can find support outside China. We can conceive the BRI as a form of building up regional cooperation without clearly delineating which states and actors can be included in the process. It is different from other kinds of regional cooperation, such as the Shanghai Cooperation Organization (SCO), which appear to be more exclusive and closed (Kaczmarski 2017a, b). One can conceive the BRI as a conceptual framework that awaits interested parties to give it substance and inject real meaning. As several recent studies have pointed out (Chen and Günther 2020; Chen and Jiménez-Tovar 2017; Liu and Lim 2018), local elites (e.g., political, business) along the route of the "Road" or "Belt" play important roles in making sense of the BRI in their own countries. What this means in practical terms is that domestic stakeholders need Chinese capital and/or expertise to help them advance their own agendas. Accordingly, they have an interest in helping to justify and to legitimize the passage of the BRI through their own countries. Currently, there are few studies of how domestic stakeholders in various countries perceive the BRI and their efforts to give it real local meanings (Liu and Lim 2018). This article uses the example of Finland to fill this empirical gap. In essence, we aim to uncover the main actors supporting the BRI and the Polar Silk Road in Finland. Why and how do these actors show support? How exactly has the BRI manifested its influence in Finland?

The domestic stakeholders that this study aims to examine should not just be actors that use the banner of BRI or the Polar Silk Road at some of their events. Hence, Confucius Institutes are excluded from our examination here. As of 2019, there has been a Confucius Institute at the University of Helsinki for 11 years. The University of Lapland was planning to establish one but decided not to proceed after years of negotiation. Due to this Confucius Institute's nature as a joint venture between the Chinese Hanban and the Finnish host university, it is no surprise that it might from time to time use the banner of the BRI or Polar Silk Road at its events. These events might make their attendees aware of the existence of the BRI, but they are not sufficiently significant for the Confucius Institute to be included in this analysis. This study seeks to focus on non-Chinese actors in Finland who have taken up the BRI banner to advance their cause. We need to ask why they have an interest in advancing China's BRI and how they do this. This naturally leads us to two highly debated projects and their initiators in Finland: the Arctic Corridor and the Helsinki–Tallinn tunnel. Ideas for these projects predate the birth of China's BRI. However, for a variety of reasons including a lack of money, concerns about returns on investment and their impact on the lives and environments of local populations (e.g., reindeer herders, indigenous Sami people), they have remained purely as ideas for decades. In recent years, their current Finnish advocates have come to notice the BRI and its potential and are trying to garner resources from China in the hope that these ideas can be given real substance. One of the prime players in making this happen is the Finnish entrepreneur Peter Vesterbacka, who is known internationally as the founder of the Angry Bird video game company.

In the following section, I will begin by introducing the Arctic Corridor and Helsinki–Tallinn tunnel projects. The third section will move on to elaborate on my hypotheses of how China's BRI can be realized in different countries. The fourth section will explain my research method and data, and the fifth section uses the Finnish case to test the hypotheses. It is this fifth section that will discuss who Peter Vesterbacka is, his agenda, and his China linkage. I should caution readers in advance, however, that this study can only present the current (as of spring 2019) status of the initial plans to construct the Polar Silk Road in Finland. None of these have yet borne fruit, but, as my report will show, at least significant steps seem to have been taken because of Peter Vesterbacka's efforts. The most recent step was Peter Vesterbacka's announcement that his firm has garnered €15 billion from China to advance his tunnel project between Helsinki and Tallinn (Yle News 2019; Pohjanpalo 2019).

By looking at the Finnish experience, it is hoped that this article can contribute further empirical evidence of the BRI's impact on developed countries. China frequently portrays the BRI as contributing to peace and development. This often leads scholars to examine its influence in developing countries, such as those in Central Asia and Africa (Chen and Günther 2020; Chen and Jiménez-Tovar 2017). However, China is also interested in developed countries because in these, areas such as the Arctic require further development. Even developed countries do not necessarily have enough funding for such huge projects, and Chinese capital can thus make a contribution. Toward both developing countries and developed countries, China uses the same tactic of becoming a cosponsor rather the sole sponsor of these countries' development (Hodzi and Chen 2017, p. 33; Blaxekjær et al. 2018, p. 442). This is practical for China, as it is difficult for Beijing to simply invent a project for construction in a foreign land. Being a cosponsor allows China to gain the trust of cooperators, boosting the image that the BRI is for the common good of both China and the states engaged (Hodzi and Chen 2017, p. 33). In the next section, we introduce the two projects that could make the Finnish side of the Polar Silk Road a reality.

9.2 The Finnish Side of the Polar Silk Road

9.2.1 The Arctic Corridor and Arctic Railway

Various Arctic states, including Finland, have been conceptualizing and discussing the Arctic Corridor for years. The term "Arctic Corridor" in Finnish is *Jäämeren käytävä*, which is thought to have been coined over 100 years ago and literally means "Finland's connection to the Arctic Ocean." Timo Lohi, spokesperson of the contemporary Arctic Corridor project, has said that he updated the concept in April 2008 and invented the English name the "Arctic corridor" around 2009–2010. The authorities in northern Finland liked the idea and decided to prepare an action plan for it in 2009. The first study for the Arctic Railway was published in February 2010, and the authorities subsequently started to prepare marketing material for both the Arctic Corridor and the Arctic Railway. According to the project's self-definition, the Arctic Corridor is a "global economic region" and a "transport and development corridor" that connects Finland and Europe to the deep-water ports of the Arctic Ocean, large production areas of oil and gas, and the western end of the Northern Sea Route (Arctic Corridor 2018).

The Finnish and Norwegian Ministries of Transport believe that the most realistic plan would entail a railway between Finland's Rovaniemi and Norway's Kirkenes, as this would complete the rail route connecting the Arctic Ocean to the Mediterranean (Arctic Corridor 2018; see also Fig. 9.1). Kirkenes is ice-free and is the closest Western port to Asia.

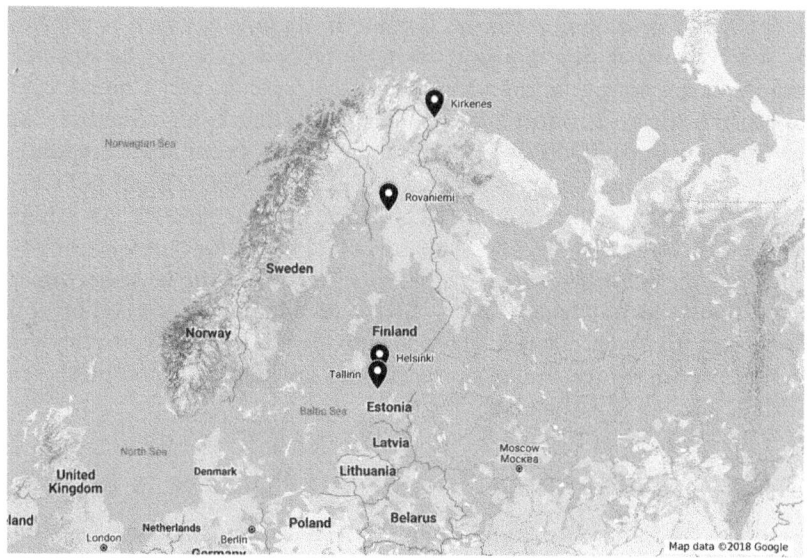

Fig. 9.1 Kirkenes, Rovaniemi, Helsinki, and Tallinn (*Source* Map drawn using Google's My Map)

Chinese goods as well as oil and gas from the Arctic fields in Russia could be transshipped at Kirkenes for movement by rail southward to Helsinki and other Scandinavian countries, the Baltic states, and the rest of Europe. The cost is estimated to be between €5 and €1.5 billion. The wide range of this estimate is related to issues such as whether to use existing tracks or not, routing and other options (Vauraste 2018). It is estimated that construction could commence as soon as the 2020s and be completed by 2030 (Arctic Corridor 2018). The railway project is still in its infancy, as the Finnish and Norwegian authorities need to study not only issues of financial viability but also environmental impacts and reindeer husbandry and take the life of indigenous Sami population into account (Finnish Ministry of Transport and Communications 2019; Vauraste 2018).

As noted earlier, observers have been aware of China's interest in Arctic shipping routes for many years (Huang et al. 2015; Peng and Wegge 2015), but it is only in the 2018 Arctic policy paper that the Chinese government officially proposed that it wishes to support all parties interested in developing the Arctic shipping routes. The Arctic Corridor is perceived by the Chinese Arctic policy paper as the Polar Silk Road. However, so far there has been no real action, including political decisions and financial plans for the construction of the Arctic Railway (Lindström 2018). As a 2019 report from the Finnish Prime Minister's Office stated, so far there is no formal Chinese involvement, but there have been "interests from Chinese media and informal expression of interests from Chinese business actors" (Koivurova et al. 2019, p. 73). It could be that if the railway project can move further to an implementation stage, formal interests from Chinese companies would arrive (Koivurova et al. 2019, p. 73).

In contrast, although the Helsinki–Tallinn tunnel project was not specifically noted by the Chinese Arctic policy paper as a part of the Polar Silk Road, it appears that it will be built sooner than the Arctic Railway. As noted earlier on, in spring 2019, there is official news that Chinese investment will be involved in the tunnel project. This could offer very preliminary evidence of the Chinese intent to construct the Finnish/Estonian section of the Polar Silk Road. The following discussion further introduces the tunnel project.

9.2.2 The Helsinki–Tallinn Tunnel

The Helsinki–Tallinn tunnel has been planned by Finnish and Estonian governmental agencies and businesses for many years. In an opening speech at a seminar on the link between Helsinki and Tallinn in 2016, the then mayor of Helsinki, Jussi Pajunen, said that the idea of building a fixed link in the form of a bridge had been discussed as long ago as 1871 (Nordic Investment Bank 2016a). At present, Helsinki and Tallinn are seen jointly as an economic area with a population of 1.5 million. People from both sides frequently move between them for work and leisure. Traffic between the two port cities has grown. According to the Port of Helsinki's 2017 annual report, Helsinki had become the busiest passenger port in Europe with 12.3 million passengers, and the Helsinki–Tallinn route in particular carried the most traffic.

In 2016, authorities from Helsinki city, Tallinn city, the Helsinki-Uusimaa Regional Council, Estonia's Harju County, the Finnish Transport Agency, and the Estonian Ministry of Economic Affairs and Communications applied for EU funding and received €3.1 million to commence a comprehensive feasibility study of the viability of constructing a fixed link between Helsinki and Tallinn (Nordic Investment Bank 2016a, b; Tsurouka 2017). A consortium of interested business entities subsequently took up the task of the feasibility study, which included cost–benefit analyses, impact assessments for both the rail and marine options, technical proposals of how the undersea tunnel could be built, and price tag determinants for construction, maintenance, and rail traffic. It also laid out the main features, such as routes and stations. In the feasibility study, the undersea tunnel was proposed to be 90 kilometers long. At present, it takes about two hours to travel by ferry from Helsinki to Tallinn, if the weather permits. The tunnel and a high-speed train would remove the uncertainty of weather conditions and shorten the journey to only 30 minutes.

China's 2018 Arctic policy paper did not specifically mention this tunnel project, but internationally known Finnish entrepreneur, Peter Vesterbacka, the former co-founder of Angry Birds, had been actively promoting the tunnel project and lobbying various stakeholders to let Chinese investors be involved. In Vesterbacka's narrative, the tunnel is a "natural" project of China's BRI (Valtonen and Vesterbacka 2018). The necessity of building the tunnel and how it should be constructed have been hotly debated in Finland. Against this background, the tunnel project is included in this study.

9.3   Conceptual Frameworks and Hypotheses

Because neither of the above two projects has been constructed and only very recently (spring 2019) has Peter Vesterbacka announced that his firm "FinEst Bay Area Development Oy" will receive Chinese funding of €15 billion Euro to construct the tunnel, our main research question focuses on what has sparked the BRI's involvement in these two projects. This is essentially connected to who or what kind of stakeholders have an interest in linking the BRI to these (originally) purely European infrastructure projects and what actual efforts they are making.

Two streams of political science theories are relevant here: interest group theories and international relations (IR) theories. This is because, ultimately, we seek to explore what kind of Finnish non-state players would make efforts to link the BRI to the Arctic Railway and Helsinki–Tallinn tunnel projects. How are they mobilized? What is their connection with Finnish and/or Chinese state actors and under what conditions would they make real impact by realizing the Polar Silk Road?

Finnish non-state actors, such as Arctic Economic Council, Peter Vesterbacka's firms and other firms that cooperate with him, are all acting in nature as interest groups to advance the building of Arctic Railway and the Helsinki–Tallinn tunnel. Various schools of interest group theories can help us conceptualize the importance of entrepreneurship, resources, and collective interests in making these Finnish non-state actors successful or not successful in their work. The reason why IR theories, particularly those on transnational non-state actors are relevant here is that Finnish non-state actors also coordinate with non-state actors and state actors from China, Estonia, Norway, Germany, and others to prepare for these ambitious construction projects. As Willetts (1982) and Risse (2001, p. 258; also cited as Risse-Kappen elsewhere in this article) have both pointed out, literature on transnational non-state actors is, to a certain degree, "commensurate with the study of interest groups."

Pertaining to a larger contention between the state-centered theories and society-centered theories in the study of Political Science, researchers have long debated the influence of non-state actors in international relations. State-centered theories (Evans et al. 1985; Skocpol 1992) highlight the "autonomy" of the state in the policy-making process, while society-centered theories (Dahl 1967, 2005; Lipset 1969) stress the demands or interests of collective societal actors in affecting the process. Society-centered theories have a strong root in the pluralist school of perspectives prevalent in the United States during the 1950s and 1960s (Risse-Kappen 1999, p. 17; Evans et al. 1985, p. 4). This debate, in Risse-Kappen's (1999, pp. 14–15) view, is misleading. Regarding the state-dominated view, Risse-Kappen (1999, p. 15) criticizes that "there is no logical connection between the argument that states remain dominant actors in international politics and the conclusion that societal actors and transnational relations should, therefore be irrelevant." In criticizing the society-centered view, Risse-Kappen (1999, p. 15) comments that "confusing the impact of transnational relations on world politics" with such a view "leads one to overlook the more interesting question of how inter-state and transnational relations interact" (Risse-Kappen 1999, p. 15). We do not have to do away with the "state" in research (Risse-Kappen 1999, p. 15). The solution Risse-Kappen (1999, pp. 19–25) proposes is a domestic structure approach, permitting the "differentiation between various degrees of state strength and autonomy vis-à-vis society to go beyond the generalities of *statist* versus *pluralist* approaches to the state" (Risse-Kappen 1999, p. 19).

Risse-Kappen's (1999, pp. 19–25) domestic structure approach suggests that researchers should look into the arrangement of political institutions, policy networks, and the structure of demand-formation in civil society inherent in a particular state. Examination of these domestic structures will help shed light on what stimulates the formation of a particular interest group in a particular state. In discussing the question of under what conditions could transnational non-state actors exert influence, Risse-Kappen (1994, p. 187) proposed that accessing the right policy-making body and cooperating with the right allies are crucial.

Keck and Sikkink (1998), however, pointed out the shortcoming of the domestic structure approach. The key problem is that this approach has so far primarily stressed the formal aspects of political and social arrangements in the studied state (Risse 2001, p. 266). Keck and Sikkink (1998, p. 202) raised the question of why human rights groups were more successful than environmental groups in changing the US policies under Presidents Carter and Reagan, given that both types of groups operated in the same American political and social settings. To remedy this flaw, Keck and Sikkink (1998, p. 202) took a constructivist approach and suggested that researchers should consider alternative explanations such as the factors of norms and values in determining interest groups' impact. The successful framing of issues by interest groups will reflect the norms and values of the society that they wish to influence. Whether Risse-Kappen's or Keck and Sikkink's theories are valid will be tested in this study. Below, I first propose three hypotheses derived from these theories.

9.3.1   Hypothesis of the Importance of a Local Champion in BRI Recipient States

Risse-Kappen's (1999) domestic structure approach suggests that gaining access to policy-making apparatus and cooperating with the right domestic actors have strong impacts on the success of interest groups. Several recent surveys of people in Central Asia and Central and Eastern Europe indicate that locals usually have little knowledge of China's BRI (Hodzi and Chen 2017). This shows that Chinese influence through the BRI is mostly at the elite level, with either business or political elites (Chen and Günther 2020; Chen and Jiménez-Tovar 2017). Although the BRI is often seen as part of China's charm offensive, its soft power influence is actually quite limited (Hodzi and Chen 2017). I therefore hypothesize that if the BRI can find a champion (or champions) in countries where it seeks to have influence, its projects are more likely to come to fruition. Hence, I first postulate the importance of a local Finnish champion (or champions) who can cooperate with the right domestic stakeholders to make the Polar Silk Road a reality.

9.3.2   Hypothesis of the Importance of Governmental Support from BRI Recipient States

My second hypothesis concerns a positive relationship between the support of the BRI recipient states and the successful implementation of the BRI. Again, this hypothesis is drawn from Risse-Kappen's (1999) domestic structure approach, which suggests the significance of winning allies in affecting the outcome of interest groups' politics. In this respect, the Finnish government's support is vital for the BRI to be realized in Finland.

9.3.3   Hypothesis of the Importance of the Nature of the BRI or the Polar Silk Road

As noted above, Keck and Sikkink (1998) took a different approach from Risse-Kappen by underlining the importance of norms and values in determining the influence of transnational networks. They believed that the nature of an issue proposed by transnational networks is crucial to the success or demise of a campaign. The most successful networks in Keck and Sikkink's (1998) study were those that focused on issues that involve bodily harm to vulnerable individuals or the rejection of legal equality of opportunity. This proposition is similar to the resonance hypothesis developed by Finnemore and Sikkink (1998), which argues that if transnational networks can create an issue or idea that resonates with preexisting beliefs in the target state, they are more likely to be influential. These ideas, in essence, come from the constructivist line of thought and echo a greater theoretical debate within social science about the influence of norms and values on the behaviors of states. In this study, the target state is Finland and I postulate that if the nature of the BRI or the Polar Silk Road resonates or is compatible with the preexisting beliefs of the Finnish government or society, the BRI (or more specifically, the Polar Silk Road) is more likely to be constructed.

9.4   METHODS AND DATA

The primary method was the qualitative analysis of policy documents, speeches, news reports, marketing materials, and press releases. Focused interviews with key actors or, in some cases, email correspondence with them was used to cross-examine preliminary findings.

9.5   EMPIRICAL ANALYSIS

The following discussion reports and analyzes the development of the two projects studied as of spring 2019. Progress before then was quite slow, but as we can see, in 2018 it appears that government-led studies and private entrepreneurship pushed the discussion of these two projects to a new and positive level. The environment is also becoming slightly more favorable for BRI to find its connection to these two European projects.

9.5.1   Development of Domestic Opportunities: Governmental Support for Private Entrepreneurship

Peter Vesterbacka is one of Finland's internationally known entrepreneurs. He is the co-founder of the Angry Birds video game franchise and the founder of Slush, an international initiative that organizes startup-related events in Helsinki and other countries, including China. Peter Vesterbacka has a keen interest in China and visits the country frequently. In 2011, *Time* magazine nominated him as one of the world's most influential people.

After his successful career in Angry Birds, Peter Vesterbacka was looking for new projects to work on. In 2016, the idea of constructing the Helsinki–Tallinn tunnel attracted him. He took up the cause and endeavored to make it happen (Breum 2018). In the summer of 2016, Peter Vesterbacka and his team attended Latitude 59, the flagship tech event of Estonia, where he approached the Estonian Foreign Minister Marina Kaljurand and declared his determination to take up the tunnel project. Not knowing about Peter Vesterbacka's involvement, the Estonian minister was bewildered (Valtonen and Vesterbacka 2018). His bewilderment actually speaks to the core of the problem. Who is the main actor in the tunnel project? Is it the government or private business?

As already noted, governmental authorities had been weighing the pros and cons of both the Arctic Railway project and the Helsinki–Tallinn tunnel project. As of spring 2019, however, the Finnish government had not made any political decision to start planning or building the Arctic Railway or the tunnel. Despite this, years of debate and studies of the possibility of building these projects had prepared the ground for private entrepreneurs such as Peter Vesterbacka to involve themselves in the projects. This is because it became clear that these projects simply could not be built with public funding.

Pre-feasibility and feasibility studies have pointed out that the tunnel project is mega in its scale (Finnish Ministry of Transport and Communications 2018a; Finest Link 2019). Public funding from both Finnish and Estonian governments is insufficient for such a giant project. It may be possible to look to the European Union (EU) for funding, but solely relying on the EU would not be viable either. Studies have found that private investment for the project is necessary, and public–private partnership might be an option (Finnish Ministry of Transport and Communications 2018b). However, a private-led model would be even more realistic. Governments, in a private-led model, should act as "enablers" to "support, give commitment, facilitate, monitor, authorize, and accept" the project, as laid out in the report of the tunnel task force issued by the Finnish Ministry of Transport and Communication in 2018.

The development of an understanding like this is critical, as it allows the Finnish and Estonian authorities to correctly understand where they should stand in such an issue. Instead of being the initiators of these projects, governmental authorities come to understand that their roles should be as the enablers of private businesses involvement. This environment, or what Risse-Kappen (1999) termed "domestic opportunity structure," thus became more and more favorable for Peter Vesterbacka to advance his agenda.

In an *EUobserver* press report in February 2018, Risto Murto, deputy director-general of the Networks Department of the Finnish Ministry of Transport and Communications, "confirmed that the governments of Finland and Estonia are studying how they may act as enablers of Vesterbacka's efforts – basically forsaking earlier suggestions of a publicly-funded tunnel" (Breum 2018). As the government moved from being a potential competitor of Peter Vesterbacka to becoming an enabler, his role as a champion for the tunnel project could be established.

Since 2016, Peter Vesterbacka's team has been garnering funding and preparing vital first steps, such as obtaining licenses and permits. For instance, a comprehensive environmental impact assessment is essential to obtaining governmental approval and licenses. Peter Vesterbacka's team cooperated with Pöyry, a consulting and engineering firm, to work on obtaining the necessary permits. Meanwhile, the tunnel project was included in the governmental regional plan. This signaled government support to progress the tunnel project. Until thus far, empirical evidence has supported the first and second hypotheses mentioned previously.

9.5.2   Entrepreneur Peter Vesterbacka's Vision

Peter Vesterbacka called his project the FinEst Bay Area project. FinEst is pronounced as "finest," the superlative of "fine." In Peter Vesterbacka's vision, the tunnel project would be based on the private funding that he can pull together. If governments wish to join his project, the project would then become public–private. The same applies to the construction of the Arctic Railway, which is also included in Peter Vesterbacka's long-term plan.[1]

The FinEst Bay Area project estimates that the tunnel will cost €15 billion, while the government-led feasibility study has estimated that the cost will range between €13 and €20 billion. Peter Vesterbacka's team believes that the FinEst Bay Area project's estimation is more accurate and is lower than the one estimated by the government's feasibility study. The FinEst Bay Area project proposes the opening of the tunnel in December 2024 while the government-led feasibility study predicted the opening year to be in 2040. The FinEst Bay Area project is actually larger than the railway project in that it is proposed to build two artificial islands along the tunnel. The islands will house 50,000 inhabitants, and financing for building these could be private. While the government-led feasibility study suggested the use of trains that would run at 200 kilometers per hour, Peter Vesterbacka has proposed using Chinese technology for a very fast train with speeds of up to 389 kilometers per hour.

As the FinEst Bay Area project and the government-led studies have different visions of the routing, timetable, modes of transportation, and other issues concerning the tunnel, some media reports have framed this

---

[1] The Finnish authorities have not held any discussion with Vesterbacka regarding his plan for the Arctic Railway and is not aware of his plan (Lindström 2018).

as two competing projects (Jarvia 2018; Oja 2018). In a press event on December 3, 2018, however, Peter Vesterbacka had tried to reject such framing. He understands the importance of governmental support to make his project come true. As he becomes capable of garnering sufficient funding for this project, he expects to turn the situation in his favor in the sense that he could negotiate differences such as routing, timetable, modes of transportation, and other issues directly with the government.

Peter Vesterbacka's current goal is the Helsinki–Tallinn tunnel, but his larger ambition is to use this to attract investors to stimulate the growth of the metropolitan areas of Helsinki and Tallinn and, in the much longer term, to build the Arctic Railway (Valtonen and Vesterbacka 2018). As Peter Vesterbacka declared in a press event on December 3, 2018: "It is not about the tunnel, but what it enables." He sees the tunnel as an enabler of drawing future talents, investments, and growth. Peter Vesterbacka believes that the tunnel will create a center of gravity that leads to the metropolitan area linking Helsinki and Tallinn becoming a region of rapid economic growth.

9.5.3 Entrepreneur's Efforts in Framing the Finnish Projects as Part of the BRI

There is interest in utilizing Chinese capital to help realize the Arctic Railway and Helsinki–Tallinn tunnel projects, both from Peter Vesterbacka's team and other stakeholders (Valtonen and Vesterbacka 2018; Lohi 2018). Most of this interest remains as expressions of interest. Peter Vesterbacka's team is the exception; they have been actively visiting Chinese investors but are not able to reveal details of current negotiations.

The fact that China's BRI has an open and inclusive nature is important. There are no geographical or spatial boundaries to the BRI's outreach. China defines the BRI in functional terms, supporting any international project that has the potential to become part of the BRI (Kaczmarski 2017a, pp. 1364–1366; 2017b, p. 1040). There is no concrete definition of what kind of cooperative engagement there should be (Kaczmarski 2017a, p. 1359). This opens the door to many possibilities, encouraging interested stakeholders in Finland to justify how their projects can be part of the BRI and thus obtain Chinese investment (Kaczmarski 2017a, p. 1359).

For instance, Timo Lohi, the spokesperson of the Arctic Corridor project, became aware of China's BRI around 2015–2016. In his view, the BRI might take part in "financing, building, and operating the Arctic Railway" in the long term. However, as of late 2018, there has been no direct BRI investment in transport and logistics in northern Finland (Valtonen and Vesterbacka 2018; Lohi 2018). Similarly, feasibility studies and reports have noted the potential connection of the tunnel project to China's BRI. Peter Vesterbacka is by far the most active actor by taking real steps to negotiate with potential Chinese stakeholders to attract investment (Breum 2018).

Peter Vesterbacka's active engagement with China is not only shown by his very frequent visits to the country. His team's office at the We+ co-working space in Helsinki is actually a Chinese-owned share-space office. He has been using We+ to help Finnish industry start-ups interested in the Chinese market. In addition, he was also said to be one of the main people pushing the Finnish tax administration to offer services in Chinese. In 2017, the Finnish tax office launched its first China desk, making Finland the first foreign tax administration in the world to offer Chinese services.

At a press event on December 3, 2018, Peter Vesterbacka explained that he spent a lot of time elaborating on one particular slide of his pitch presentation to potential Chinese collaborators. His pitch to investors was encapsulated by four bullet points on this slide: Finland's clean air, high education, low corruption, and the fact that Finland is ranked the happiest country in the world by the United Nations 2018 World Happiness Report.

By framing Finland as a Eurasian country, Peter Vesterbacka repeatedly reminds investors that Finland, albeit on the northern periphery of Europe, is actually the "closest neighbor of China, India, and Japan in the EU" and that Finland has direct air connections putting it 6–8 hours from China, India, Japan, and the rest of Asia. It is interesting to note that a similar Eurasian discourse is used by promoters of the Arctic Corridor project to create a sense of spatial closeness with Asia and thus legitimize the project's natural contribution of Asian investors. For instance, in a report by Breum (2018), Risto Murto, deputy director-general in the Networks Department of the Finnish Ministry of Transport and Communications, said "When we think of new corridors to China, we are halfway between Europe and Asia. Finland is not an island anymore. We look at our geopolitical position in a whole new way."

It is clear that the entrepreneurial efforts of Peter Vesterbacka have helped establish the relevance of these two seemingly European-based projects to China's BRI, thus making the Polar Silk Road from imagination to reality. This is particularly remarkable since China's Arctic Policy initially did not mention the tunnel project, but the open and inclusive nature of the BRI or the Polar Silk Road concepts has been useful for Vesterbacka to make the linkage to his own project. This supports the validity of the third hypothesis mentioned previously.

It is vital to note, however, not all of the affected local individuals and elites would necessarily understand nor accept that Finland is a part of China's metaphorical Silk Road as this seems to go against common geographic knowledge and perception. Moreover, the principal–agent problem mentioned at the outset of this paper still exists at this stage. Although Peter Vesterbacka's entrepreneurship has shown some preliminary evidence of success in making the Polar Silk Road closer to reality, anonymous officials from the Finnish Ministry of Foreign Affairs have revealed that they do not support the narrative that Polar Silk Road has found its Finnish route. The fundamental problem for them is that Finland has not officially joined the BRI. As one of the anonymous officials from the Ministry of Foreign Affairs explained to the author, the ministry does not have a position on the tunnel project and is generally supportive of increasing connectivity between Europe and Asia. Such connectivity, however, does not need to be seen in the context of BRI at all. To some extent, I have observed that Peter Vesterbacka does understand this point. Yet, he adds the concept of the Silk Road to his campaign for clear reason: to attract Chinese capitals and legitimize Chinese involvement.

9.5.4 First Sign of Success in Spring 2019?

Although Peter Vesterbacka is not willing to disclose details of his ongoing negotiations in China, there is some evidence to suggest that the process might have not been easy. In an *EUobserver* report published in February 2018, Peter Vesterbacka claimed that "Chinese investors will cover two-thirds while northern European pension funds will probably cover most of the rest of the €15 billion" (Breum 2018). This funding plan and the proportion of Chinese investments seems to have decreased over time. In a press event held in Helsinki on December 3, 2018, Peter Vesterbacka said that 50% of the funding would be from Europe with the other 50% coming from Asia, where countries such as Japan, China, India, and others could play a role. This plan differs from the February *EUobserver* report that Chinese involvement would be greater. At the same press event, Peter Vesterbacka proposed that 30% would be equity funding while 70% would be loans. He announced that he had secured seed funding from the first outside investor; Dubai-based ARC Holding would finance the seed stage of funding in the amount of €100 million. No Chinese investment had been secured as of late 2018.

One should bear in mind that in other countries with China-funded projects, the projects are normally implemented by Chinese companies and China typically offers loans not investments. The current development shows a different arrangement in the case of Finland. In spring 2019, Peter Vesterbacka officially announced his success in obtaining €15 billion for his project. A private equity firm called Touchstone Capital Partners Ltd. will contribute one-third of the money through equity investment, thus getting a minority stake in this project. The remaining two-thirds will be a loan.

Although Touchstone Capital Partners Ltd. claims to be a private equity firm, it has an OBOR Consortium Group that including 15 China's leading state-owned enterprises (SOEs) and 15 international firms. With this, the firm has €100 billion USD One Belt One Road Fund to expand OBOR's related business.

Current arrangement means that the FinEst Bay Area project will be able to remain majority Finnish-owned. In a report by the Finnish state media Yle News, Peter Vesterbacka explained this arrangement as a result of the Finnish side's plan to restrict the amount of Chinese investment and makes the Finnish side to still obtain a majority stake in the project. As Vesterbacka clarified, "At the moment there is a global discussion in Finland and elsewhere, there is a desire to not have too much Chinese money" (Yle News 2019).

In addition to Chinese funding, Peter Vesterbacka has talked to major Chinese state-owned entities that have already had funded BRI projects in other countries, such as the China Railway Group Limited (CREC). It is unclear to outsiders what CREC's role might be, but from the limited information that his team is willing to disclose, we know that Chinese technologies and expertise, along with technologies from other countries, will be used in building the tunnel and operating the very fast train. In sum, Chinese involvement in the tunnel project means bringing in Chinese capitals and contracts for Chinese companies and operators of infrastructure.

Lastly, I shall mention that the Chinese Embassy in Finland has had discussions with Peter Vesterbacka's team about the tunnel project and with the Finnish Ministry of Transport and Communications about the Arctic Corridor project. However, this study does not have further details of their communications. Sabina Lindström, leader of the Task Force Study for the Arctic Railway, advised that the discussion remains "on a very general level, and no concrete proposals have been presented by either side" (Lindström 2018). In an interview that Blaxekjær et al. (2018, p. 442) conducted with Chinese Arctic ambassador Gao Feng, the ambassador also indicates that the Chinese approach is to let Nordic actors form their ideas to see how they wish to be part of the Polar Silk Road first before the Chinese embassy would get involved in further discussion. These evidence supports the kernel of this article's argument that a localized approach is the right approach to evaluate whether BRI can be realized in target states or not.

9.5.5   Summary

Current progress seems to suggest that domestic opportunity structure matters. A local champion such as Peter Vesterbacka in BRI recipient states makes a difference, as he can act to develop the tunnel project more quickly than the Finnish authorities. His team has indicated that looking for EU funding would delay the process. This stance differs from the feasibility studies pointing to potential support from the EU. Although his team has noted that obtaining public funding would slow the process, this team takes pains not to criticize the government, because it understands the importance of obtaining governmental support. The stance of the Finnish authorities to act as enablers of Peter Vesterbacka's plan is crucial. He needs the governmental support to put the tunnel in the government's development plan and to get all the necessary licenses and permits to start the construction.

The development of the domestic environment in Finland, moving the government from a potential competitor to an enabler of private entrepreneurship, and the championship of Peter Vesterbacka's team facilitates the realization of the tunnel project and the potential connection of the BRI with Finland. This supports the use of Risse-Kappen's domestic opportunity structure approach to look at how the BRI can find relevance in potential target states.

In general, the BRI's space-free and functional approach to cooperation and Finland's desire to position itself as a major connecting point linking Asia and Europe match well. The BRI's promise of economic benefits for participants and openness to regional cooperation are also generally in line with Peter Vesterbacka's discourse of using infrastructural initiatives to revive regional economies. This allows Finnish stakeholders to justify attracting BRI capital and opens the door for BRI to construct its Polar branch. The Polar Silk Road is gradually being imagined, articulated, and realized, despite its slow process.

It is important to note, however, that although the third hypothesis concerning the nature of the BRI is valid, it is only of secondary importance. It only provides a condition that can allow interested stakeholders to justify their projects' relevance to the BRI. Local championship and governmental support are integral to the realization of projects. Hence, Risse-Kappen's (1999) domestic structure approach allows a better interpretation of the Finnish case than the constructivists' concern for the nature of issues, values, and norms. Knowing the nature of the issue is a necessary but not a sufficient condition for the BRI concept to become reality in a target state.

9.6   Conclusion

This study shows the very preliminary development of two infrastructure projects in Finland that have the potential to be part of the Polar Silk Road of the future. In Finland, domestic discussion about these two projects and preparations for them became more active in 2018 than in any previous year. As the process is still embryonic, it is hard to be precise about the real Chinese involvement beyond our tentative knowledge of the potential arrival of Chinese capitals, technology, and expertise in the tunnel project. But what is clear is that for the BRI to make its way to Finland, local champions and support from the Finnish authorities are needed to sow the seeds of further cooperation. Framing and justifying the BRI as relevant to the Finnish projects demands substantial effort. This framing should allow potential Chinese investors to feel comfortable with these projects and be willing to contribute to them. These framing processes are as important as the actual negotiations between the Chinese and the Finnish stakeholders. The very preliminary findings that this study offers to reveal the challenges faced by the BRI in making a real impact on target states. Future studies could take a more recipient-centered approach in looking at the influence of the BRI, which would give a more balanced picture of exactly the kind of impact that China can have on world politics and business.

REFERENCES

Blaxekjær, L. Ø., Lanteigne, M., & Shi, M. (2018). The Polar Silk Road & The West Nordic Region. In L. Heininen & E.-P. Heather (Eds.), *Arctic yearbook 2018* (pp. 437–455). Akureyri, Iceland: Northern Research Forum.

Breum, M. (2018, February 28). Finland plans Arctic Corridor linking China to Europe. *EUobserver*. https://euobserver.com/nordic/141142. Accessed 10 Nov 2018.

Chen, Y.-W., & Günther, O. (2020). Back to normalization or conflict with China in greater Central Asia? Evidence from local students' perceptions. Special issue "Encounters after the soviet collapse: Chinese presence in the former soviet union border zone". *Problems of Post-Communism*. https://www.tandfonline.com/doi/full/10.1080/10758216.2018.1474716.

Chen, Y.-W., & Jiménez-Tovar, S. (2017). China in Central Asia: Local perceptions from future elites. *China Quarterly of International Strategic Studies, 3*(3), 429–455.

Dahl, R. A. (2005). *Who governs? Democracy and power in American city* (2nd ed.). New Haven: Yale University Press.

Evans, P. B., Rueschemeyer, D., & Skocpol, T. (1985). *Bringing the state back in* (P. B. Evans, D. Rueschemeyer, & T. Skocpol, Eds.). New York: Cambridge University Press.

Finest Link. (2019, February 7). *Helsinki–Tallinn transport link: Feasibility study-final report*. http://www.finestlink.fi/wp-content/uploads/2018/02/FinEst-link-REPORT-FINAL-7.2.2018.pdf. Accessed 27 Feb 2019.

Finnemore, M., & Sikkink, K. (1998). International norm dynamics and political change. *International Organization, 52*(4), 887–917.

Finnish Ministry of Transport and Communications. (2018a, May 15). *Helsinki–Tallinn tunnel task force: Report of the main findings*. https://www.lvm.fi/asiat-aikajarjestyksessa/-/mahti/asianasiakirjat/75814. Accessed 10 Nov 2018.

Finnish Ministry of Transport and Communications. (2018b, May 15). *Tallinn tunnel task force: Unique mega-project requires private sector participation*. https://www.lvm.fi/en/-/tallinn-tunnel-task-force-unique-mega-project-requires-private-sector-participation-972876?from=timeline&isappinstalled=0. Accessed 31 Mar 2019.

Finnish Ministry of Transport and Communications. (2019, February 11). *Final report of the joint working group between Finland and Norway on the Arctic Railway*. http://julkaisut.valtioneuvosto.fi/handle/10024/161367. Accessed 31 Mar 2019.

Hodzi, O., & Chen, Y.-W. (2017). *The great rejuvenation? China's search for a new 'global order'* (pp. 1–41). Stockholm: Institute for Security and Development Policy.

Huang, L., Lasserre, F., & Alexeeva, O. (2015). Is China's interest for the Arctic driven by Arctic shipping potential? *Asian Geographer, 32*(1), 59–71.

Jarvia, H. (2018, May 23). Helsinki–Tallinn: Two competing tunnel projects. *Standby Nordic*. https://standbynordic.com/helsinki-tallinn-two-competing-tunnel-projects/. Accessed 1 Apr 2019.

Kaczmarski, M. (2017a). Non-western visions of regionalism: China's New Silk Road and Russia's Eurasian Economic Union. *International Affairs, 93*(6), 1357–1376.

Kaczmarski, M. (2017b). Two ways of influence-building: The Eurasian Economic Union and the One Belt, One Road Initiative. *Europe-Asia Studies, 69*(7), 1027–1046.

Keck, M., & Sikkink, K. (1998). *Activists beyond borders: Advocacy networks in international politics*. Ithaca, NY: Cornell University Press.

Koivurova, T., Kauppila, L., Kopra, S., Lanteigne, M., Shi, M., Smieszek (Gosia), M., et al. (2019). *China in the Arctic and the opportunities and challenges for Chinese–Finnish–Arctic co-operation*. Helsinki: Prime Minister's Office.

Lipset, S. M. (1969). *Political man*. London: Heinemann Educational Books.

Liu, H., & Lim, G. (2018). The political economy of a rising China in Southeast Asia: Malaysia's response to the Belt and Road Initiative. *Journal of Contemporary China, 28*(116), 216–231.

National Development and Reform Commission and the State Oceanic Administration of the People's Republic of China. (2017, June 20). *Vision for maritime cooperation under the Belt and Road Initiative*.

Nordic Investment Bank. (2016a, November 21). *Seminar debates fixed connection between Helsinki and Tallin*. https://www.nib.int/who_we_are/news_and_media/news_press_releases/1994/seminar_debates_fixed_connection_between_helsinki_and_tallinn. Accessed 6 Dec 2018.

Nordic Investment Bank. (2016b, December 1). *The Helsinki–Tallin tunnel: A silk road in the slush*. https://www.nib.int/who_we_are/news_and_media/articles/2005/the_helsinki-tallinn_tunnel_a_silk_road_in_the_slush. Accessed 25 Oct 2018.

Oja, T. (2018, May 8). Helsinki–Tallinn: One tunnel, two projects. *Postimees*. https://news.postimees.ee/4485267/helsinki-tallinn-one-tunnel-two-projects. Accessed 1 Apr 2019.

Peng, J., & Wegge, N. (2015). China's bilateral diplomacy in the Arctic. *Polar Geography, 38*(3), 233–249.

Pohjanpalo, K. (2019, March 8). *World's longest undersea rail tunnel gets $17 billion in funding*. Bloomberg. https://www.bloomberg.com/news/articles/2019-03-08/world-s-longest-undersea-rail-tunnel-agrees-17-billion-funding. Accessed 8 Mar 2019.

Port of Helsinki. (2017). *Annual report 2017*. https://vuosikertomus2017.portofhelsinki.fi/en/. Accessed 8 Dec 2018.

Risse, T. (2001). Transnational actors and world politics. In W. Carlsnaes, T. Risse, & B. A. Simmons (Eds.), *Handbook of international relations* (pp. 255–274). London: Sage.

Risse-Kappen, T. (1994). Ideas do not float freely: Transnational coalitions, domestic structures, and the end of the Cold War. *International Organization, 48*(2), 185–214.

Risse-Kappen, T. (1999). *Bringing transnational relations back in: Non-state actors, domestic structures and international institutions* (T. Risse-Kappen, Ed.). Cambridge: Cambridge University Press.

Skocpol, T. (1992). *Protecting soldiers and mothers: The political origin of social policy in the United States*. Cambridge, MA: Belknap Press of Harvard University Press.

State Council Information Office of the People's Republic of China. (2018, January 26). *China's Arctic Policy*.

Tillman, H., Jian, Y., & Nielsson, E. T. (2018). The Polar Silk Road: China's new frontier of international cooperation. *China Quarterly of International Strategic Studies, 4*(3), 345–362.

Tsurouka, D. (2017, July 2). Finland could serve as China's Arctic Gateway for OBOR. *Asia Times*. http://www.atimes.com/article/finland-serve-chinas-arctic-gateway-obor/. Accessed 25 Oct 2018.

Willetts, P. 1982. *Pressure groups in global system: The transnational relations of issue-oriented non-governmental organizations* (P. Willetts, Ed.). London: Pinter.

Yle News. (2019, March 8). *€15bn Chinese funding deal for Helsinki–Tallinn tunnel: A proposed link between the Estonian and Finnish capitals is set for a boost from China's Belt and Road Initiative*. Yle News. https://yle.fi/uutiset/osasto/news/15bn_chinese_funding_deal_for_helsinki-tallinn_tunnel/10680376. Accessed 8 Mar 2019.

Websites

Arctic Corridor. (2018). http://arcticcorridor.fi/.
FinEst Bay Area Development. https://finestbayarea.online.
FinEst Link Project. http://www.finestlink.fi/en/.
Silk Road Briefing. https://www.silkroadbriefing.com/.

Face to Face Interviews, Phone Interviews, and Email Correspondences with Key Stakeholders

K. Valtonen, & Vesterbacka, P. Founders of FinEst Bay Area Project, Interviewed by Yu-Wen Chen, October 29, 2018.

T. Lohi, Spokesman of Arctic Corridor, Interviewed by Yu-Wen Chen, October 30, 2018.
S. Lindström, Chair for Task Force Study for Arctic Railway, Interviewed by Yu-Wen Chen, November 9, 2018.
T. Vauraste, Chair of Arctic Economic Council & President and CEO of Arctia (Finnish state-own company operating the Finnish icebreaker fleet), Interviewed by Yu-Wen Chen, November 12, 2018.

PART III

History and Geography

Between Adoption and Resistance: China's Efforts of 'Understanding the West', the Challenges of Transforming Monarchical Legitimacy and the Rise of Oriental Exceptionalism, 1860–1910

Christian Müller

10.1   Introduction: China's Efforts of 'Understanding the West' and the Missing Vision for Reforming the Qing Empire, 1860–1910

When China was invited to take part in The Hague Peace Conference of 1899, the Imperial Court under Empress Dowager Cixi had only one question—what is in it for us? The Court questioned the Foreign Ministry, the *Zongli Yamen*, and the envoy to The Hague in great detail about

C. Müller (✉)
University of Nottingham Ningbo China, Ningbo, China
e-mail: Christian.mueller@nottingham.edu.cn

Visiting Research Fellow, Rothermere American Institute,
University of Oxford, Oxford, UK

© The Author(s) 2020
H. K. Chan et al. (eds.), *International Flows in the Belt and Road Initiative Context*, Palgrave Series in Asia and Pacific Studies,
https://doi.org/10.1007/978-981-15-3133-0_10

the benefits for the Empire and for the Manchu dynasty: 'Does China have to take part in this? Can we gain any benefit from it?'[1] The correspondence between the Court, the *Zongli Yamen*, and the plenipotentiary envoy, Yang Ru, to The Hague reveals that China's efforts of 'understanding the West' were designed to identify direct benefits if Western concepts should be adopted and framed for Chinese politics. The memorials to the throne further point towards a 'Great Wall of Prejudices' and misconceptions about the mechanisms of European political, diplomatic, and symbolic interaction that strongly influenced the way in which Qing China meandered around the topic of active 'Westernisation' since the 1840s, without a coherent and proper cause.[2]

From the late eighteenth century onwards, but more specifically from the turmoil and crisis of the Empire as it emerged from the Taiping Rebellion in the early 1860s until the end of the Qing dynasty, China followed a utilitarian approach to adopting Western concepts in order to strengthen the Confucian Empire. Chinese administrative and intellectual elites were eager to understand Western definitions of the international system, statehood, and society, as well as political and social rights. However, they were less eager to adopt those and included them in a reform plan for the Chinese Empire that looked for a middle ground between Western forms and Chinese content that would support the existing imperial legitimacy. Most transfers imitated Western forms of politics to adhere to an international, Euro-centric standard, but the contents were radically transformed for domestic purposes.[3] As in the case of the reforms to the Geneva Conventions discussed in The Hague in 1899, the Chinese delegate Yang Ru argued 'China cannot be the only country that runs counter to the current trend of politics'.[4] However, China questioned the rationale of restricting its own means of warfare by adhering to the propositions made

---

[1] *Qingji waijiao shiliao* (2015), Vol. 140, 18. The volume pagination of the original 1934 edition is used.

[2] Gustave Moynier to W.A.P. Martin, Geneva 30 April 1885, in *Archives du Comité International de la Croix Rouge* [*ACICIR*], *Personel Gustave Moynier* [*PGM*], Box 14, fols. 109–110. See more general: Reeves (2005), 64–93.

[3] No one, not even from the reformers wanted a whole Westernization of the country in the late nineteenth century. Chevrier (1989), 97.

[4] *Qingji waijiao shiliao* (2015), Vol. 140, 18.

in The Hague, and tacitly ignored the conventions while publicly consenting to the forms of diplomacy with humanitarian goals.[5]

To capture the relationship between 'foreign examples', their transfer from the constructed 'West' to China, and the changes of concepts when adopting and implementing them, this study utilises the approach of strategic 'framing'.[6] Benford and Snow have shown that concepts and practices are not transferred by individuals and collective actors free of purpose, but that the act of transfer follows the rationale of 'who benefits how from a transfer'.[7] Although this concept about different social nuances of communication between 'sender' and 'receiver' is not new, this conceptual framework helps heuristically to identify the mechanisms of cultural transfer. Thus, research has shifted from studying mere similarities between social and political aspects of two or more countries, and has abolished the naïve idea that by studying social, political, or national 'images' of one country in another country's discourse, one would understand the dialectic of adoption and resistance in the transfer and purposeful framing of foreign concepts and practices.[8] In the context of importing and exporting ideas, goods, and even sets of normative institutions and practices, the Chinese elites as the main actors are identified as a sometimes eager, sometimes reluctant, yet always active receiver and importer of European ideas.

Two questions emerge from this observation: (1) What purpose did different Chinese elites have to import and adopt Western concepts? and (2) How did those elites—conservative or reforming—frame and alter Western imports in a Chinese context to make them usable in a contested process to reform Qing China? These questions also address the diversity of actors, namely the Chinese administrative and intellectual elites who could shape the 'West' towards supporting or undermining the legitimacy of the Confucian order. The adoption of European elements regarding state and society had the potential to facilitate or speed up the waning of the imperial power. Thus, the aim of this study is to contextualise the transfer of Western concepts within the reform discourses of the late Qing Empire.

---

[5] *Qingji waijiao shiliao* (2015), Vol. 140, 18, 20.
[6] See Paulmann (2004), 169–196.
[7] Benford & Snow (2000), 611–639.
[8] Muhs, Paulmann, & Steinmetz (1998); Paulmann (1998), 649–685.

10.2   LITERATURE REVIEW—CHINA'S 'MANIFEST DESTINY' AND THE LOST LEGACY OF A HARMONIOUS WORLD ORDER REVISITED

The literature on the influence of the 'West' and foreign ideas in China and on Chinese-Western encounters in the late Qing dynasty is vast.[9] The scholarship has argued in detail the complexities of conceptual transfer in international relations, and concepts of state, society, and rights; however, it appears that, predominantly, the Chinese people's 'sole aim [was...] to make use of Western technology'.[10] Scholars during the self-strengthening movement, such as Feng Kuei-fen in 1861, brought it to a simple formula: 'What we then have to learn from the barbarians is only the one thing, solid ships and effective guns'.[11] However, the transfer of political concepts is much more complex than a simple copy of technology, as recent scholarship has highlighted. The context of many adoptions of European ideas related to the basic understanding that Chinese elites thought of a dichotomy of the Chinese essence as opposed to European utility of basic concepts in state, society, governance, and international relations. This dichotomy of *t'i-yong* was dominant in judging Western ideas against the yardstick of a Confucian Imperial Order and of the Chinese civilisation as the alleged crown of human development over time.[12] Orthodox Chinese historiography has marked the historical necessity of Chinese modernisation by adopting 'Western' elements during the 'imperialist period' of the 1840s to the 1940s to sketch the rising national and popular 'resistance' against the bourgeois, imperialist foreign domination.[13] Here the 'West' serves the purpose of radically transforming China by abolishing the 'feudal' Qing Empire and eventually the 'bourgeois' Republic with modernising means.

[9] See for example the classical account in Wang (1966).

[10] Ch'en (1969), 3–4.

[11] Feng Guifen, 'On the Manufacture of Foreign Weapons' (1861), quoted as in: Têng & Fairbank (1979), 52–54, 53.

[12] Ch'en (1969), 4; Liang Qichao, 'Die Evolution Chinas in den letzten 50 Jahren' (1922), quoted as in Lei (2009), 17.

[13] Osterhammel (2014), 52.

Modernising with Western forms served a necessary function in history towards the formation of the People's Republic of China in 1949.[14]

This crude materialist orthodoxy overlaps with new narratives about the continuity of a Chinese manifest destiny spanning from the Empire to the People's Republic. Interestingly, the moral dichotomy between 'bad' European imperialism and 'good' Chinese nationalist resistance has recently taken a turn towards considering the 'West' as the greater evil by brushing over the 'feudal' legacy of the Empire. The invention of ethnic 'Chineseness' as the essence of the Chinese Empire supersedes the ideological conflicts between the 'feudal' Empire and the Communist People's Republic. Recent contributions overemphasise the potential benefits of an imagined benevolent Chinese world order under the Qing Empire that was destroyed by the imperial expansion and dominance of European powers, Japan, and the United States of America.[15] Other historians have focused on the international regional system of China in Asia in the early nineteenth century and on the foreign invasion of mighty European concepts like international law, statehood, and civil society. They have depicted the 'forced' learning of European concepts as key to the destruction of a harmonious regional system in which Imperial China was both the core and the guardian for peaceful coexistence.[16]

In these narratives, the Qing Empire is framed as a peaceful and benevolent, disinterested and harmonious giant. This narrative bears striking similarities to the recent Chinese Belt and Road Initiative (BRI).[17] By tracing the origins of the BRI back into the early nineteenth century, the ideological differences between Empire and People's Republic give way to an ethno-centric narrative of harmonious progress under a Chinese Han shepherd with Manchu overtones. The damage was supposedly done by the European Imperial powers who forced the benevolent international giant China into a Euro-centric system on the terms of the imperial powers that pressed into East Asia with might and modernising concepts. This rather dubious and naïve narrative implies that the BRI is reinstating the

---

[14] Osterhammel (2014), 53; Troeltsch (1922), 756, 765.

[15] Zhao (2015), 961–982.

[16] Carty & Nijmann (2018). Many of the Chinese contributions on China in this recent prominent essay collection highlight this.

[17] See the invention of Zhang Qian's mission to the West in 138 BCE as a 'mission of peace and friendship' and not as a repeated attempt to secure Xinjiang as a vassal tributary state. Speech by Xi Jinping (2013), Nazarbayev University, Astana, 7 September 2013.

manifest destiny of China and its central role in global politics from the point in time around 1840, where the course of Chinese history diverted from its teleological course in the Marxist or Hegelian sense, through the intervention of European imperial interests. This type of scholarship appears to support the history of Chinese exceptionalism as an—only temporarily interrupted—eternal mission for global harmony.

This article addresses the problem of BRI-related narratives of the past to question the assumption that Qing China in fact provided a viable solution for a peaceful world order in the nineteenth century that was suppressed by the Europeans. Furthermore, it criticises the hidden ideological agenda that global harmony will flourish anew under the BRI in the twenty-first century with historical legitimisation. Chinese elites actively longed to import Western concepts to reform, transform, or revolutionise China until 1911. Yet, it remains unclear why so much of their purposeful efforts to understand and adopt Western concepts failed to translate into a comprehensive transition of the Qing Empire to counter the West.

This article, far from proposing to offer new sources or fundamentally question previous findings, argues that the process of learning from the 'West' was complex and competitive as to the purposes of how to reform the Chinese order of governance. Different actors would contest the 'Chinese World Order' when identifying and adopting specific 'Western' elements.[18] However, the biggest problem was the lack of coherent alternative visions and blueprints for a comprehensive reform of China to substitute the Qing world order based on Confucian traditions.[19] The internal struggle between competing world orders that juxtaposed the Qing order against the well-being of country and people has contributed to the dilemma of the Qing reform period and made purposeful adoptions of Western concepts much more complicated.[20] Yet, it would be erroneous to assume that the Manchu government only knew the alternatives between strict conservation of the Confucian order and Western modernisation.[21]

---

[18] Fairbank (1968), 12.

[19] Svarverud (2007), 45; Kayaoğlu (2010), 13.

[20] The Imperial Edict of 29 September 1898 condemned the 100-Day Reforms as treason because they substituted the preservation of the Great Qing Order with the preservation of China. Ch'en (1969), 6.

[21] Smith (1994), 285; Spence (1990), 140.

The efforts of Western conceptual transfer are regrouped anew around the following questions: who transferred, what was transferred, how was the transferred element adopted, and for which specific purposes was the transfer framed, and at times, altered? Knowledge exchange between Europe and Asia did not work as a one-way street where imperial and expansive European senders met wilfully obedient Chinese receivers. Chinese elites outside of or within the imperial hierarchy actively sought out aspects of 'Western' knowledge in international relations, constitutional and social politics, and the human rights discourse that would potentially help to reform the Qing Empire. The end of reform was and remained contested until the end of the Empire and reached from a defensive modernisation of technical means to a comprehensive revolution of the very basis of the imperial monarchy. All reforms (no matter the aim) that comprised transfers shared the problem of domestic framing. In order to be adaptable, the context or even the very meaning of Western concepts needed to be changed so that they would fit in a Chinese understanding of being the exceptional Middle Kingdom and the First Empire in the East and ultimately, the Centre of the Civilised World. Emphasising this particular worldview of Chinese exceptionalism, the *Zongli Yamen* claimed in 1899 that 'the treaties and declarations concluded [in The Hague] all aim at clarifying regulations of the West, which are different from China's laws and traditions'.[22] China was eager to adopt forms and discourses to satisfy the formal aspect of adhering to a Western standard while it aimed at including the function of these concepts into a distinctly exceptional Chinese interpretation of the world.[23]

In conclusion, this imperial project ultimately failed because it relied on the overly-optimistic assumption of a strong and equal China facing the Western powers that mirrored the history of the Qing dynasty from the late seventeenth century until the 1820s. Given the shrinking power of China, and the Manchu dynasty in particular; with a view to the European powers after 1840, this led to massive problems, failed transfers, and wilful misunderstandings.[24] Unlike the omnipresent example of Japan that wilfully adopted Western forms to strengthen its own modernising imperial project after 1870, China faced the challenge of lacking

---

[22] *Qingji waijiao shiliao* (2015), Vol. 140, 20.

[23] See for example Eyffinger (1999), 137–138; Eyffinger (2008), 7–46.

[24] Chang (2014), 287, 329.

a coherent defensive modernisation project that is backed by all parts of the imperial hierarchy in which different aspects of 'the West' could be included, transformed, and framed. Transfers of 'Western' concepts that would have any chance of implementation had to strengthen the imperial monarchic legitimacy of the Qing order. However, many transfers of the 'West' led to conclusions that had a reforming or revolutionary potential of undermining this very legitimacy. This tension around the purposes of 'framing' Western conceptual transfers opened the field for contested discourses about purposeful adoptions of the 'West' that claimed to offer a coherent blueprint for a future China.

10.3   WESTERN AND CHINESE VISIONS OF WORLD ORDER

In the beginning there was Prince Kung (Gong). The strong impetus on 'Understanding the West' as a model for Chinese defensive modernisation started with the so-called 'self-strengthening movement' under the *Tongzhi* Restoration in 1861/2. Prince Kung was the leading figure to order and consolidate the Empire after the Taiping Rebellion and other uprisings in the north and central provinces had brought China and the Manchu dynasty to the edge of extinction in the 1850s and early 1860s.[25] His programme was built upon the idea that in order to match the Western powers and to strengthen the Chinese Empire, it had to learn from the 'West'.[26]

The *Tongzhi* programme to understand the 'West' has been judged ambivalently by historians because, ultimately, China did not modernise in the way Japan did under the Meiji Restoration around the same time.[27] The efforts to 'imitate' European knowledge and institutions were judged as either too timid or simply a failure. However, these verdicts do not take into account the purpose of the Chinese attempts to incorporate 'Western' forms. Unlike the revolutionary creation of modern Japan under the

---

[25] Osterhammel (2014), 547–551.

[26] Kuo & Liu (1978), 491–542, 493f.; Chu & Liu (1994); Pong (1994), pp. 299–311; Imperial Memorial, January 13, 1861 ['The New Foreign Policy of January 1861'] and Feng Guifen, 'On the Adoption of Western Knowledge' (1861), quoted as in Têng & Fairbank (1979), 47–49, 51.

[27] Sun (2013).

Meiji era, the *Tongzhi* reforms and subsequent attempts from above constituted an essentially conservative programme to elevate the status of the Confucian Manchu monarchy. In essence, late Qing diplomacy and domestic politics were contested sequences of resistance and adaption to the 'West' that were at odds with the prevalent chauvinistic 'othering' of non-Chinese states, empires, and traditions of thought. Those foundations, stemming from the traditional tributary system and the worldview of superiority of the Middle Kingdom, were supposed to be reinforced rather than questioned. The rationale of 'understanding the West' was not a radical way of reform, but a deeply conservative enterprise to reinforce traditional monarchic legitimacy.

The fiction of Chinese superiority regarding every 'other' nation remained valid throughout the nineteenth century. The Chinese defeats in the two so-called 'Opium Wars' of 1840–1842 and 1858–1860 resulted in the increasing power of European states and established a Euro-centric international law of nations as the 'rules of the game' in international relations.[28] These new political developments triggered a Chinese reaction to become an active receiver of Western ideas after the Treaty of Tientsin 1860. Prince Gong initiated a new Foreign Ministry (*Zongli Yamen* or *Tsung-Li Ko-Kuo Szu-Wu Ya-men*) that imitated European practices of diplomacy and mirrored *prima facie* government responsibilities for international relations.[29] While this institution superseded the old Court Office for Tributary affairs, the *Zongli Yamen* remained an ambivalent institution between Court responsibilities and hierarchies, although it displayed notions of representing a 'state' as a sovereign institution. However, the *Zongli Yamen* was far from being the central ministry of foreign affairs (the *Wei Wu Pu* was established only in 1901) and fought for influence within the Court hierarchy under the sovereign emperor. European scholars have had difficulties describing the exact nature of the *Zongli Yamen* because it exemplified the lack of a sovereign Chinese state according to the European 'norm' and the multiplicity of competences in foreign policy that ultimately depended on the individual decision of the emperor as the ultimate source of power, authority, and sovereignty.[30] While the European state embodied sovereignty in a legitimate power monopoly

---

[28] See Bluntschli (1874), 444.

[29] Banno (1964), 219–236; Meng (1962), 5–26; Zhang (1991), 3–16.

[30] Tsai (1983), 1.

located in an abstract body politic, this embodiment of plenipotentiary power lay with the Chinese Emperor as a person. Thus the body politic was identical with the body natural and not conceptually separated into two bodies.[31]

This ambivalent nature of the *Zongli Yamen* as a Foreign Ministry and a Court Office became apparent already in the name. 'The Office in Charge of the Affairs of All Nations' (the official translation of the *Zongli Yamen*) mirrored the former 'Board in Charge of Tributary Nations' (*Li Fan Yuan*) and alluded with the use of 'Li' to the fact that the Foreign Office only gradually changed in dealing with different types of barbarian nations.[32] Prince Kung adhered to the idea that the *Zongli Yamen* mirrored the Chinese worldview of *Tiānxia* (天下) ('All under One Heaven') with the Chinese Emperor and his heavenly mandate (*tiānmìng*, 天命) at the centre of international affairs. The Prince insisted that China had its own laws, notably the Qing code, and therefore would not integrate itself into the system of 'Western' international law.[33] The adoption of a quasi-Foreign Office simply served as a useful tool 'of considerable value for defence against the West'.[34] Prince Kung stressed, much to the liking of the administrative Court hierarchy, that Confucianism was autarkic and isolated as it presented a whole world order and did not need Western learning.[35] In the same sense, the *Tongwen Guan* (同文館, College of Combined Learning) was founded in 1861 as a school for translations in order to understand European writings on International Law to counter the West.[36]

Under the guidance of the American missionary-turned-social scientist W. A. P. Martin, Henry Wheaton's *Elements of International Law* served as the primary source for training the officers in the *Zongli Yamen*.[37] However, the translation blurred, rather than highlighted, the differences

---

[31] For the separation of body natural and body politic see Kantorowicz (2016).

[32] Ching (1901), 251–254.

[33] 'Prince Kung's Discovery of International Law' (1864), in: Têng & Fairbank (1979), 97–99.

[34] Fairbank (1968), 2; Têng & Fairbank (1979), 97.

[35] Fairbank (1968), 2; Tsai (1983), 1–2; Cheung & Fung (2018), 331; Carty & Tan (2018), 439.

[36] Covell (1978), 169–198.

[37] Covell (1978), 167–178; Svarverud (2007), 62, 66; Têng & Fairbank (1979), 98. See Wheaton (1864).

between Chinese legal thought and natural law that formed the foundations of European international law discourses since Vattel and Grotius.[38] Further, the translation seemed to support the compatibility of European law with Chinese perceptions of the world. The transfer did not aim at internalising or altering the normative foundations of the Qing Code as the basic law for the domestic, and ultimately Confucian, world order.[39] Rather, the study of European classics was encouraged as useful 'examples' for learned arguments with the 'eloquent' foreigners to contest the might of the European powers in East Asia.[40]

This instrumental use of European International Law is mirrored in the legal discourse pursued by the institutions responsible for the lines of foreign policy. Chinese foreign policy from the 1860s to the 1890s depended on an active role of the *Zongli Yamen* that showed a remarkable mixture of competence and complete amateurism in charge of affairs. Yet, China was by no means powerless or inflexible when it came to negotiating complex nuances of sovereignty and treaty rights.[41] The *Zongli Yamen* forged relations to the new emigration centres and resolved problems of the Coolie trade with the Americas rather competently. The learning process of adopting Western norms occurred smoothly when it served a direct Chinese purpose, as the Cuban mission in the early 1870s shows.[42]

However, China acted in an amateur manner towards the European Concert of Power in the 1860s and 1870s. Due to a lack of modern embassy and envoy relations, 'friendly' foreigners like the American, Burlingame, were recruited by the Imperial Court to carry out foreign missions to revise the commercial treaties on behalf of the Empire.[43] Yet Burlingame used his European tour to St. Petersburg, Berlin, and London from 1867 to 1868 to talk about American interests in Europe rather than about Chinese questions abroad.[44] The German envoy to

[38] Cheung & Fung (2018), 316–326.

[39] Cheung & Fung (2018), 329–332.

[40] Feng Guifen, 'On the Manufacture of Foreign Weapons' (1861) in Têng & Fairbank (1979), 53.

[41] Martinez-Robles (2016), 729–740.

[42] Ng (2014), 39–62.

[43] Foster (1903), 263, with the Imperial Edict of November 1867 in English translation that gives plenipotentiary powers to Burlingame.

[44] Yü (1981), 152–153.

Peking, Rehfues, informed the Prussian Chancellor and Leader of the North German Confederation, Otto von Bismarck 'the whole mission appeared to be more an American than a Chinese, because the negotiations [of Burlingame] mainly served the interests and goals of the United States [of America]'.[45] Learning from these failed attempts to enter negotiations on treaty revisions, from the 1870s onwards the Chinese Court started to send envoys like Kuo Sung-T'ao to London to learn European forms of diplomacy, attend expert conferences on international law, and become accustomed to the practices of European diplomacy that bookish studies in Peking simply could not convey to the ardent disciples in international affairs.[46] Kuo Sung-T'ao reported from London in 1878 that 'since the [Europeans'] knowledge and their strength are both preeminent, we must study ways of dealing with them'.[47]

This semi-integration of China in international practice is reflected in the late nineteenth century concepts of international law. China considered itself exceptional and the 'Centre of the Civilised World', with the European 'barbarians' from the fringes of the 'Oriental Civilised World' pressing with might into East Asia.[48] Meanwhile, European powers were eager to consider China a viable partner in trade and commerce but were increasingly weary as to the future political relations with the Empire. Doubts prevailed whether China could be considered an equal member of the Euro-centric international system because the Empire did not share the normative and moral basis of European international law.[49] Wheaton's assumption in his *Elements of International Law* that the morals of international law were based on Christianity found its way into the definitions of 'civilisation' as the main yardstick for full membership of the international system.[50] 'The progress of civilization, founded on Christianity, has gradually conducted us to observe a law analogous to this in our

---

[45] Rehfues to Bismarck, Peking 18 January 1870, quoted as in: Yü (1981), 154–155.

[46] International Association for the Reform and Codification of the Law of Nations (1879), 209. See also Frodsham (1974).

[47] Kuo's Journal, Entry 2 January 1877, in Frodsham (1974), 43.

[48] Hodgkin (1923), 69 on the Reform Edict of 1898; Liu (2004), 31–69, 33–35; Liu (1999), 127–164; Lei (2009), 37–39.

[49] Svarverud (2007), 61, 66.

[50] Liu (1999), 129, 141.

intercourse with all the nations of the globe, whatever may be their religious faith, and without reciprocity on their part'.[51] Europeans identified religiously defined, yet universally promoted, morals and rational modernisation as the backbone of civilisational progress in history.[52] China, as much as the Ottoman Empire and other African and Asian 'states', did not match this ideology of shared and progressive values that lay at the normative heart of late nineteenth century European internationalism: 'The Law of European Nations has itself always been exceptional in its application to Mahommedan [sic!] and other non-Christian nations'.[53] To play an active and equal part in international relations, non-European states were expected to adopt moral and political criteria of 'civilisation' as defined by the European powers. The purposeful adoption of Western norms and institutions in Japan worked towards this international recognition since the late 1860s.[54] China's rhetoric and practice of exceptionalism and half-hearted adoption of forms was perceived in Europe with doubt and concern.[55] China was seen as the searching apprentice who needed more guidance, especially in its ignorance of international humanitarian law and the Geneva Conventions of 1864, 1887, and 1899 as the new international gospel of civilisation.[56]

The defeat against Japan, manifest in the Treaty of Shimonoseki 1895, hit China in its assumption of international superiority to the core. Chinese elites actively looked for explanations of how the long-time inferior brother nation, Japan, was able to defeat the Chinese Empire, and found ample reasons in the rapid Western modernisation of their neighbour. After 1895, Chinese diplomats looked both to the European nations and to the successful apprentice Japan to understand the West and how to use the lessons presented by Japan for Chinese purposes that would go beyond superficial learning of forms and technicalities. Students returning

[51] Liu (1999), 140–141.

[52] Koskenniemi (2001), 131–135; Anghie (2004), 32–114; Oberleitner (2013), 275–294, 286.

[53] Twiss (1892), 267; Twiss (1879–1880), 301; Bluntschli (1870), 17–19.

[54] Käser (2016), 16–32.

[55] Reeves (2005), 63–93, 71. See Gustave Moynier to W. A. P. Martin (Peking), Geneva 30 May 1873, in: *ACICR Ancient Fond [AF]* 03/05.1/01-02; Moynier to Martin, Geneva 30 April 1885, in: *ACICR, P GM*, Box 14, fols. 109–110.

[56] Moynier to Dr. Peck of Tientsin, Geneva 6 October 1894, in: *ACICR AF* 03/05.1/03.

from Japan brokered their Japanese understanding of the West in China, and their translations of Western thought from Japanese were much more appreciated in China than the rather pedantic translations by the missionaries. However, the reforming fractions among Court officials and within the intellectual and administrative elites engaged in multifarious and diverging reform discourses that did not define an overarching coherent concept in which ways China would adopt and make use of learning from the West. While intellectuals like Kang Youwei praised The Hague Conferences and China's recognition as equal member state of the conference as a new Confucian world order of peace, more critical contemporaries looked out for a way of adopting European standards to counter European efforts of 'dominating the nations beyond Europe' on the basis of international law.[57]

The watershed moment for China in its attempts to utilise the West in order to boost the Chinese standing in the international system came in 1899. The domestic 100-Day 'Reforms' had been suppressed, and it left the Empire in a state of disorientation. The 'Reformers' had used the rhetoric of learning from the West to implement radical changes in the imperial structure of power, yet had been crushed by the Empress Dowager.[58] The conference at The Hague offered another chance to encounter the West and implement reforms that had the potential to increase China's standing with a view to the European powers.[59] The Court recognised the huge chance and agreed to take part, yet with a cautious eye to the immediate application of the specific results. While the great powers negotiated on the ban of warfare and its atrocities and thus provided the rhetoric for civilisation in international diplomacy, China very much looked at the direct gains of the debates, conventions, and treaties that seemed to hamper and restrict the free exercise of power in times of war.[60]

The Court, and the *Zongli Yamen* in particular, were not concerned with the question of how liberal internationalism was shaping the world order by adding a layer of civilising rhetoric on power politics. The Court 'misunderstood' the West to the extent that China would neither use

---

[57] Liang Qichao, 'Congratulations' (1901), quoted as in Tao (2018), 347.

[58] Chang (2014), 237–246.

[59] Reeves (1998), 80–84; Reeves (2005), 75–76; Eyffinger (1999), 137–138.

[60] *Qingji waijiao shiliao* (2015), Vol. 140, 18.

nor adopt the civilising efforts of benevolent and humanitarian internationalism. China failed to see that around 1900, nations could elevate their status in the international order through showing or rhetorically staging benevolent humanitarianism. The Qing Empire missed out on this genuine opportunity in the aftermath of The Hague Conference. Despite persistence from the delegate Yang Ru, China failed to sign the revised Geneva Conventions as they appeared to 'restrict' the free and sovereign decision over the *ius ad bellum* and the *ius in bello*. China remained within the conservative and traditional thinking that might of arms and direct benefits for the Empire within the traditional order would determine the fate of the Empire, and not the politics of softer rhetoric to turn humanitarianism into an outward-looking, benevolent, and universal cause. For Chinese officials in Court, the Middle Kingdom, with its military power was still the exceptional centre of the civilised world that would only subscribe to international rules if the material gains of treaties could strengthen China's power position.[61] The European idea that benevolent internationalism and humanitarian politics would supplement the status of a nation and eventually become the crown of the edifice of a system of civilised states was completely misunderstood and thus ignored.[62] Similarly, the atrocities conducted by parts of the imperial army and renegade troops from the 'Boxers' that were supported by the Imperial Court added to the European impression that China did not want to adhere to the yardstick of civilisation or to learn from the West, and thus could not be regarded as equal partner of the civilised world.[63] In the international system, China was not eager to understand the emerging changes in 'soft' power but tried to adopt piecemeal direct benefits into its traditional order while the contradicting Confucian interpretation of international relations remained the yardstick.[64] Thus, the competing visions of world order resembled a dialogue of the deaf divided by the 'Great Wall of Misunderstandings', yet with the more powerful position resting with the European powers to influence the Chinese Empire after 1900.

[61] *Qingji waijiao shiliao* (2015), Vol. 140, 20.

[62] Fried (1908), V, 32–33.

[63] Svarverud (2007), 66, 70. See already Moynier to Peck, Geneva 6 October 1894, *ACICR AF* 03/05.1/03.

[64] *Qingji waijiao shiliao* (2015), Vol. 140, 18 and Vol. 141, 4.

It remained a dilemma that the source of authority, the Imperial Court, had no concerted reform plan for China in which Western concepts could be framed or integrated. The 100-Day Reform was a short-lived adventure that contributed more to discrediting the 'West' in China than it would actually have adopted and framed Western principles.[65] The most obvious case of a complete lack of genuine understanding of European International Law occurred in early 1904 at the beginning of the Russo-Japanese War in Manchuria. China hoped to stay neutral in the conflict despite the war being fought on Chinese territory, but it could not actively protect its civilians (mostly migrant workers from Shandong and local families) under international law.[66] For that, China would have had to sign the Geneva Convention and be a recognised member state in order to send its own Red Cross personnel and hospitals for disaster and distress relief of civilians on the battlefield.[67] It appears that during the Boxer Uprising after The Hague conference, China simply had forgotten to sign the Geneva Conventions, and the Court had assumed that the public consent of its envoy in 1899 and the Court's approval later that year had been enough to gain international protection.[68] Thus, the direct use of Western principles dictated and dominated its adoption in China, and the apparent misunderstanding of the West also coined the lack of adoption and transfer into a system that lacked a coherent plan of how to integrate and use the West for purposes of reforming Imperial China.

Humanitarianism as a principle of politics was not new to China, yet its application as a tool for power rivalry in the international system was. This was totally at odds with a strict hierarchy of tributary states that was not subject to rivalry and change. Although 'Li' and 'Ren' (benevolence) as the new yardstick for civilisation could be seen as the common centre of both universalist traditions, the implications of acknowledging the

[65] Chang (2014), 287–289.

[66] International Committee of the Red Cross to Prince Kang (President Wei Wu Pu), Geneva 13 January 1904, *ACICR AF* 03/05.1/05; Fairbank (1975), II, 1405; *Report of the International Red Cross Committee of Shanghai, 1904–1906* (1906), 1–3.

[67] *Qingji waijiao shiliao* (2015), Vol. 140, 18: China did not want to treat enemies if 'there is warfare taking place on China's territory', but forgot about treating their own civilians.

[68] *Qingji waijiao shiliao* (2015), Vol. 140, 18; Correspondence between the ICRC, the reformed Foreign Office of China [Wei Wu Pu] and Prince Qing, Geneva 11 and 13 January 1904 and Peking 3 April 1904, *ACICR AF* 03/05/05-08 and 03/05.1/05. See Reeves (2005), 82–84.

superiority of the 'i' (barbarians) from Europe strongly hampered the purposeful adoption of Western principles.[69] The general dilemma stemmed from the fact that Chinese elites did not have a coherent vision of the purpose and benefits of implementing these new forms of politics in Chinese international policies. Unlike in Japan, where the domain of foreign policy was closely linked to the strengthening and legitimacy of a newly designed Imperial Hierarchy, China developed in its chaos of competencies, actors, and discourses with no single coherent plan on how to purposefully and strategically adopt elements of Western, European international law into an outward-looking reforming vision of the Empire. Thus, the cultural transfer triggered a patchwork of discourses with contradicting adoptions of Western ideas, while displaying a growing resilience to the 'West' in discourse, form, and content after 1900.

China and its elites did not have a coherent vision of how to shape the international order on its own terms by adopting and utilising legal concepts from the West that could serve as sources of recognition, international prestige, and ultimately power. Around 1900, China finally moved from 'obscurity to distrust in international matters' and lost its equal standing in the international community.[70] China found itself in the awkward position after it had gambled away most of the international esteem that Yang Ru had gained in The Hague in 1899. Empress Dowager Cixi tried to embark on a comprehensive reform of the Empire to secure the stability of the country and the legitimacy of the monarchy against rising nationalism and anti-Manchu sentiments. At the core of this delayed reform was the transformation from Empire to state.

10.4   SERVING THE STATE—WESTERN CONCEPTS OF STATE AND SOCIETY IN CHINA

China's encounters with the West were due to the European presence in East Asia. After 1842, Great Britain and France, but increasingly also Germany, Italy, and other countries, embarking on the trading route to China, pushed with might into the former Chinese sphere of influence. While in the international arena, China reluctantly accepted elements of international law into their own concept of world order, the rhetoric of

---

[69] Hsü (1960), 111; Yin (2016), 1005–1023; Li (2016), 2274–2291.

[70] Svarverud (2007), 66.

incompatibility and Chinese exceptionalism remained much stronger in the organisation of domestic political settings. This is related to the conservative and stabilising purposes for which the Chinese officials aimed at adopting foreign concepts in the domestic arena.

In essence, the Chinese and Japanese reform efforts starting in the 1860s were completely different from the start. China's adoption of Western concepts was meant to stabilise and strengthen the Empire; Japan's adoption was meant to legitimise the revolutionary imperial monarchy established under the Meiji. Japan followed the high route to adopting European state structures to legitimise a strong, centralised imperial monarchy with a civil and military administration focused on its monarchical centre.[71] This revolutionary and strong programme drove Japanese experts to select and broker different European concepts of state and society, administration, and citizenship.

The Chinese *Tongzhi* reforms stemming from the necessity of consolidating a deeply weakened China after 1860 were not designed to transform the Empire into a centralised state with a new centre in need of a different legitimacy. On the contrary, the reforms under Prince Kung aimed at including Western forms where a direct function of rendering China strong and more competitive was assumed, but they were conservative and anti-revolutionary in nature. The basic structure of an Empire led by the Manchu dynasty, and the dual rule of Manchu and Han officials in important posts, remained untouched. In essence, Western learning was supposed to help China modernise in form and technologies, while retaining the monarchic legitimacy of the dynasty. This proved almost impossible and made the purposeful transfer and useful framing of Western ideas increasingly difficult.

Japan was eager to implement the European concepts of state and society into its reformed monarchy in order to modify Japanese society from feudal kinship relations into a society of individual subjects guided and bound together by the imperial state. By contrast, China, until 1900, had no direct interest in taking up the dual nature of state and society to transform its imperial structure in a way that offered elements of a modern state, while relying mostly on the dynastic legitimacy of the Manchus

---

[71] See Käser (2016), 17–19, 26–27; Osterhammel (2014), 831–833, 889–894; Hill (2013), 134–158.

facing an increasing Han nationalism within the Empire.[72] Efforts after 1895, and 1901–1902 were piecemeal and limited, although the recurrent rhetoric and Cixi's reform edicts after 1895 mirrored Chang Chih-Tung's book *China's Only Hope* to adopt Western practical knowledge in order to stabilise and strengthen China internally.[73]

However, Chinese intellectuals were eager to understand how European states actually worked and what could be learned from their structures for a direct application or implementation under the assumption of Chinese Imperial exceptionalism. The constituent for the European concept was the dialectic dualism of state and society as outlined in Hegel's Principles of Law.[74] Here the state as the objective manifestation of sovereignty encountered the abstract objectivity of all social interests that manifested itself in the concept of the bourgeois society. This dualism, essential for Habermas' development of the public sphere as the discursive manifestation of bourgeois society, aimed at providing a progressive synthesis that would result out of conflicts between state and society. Those conflicts were located in the parliament as the legislative and executive arena of responsible government, with the government as the state on one side and the representatives of society on the other. This system, which found its essence in the French July monarchy under Guizot and in the German pre-revolutionary constitutions until 1848, fascinated Chinese intellectuals who wanted to conceptualise relations among subjects and between subjects and the Imperial Court to overcome the omnipotent role of the Emperor as the personal embodiment of state and society.[75]

Active reception and purposeful implementation of European concepts of state and society thus remained fractioned as the dominant powers for reform discourses—the Court and the administrative elites—were rather disinterested in 'Westernising' the imperial monarchy. At least until the turn of the century, European concepts of state and society were superficially digested under the maxim of '*t'i-yong*' to keep the essence of Chinese exceptionalism, while looking for the practical usefulness of Western concepts. However, conceptually and theoretically, Chinese intellectuals like Liang Qichao provided the basis for a transition of

---

[72] Osterhammel (2014), 583–584, 588.

[73] Chang (1900), 59–61; Hogdkin (1923), 65, 68; Chang (2014), 329–331.

[74] Hegel (1991), 220–221, §§ 182–184.

[75] Habermas (1991); Rosanvallon (1985). For China see Rowe (1990), 309–329.

China from Empire to state that would come about in the 1900s and 1910s.[76] Their main interest focused on the translation of what actually constituted a state, and how to categorise this in Chinese terms. Again, it appears that the watershed moment for the turn from intellectual curiosity about the 'barbarian West' towards purposeful adoption of concepts of state and society came with the aftermath of the lost Sino-Japanese war of 1895. Intellectuals like Liang Qichao claimed the Chinese Empire in its internal structure as 'uncivilised' and 'degenerate' and called for a belated, yet comprehensive modernisation of the Empire according to Western models of the state.[77] The traditional legitimacy of the imperial monarchy based on Confucianism lost its strength among intellectual circles that looked for alternative systems of organising and legitimising China's public order in the following decade.[78]

Facing the challenges following the defeat of 1895 against Japan and the establishment of new territorial colonies on Chinese soil, Chinese intellectuals thought to transform the universal Empire into a modern nation state along the lines of German state theory that called for the three principles of territorial sovereignty (*Staatsgewalt*), clearly defined territorial borders (*Staatsgebiet*), and a territorial population (*Staatsvolk*). This turn towards modernisation of state and society along European lines was by no means a wilful evolution, but followed patterns of a rather forceful adoption of European, or more specific, German concepts and patterns to counter imperial claims of European powers in China.[79] Chinese, as well as Japanese thinkers, were highly interested in defining what actually was a modern state and how was it 'invented' in European terms. Due to the widespread popularity of the Swiss-German international legal scholar, Johann Caspar Bluntschli, the German concept of the state became the norm.[80] Bluntschli's concept of a state and the transition from Empire to nation state were not simply adopted as a German blueprint for Chinese problems, but indicated possibilities for a radical reform by conceptualising the state in the Empire. Bluntschli argued that

[76] Metzger (2005), 16–23.

[77] Liang Qichao, 'On the Promotion of Legal Sciences in China' (1896), quoted as in Lei (2009), 17.

[78] Lei (2009), 19–25; Chang (1987).

[79] Lei (2009), 18; Metzger (2006), 33, 35–39.

[80] See especially Bluntschli (1868); Lei (2009), 44.

the state was an organic formation with different parts relying on each other and performing essential functions. Instead of an overwhelmingly powerful Emperor, in the way that the people comprised civil society and assembled in parliament served the state, similarly, the Emperor was the first servant of the state and equal to the people.[81]

The position of the Emperor as subject to the state and the well-being of the people was revolutionary for Chinese imperial thought. Yet, the idea promoted by Bluntschli that the state was a living organism with both the people and the Emperor adopting functional parts in this organism fit well into Chinese imaginations of politics. However, if practised similarly as in the Japanese Meiji Constitution in 1889, the adoption of the German state concept and its application to the Empire would mean to undermine the Chinese Emperor as the centre and substituting him for an abstract state. Thus, the Emperor was bound by a written constitution as *ultima ratio* in politics.[82] Qichao, as well as Wang Tao, in his reflections on the Franco-Prussian War (1886) argued that progress in European society depended upon a dialogue of ruler and ruled, of Emperor and People, of top and bottom within a contractual agreement of a constitution that represented the idea of the abstract state.[83] Mirroring German liberal reform writings around 1900, the emperor and the people should form a unity to serve the state. Qichao's most revolutionary idea that the people and the state would in essence be identical completely undermined the heavenly mandate of dynastic Manchu legitimacy.[84] Thus, adopting European concepts—the specific liberal German traditions of an organic unity of people and state—meant in essence a revolution of the Empire to the extent that the traditional monarchic legitimacy would either transform into a constitutional monarchy or vanish altogether. This revolutionary challenge to imperial legitimacy in Qichao's writings led to their marginalisation until after the Revolution. Translations and adoptions of German public law concepts revolutionised Chinese thinking about constitutionalism and democracy after 1911. Ultimately, this late adoption of

---

[81] Lei (2009), 48, 66–89.

[82] See Articles 1, 4 and 5 of the Meiji Constitution (1889) commented with a view towards the German tradition of the state: *Die Verfassungsurkunde für das Kaiserreich Japan (Deutsche Übersetzung)* (1890), 3.

[83] Wang T'ao, *Pu-Fa zhanji* (Hong Kong: n.p., 1886), quoted as in: Lei (2009), 42; Cohen (1987).

[84] Naumann (1917), 3–14. See Stråth (2008), 171–183.

revolutionary statehood compared to the legitimacy of the Qing Empire helped with forming the Communist foundations of the People's Republic as an abstract state.[85] However, before 1911 adopting the vital concept of the German state was essential to question the legitimacy of the old Chinese order. The cultural transfer of the 'West' in this realm proved revolutionary.

It was similarly revolutionary to suggest that the people as part of the state would constitute a more politicised civil society by free associations. Traditionally, the Emperor ordered the society in a hierarchical way through a decree from above and through privileges. Max Weber's observations on the lack of an active civil society in China proved by and large true.[86] The establishment of civil society associations and the adoption of European models of associationalism as an expression of a reform-oriented civil society found its strict limits in the belief that reforming and ordering society for benevolent purposes and the benefit of the people was connected to an official, imperial mandate.[87] The 'heavenly mandate' of a benevolent shepherd ordered the imperial hierarchy to change and improve social conditions. Society itself was not to order itself for sociable or political purposes nor entitled to do so. Chinese benevolent and relief associations, springing up during the crises of the 1870s, 1890s, and 1900s, were by and large organised by wealthy citizens who had exercised or were exercising mandates within the Imperial Order, either as *Taotais* of the local communities or imperial magistrates. The foundation of the Chinese branch of the Red Cross Society in Shanghai in 1904 to help with the social repercussions of the Russo-Japanese war for the Chinese in Manchuria was no exception. Shen Dunhe, a wealthy Shanghai merchant, formed the Chinese executive committee in exercising his imperial mandate as *Taotai* for the Shanghai port.[88] Exercising humanitarian help for others was part of civil life, yet unlike in Europe since the late eighteenth century where it was located as part of 'bourgeois' citizen duties, in China it remained—similar to early modern Christian traditions of the

---

[85] Lei (2009), 285. See more general Chang (1968), 143–184.

[86] Weber (1951); Rowe (1990); Osterhammel (2002), 71–108.

[87] For the European roots of associationalism as the bourgeois expression of civil society in the nineteenth century, see Herren (2004), 24–25, 43.

[88] *Report IRCSS* (1906), 1–2, 19; Richard (1916), 263–266; Fairbank (1975), II, 1044; *Shenbao* (Shanghai), 4 and 10 March 1904, *North China Herald* (Shanghai), 15 and 22 April 1904.

duties of Christian authority—a moral obligation attached to the offices in the imperial hierarchy. Ultimately, the pastoral overlord and its offices were bound to provide charity and care for people in need to uphold the monarchical legitimacy.[89]

10.5   Whose Rights? Confucian Values of Community Contesting Individual Human Rights

One of the most contested discourses when encountering, adopting, and translating European traditions was how to react to the concept of civil and individual rights. In the *'t'i-yong'* tradition of keeping the Chinese essence while adopting useful Western elements, intellectuals calling for reform tried to locate civic rights in Confucian ideology. Thus, the 'West' could appear in essence as a copy of already existing Chinese thought in practice.[90] He Qi and Hu Liyuan explained in the 1890s in their pamphlet, *True Interpretation of New Policies*, that Confucian goals, and especially the interpretation of 'civil rights' by Mencius, appeared to have much in common with Western concepts by referring mostly to the English tradition of liberties.[91] In 1898, the Hunan scholar Pi Xirui claimed that the European policy of philanthropy and charity that made its way to East Asia in the forms of the Red Cross, orphanages, and hospital foundations all embodied the Confucian *Ren* or benevolence.[92]

The main impetus of such analogies was to frame Western concepts of civil rights and legal order in Chinese terms so as to make the integration of principles easier. However, the contested discourses about integrating civic rights often resulted in denying the necessity of a major reform of the Confucian order. The majority of the literature around 1900 tried to legitimise the Chinese way of resilience to reform and of resistance to individual rights rhetoric with the Chinese classics. Perhaps the most cited

---

[89] Chang (2014), 329, 395.

[90] Tao (2018), 340.

[91] He Qi and Hu Liyuan, *Xinzheng Zhenquan (The True Interpretation of New Policies)* (Hong Kong: Scientific Review Publishing House, 1901), 6, quoted as in Tao (2018), 340.

[92] Pi Lumen, '*Xuezhang Nanxuehui Dijiuci Jiangyi* (by Senior Pi Xirui)', in: *Xiang Bao* (Hunan Daily, 1898), Changsha, no. 57. Quoted in Tao (2018), 340–341.

text to uphold the community traditions of the Qing society is the Confucian comment on the 'Spring and Autumn Annals' reflecting Lu state's history of the pre-Warring State Period (722–481 BCE).[93] The history was interpreted as a possible source for a generic reform of the Chinese Empire, as it could provide guidance on morals, as well as a fundamental code for State governance and individual duties and obligations. However, texts like these stress individual duties towards communities—family, society, the Empire—rather than individual positive or negative liberties that would follow the rationale of natural law theory that entitled the individual against the state or society.

The alternative was to frame citizenship as a set of moral obligations towards the Empire, similar to Japan. Drawing on the idea of individual rights and duties of subjects in the Prussian and German Imperial constitutions, the Japanese Meiji constitution of 1889 outlined less the rights, than the civic obligations of the modern Japanese subject.[94] Duties and moral obligations also formed the core of the associations of civil society in Japan.[95] While many Chinese intellectuals were fascinated by the Japanese experience, this idea of individualism in duties (or rights) ran counter to the reforming principles of constitutionalism as promoted by Qichao and Tao in the 1880s and 1890s that argued for a comprehensive reform of state and society. A reformed imperial monarchy would rely on the organic evolution of a dialogue between the people as a collective entity and the monarch. Yet, while Qichao relied to some extent on more radical interpretations of *Spring and Autumn*, the main idea remained that civic rights of the individual in society ran counter to a Confucian ethic of kinship and family obligations. They would contradict a Chinese tradition that reform of society would emanate from a pastoral power embodied in imperial decrees from above.[96]

In the end, the idea of individual rights and liberties did not strike a chord with Chinese administrative elites—neither before nor after 1911. Chang Chih-Tung severely attacked the idea of 'liberty' promoted by

[93] See Martin (1882), II.2, 71–78, 72, 75–76.

[94] *Die Verfassungsurkunde für das Kaiserreich Japan* (1890), 5–7 (articles 18–32 on the rights and duties of Japanese subjects/citizens).

[95] Käser (2016), 18, 24.

[96] For an application of Foucault's Concept of 'Pastoral Power' Zhang et al. (2018), 784–803.

Republican reformers in the late 1890s as being 'absolute' and questioning the imperial legitimacy. Instead of individual liberty, China could only be made strong against the 'foreign nations' by 'uniting ourselves under the imperial dignity and power'.[97] The English idea of positive liberty, in particular, would only serve the purpose of undermining the Manchu dynasty. Further, the concept of negative liberty, as indicated by the continental tradition of catalogues of rights and duties of the citizen (following the French declaration of the Rights of Man and Citizen of 1789), would equally bind the heavenly monarch and undermine its pastoral mandate for the people and the state.[98] In Japan, monarchical legitimacy, as well as individual civic duties and rights, were bound to the positivist document of the Meiji Constitution. In China, neither monarchical legitimacy nor individual rights or duties were legalised through a positivist covenant. Changes in the concept of individual rights deriving from any other authority than the imperial mandate (in the form of privilege) would undermine the existing order.

While those more abstract liberties would potentially threaten the imperial monarchy, the Emperor exercised his pastoral and omnipotent power on behalf of his subjects to protect specific rights of groups, especially of Chinese sojourners and emigrants. It was part of the Emperor's duty to take care of the individual and collective rights of Chinese overseas, and that practice can be traced in international agreements starting in the 1860s.[99] The Report on the Condition of Chinese Coolies in Cuba from 1874 expresses the detailed consideration of social rights of Chinese workers, yet not as rights derived from a natural law order, but as deeds granted by the benevolent pastoral power of the Emperor on their behalf.[100] Similarly, the 1904 Convention on indentured labour with Britain enumerates social rights and conditions to be fixed by contract before emigration would be granted. However, the agreement negotiated by the Emperor does not indicate specific individual rights or liberties indicated as inviolable. The daily working hours, rates of wage, and

---

[97] Chang (1900), 61.

[98] Lei (2009), 46–49, 223–258.

[99] Kuo Sung-T'ao to the Earl of Derby, London, 2 January 1878, in: Frodsham (1974), Appendix no. 3, 188–189 on the Chinese interpretation of consuls to 'protect the interest of its nationals residing in other countries.' See also Chang (2014), 329, 395.

[100] *Report of the Commission sent by China to Ascertain the Condition of Chinese Coolies in Cuba* (1876), 1–92, especially 6–17, 22–26.

modes of payment, and even the nature of the indenture were open to negotiation. They related to the needs of the family, which the migrant workers tackled.[101] Thus, the social rights framework and its protection fell under imperial care, yet not the duty to ensure individual rights and procedures for granting them in the domestic sphere.

The question of human and social rights remained problematic in the transition from the Empire to the Republican era. After 1919, the International Labour Organisation (ILO) in Geneva seriously questioned China in its adoption of international standards of social rights. Countering the normative standard of working hours upon the request of the ILO, the Chinese Republican government countered the adoption of 'Western standards' with the rhetoric of Chinese exceptionalism: 'We find ourselves unable to accept the principle of a weekly rest day because tradition and custom in China are not the same as in Western countries'.[102] The rise of nationalism in China also facilitated the rhetoric of exceptionalism as a way to counter European dominance and assumed social imperialism. In this transition from an imperial to a democratic legitimacy, China left out the people as active citizens with rights and duties in the Western tradition. Human rights as individual liberties, both positive and negative, were not adopted but denied and 'othered' in terms of anti-foreign sentiments and imperialism after 1900. This cultural practice of 'othering' forms a legacy that runs through the Republic to the People's Republic as the imagined shepherd of harmonious society changed from Emperor to Party Rule.

10.6   Conclusion—Contested Orders of Governance in the Late Qing China and the 'Othering' of the 'West'

China's efforts to convey a peaceful and benevolent model of foreign investment in the BRI rely on how it frames its past visions of regional and global world order. The narratives provided to position late Qing China as a benevolent regional hegemon with a peaceful vision of global order

---

[101] *Convention respecting the employment of Chinese labour in British colonies and protectorates*, May 13, 1904 (1921), 478–482, 480 (Art. VII).

[102] Chinese Presidential Decree 225, 29 March 1923. *International Labour Office, Official Bulletin* VIII (1924), 49, and the Director General of the ILO, Albert Thomas (1924), 47–49. See Mueller (2018).

and a harmonious society of patrimonial values to give people a sense of belonging support the new vision of China. China was not the benevolent hegemon providing harmonious relations who suffered the imperial submission of the European powers and their import of Westernisation that is at the core of Chinese narratives against the West. The historical analysis shows that Chinese approaches to the 'West' between the 1840s and 1911 need to be understood as ambivalent attempts to resist the simple copy of European political and legal forms while adopting diverse aspects of European states and societies to forge a defensive modernisation in China. The ambivalent efforts to come to terms with the West resulted from a lack of coherent reform concepts into which Western elements could be implemented and usefully adopted. The result is a broken legacy of failed attempts to broker the West in different forms of technology while ignoring or actively resisting its political essence as being useful to Chinese politics or society.

Samuel Moyn's claim that ideas are not universal seems obvious.[103] In the specific context where Asian actors adopt European ideas under the powers of discourse and influence in the nineteenth century, the purposes of adoption and transformation on the side of the active importers matter as they reconfigure the 'West'.[104] In the case of the late Qing China, the adoption and implementation of European concepts proved rather difficult, but it was the Chinese people who actively sought a way to implement aspects of European 'civilisation' into the Chinese system of governance. The main problem that Chinese importers of ideas faced was that many elements that were identified as beneficial for modernising China were fit to undermine or destroy the very legitimacy of the imperial monarchy. Most aspects proved to bear revolutionary potential for the Chinese Empire: abstract sovereignty, the universal equality in international relations based on a public moral of Christian values, the concept of the state that was the source of the Emperor's legitimacy, government and opposition of an assembled society in the parliament, and finally, the concept of individual rights derived from the state as sovereign to limit the power of the Emperor. Every one of these concepts would have challenged the Empire in its very foundations if implemented. Therefore

---

[103] Moyn (2013), 187–204.

[104] Bayly (2004), 240; Conrad (2013), 22–3; Osterhammel & Petersson (2005), 96, 101.

'implementing the West', even with adoptions to the Chinese context, proved revolutionary.

The key to analysing China's actions in regard to the transfer and adoption of Western concepts lies in establishing the different contexts of discourses and power struggles in which ideas presented as universal by the West were frames and implemented into Chinese political and social thought. Referring to Japan's discourse of furbishing the revolutionary enterprise of the Meiji Empire, one can argue that China struggled with the transfer of revolutionary ideas into what was essentially a conservative and gradual reformist context of the late Qing dynasty. Instead of questioning the fundamentals of the Empire, state, and society, as well as the legitimacy of the dynasty, the efforts of 'understanding the West' were oriented towards a mere utilitarian inclusion into practical reforms, and thus remained on a conceptual level of reform sketchy and scattered at best. Scholars have argued that there was no need to adopt Western concepts while the Confucian order was still working. The limits and problems of the Manchu dynasty in exercising authority over a disintegrating Empire shows that this was wishful thinking in 1890, as much as it is in current scholarship with a legitimising mission towards the BRI. However, the bigger obstacle towards radically adopting Western concepts and superseding older structures of the Empire and the society and of legitimacy and allegiance was the apparent lack, among both the court and other officials and intellectuals, of an overarching vision for a future order of the Empire that would integrate transformed elements of the 'West'.

The absence of an alternative concept of political order to transform the late Qing China contributed to its rapid demise after 1900. The patchwork of discourses on 'adopting the West' (whether in useful forms, technologies, or in content and essence) needed a vision that presented a compromise between the Imperial Court, administration, and intellectuals. Instead, the discourse on reform in the late Qing China was dominated both by the absence of the 'West' and by its wilful misunderstanding when the 'West' and 'Civilisation' are placed among the common enemies of people and monarchy to secure the fragile status quo of the Manchu legitimacy that faded in 1911. The rise of the discourse of Chinese exceptionalism, by framing modernisation in terms of successful anti-imperial resistance against the European powers and as defence of Chinese essence against Western forms, has its roots in the discourse on the purpose of adopting the 'West' in the late Qing China.

Reference List

Primary Sources

Archival Sources
Archives du Comité International de la Croix Rouge [ACICR].
Personel Gustave Moynier [ACICR PGM].
Ancient Fond 05/01: Correspondence CICR with China before 1914, incoming [ACICIR AF 05/01].
Ancient Fond 05/01.1: Correspondence CICR with China before 1914, outgoing [ACICIR AF 05/01.1].

Periodicals

Shenbao (Shanghai), 1904.
North China Herald (Shanghai), 1895–1905.

Printed Primary Sources

Bluntschli, Johann Caspar. (1868). *Das moderne Völkerrecht der civilisierten Staaten als Rechtsbuch dargestellt*. Nördlingen: Beck.
Bluntschli, Johann Caspar. (1870). *Le Droit International Codifié*. Paris: Guillaumin & Co.
Bluntschli, Johann Caspar. (1874). *Deutsche Staatslehre für Gebildete*. München: C.H. Beck.
Chang Chih-Tung (1900). *China's Only Hope: An Appeal by Her Greatest Viceroy* ... (Samuel Woodbridge, Trans.). New York et al.: Flemming H. Revell.
Ching, Wen (1901). *The Chinese Crisis from Within*. Rev. G.M. Reith (Ed.). London: Grant Richards.
Convention Respecting the Employment of Chinese Labour in British Colonies and Protectorates, May 13, 1904 (1904). In John V.A. MacMurray (Ed.). (1921). *Treaties and Agreements with and Concerning China, 1894–1919: Volume I: Manchu Period (1894–1911)*, 478–482. New York and Oxford: Oxford University Press.
Fairbank, John K. (Ed.). (1975). *The I.G. in Peking. Letters of Robert Hart 1868–1907*. 2 Vols. Cambridge/MA: Belknap Press.
Foster, John W. (1903). *American Diplomacy in the Orient*. Cambridge: Riverside Press.
Fried, Alfred H. (1908). *Das Internationale Leben der Gegenwart*. Leipzig: Teubner.
Frodsham, J.D. (Ed.). (1974). *The First Chinese Embassy to the West: The Journals of Kuo Sung-T'ao, Liu Hsi-Hung and Chang Te-Yi*. Oxford: Clarendon Press.

Hegel, G.W.F. (1991). *Elements of the Philosophy of Right*, Allen W. Wood (Ed.) (H.B. Nisbet, Trans.). Cambridge: Cambridge University Press.

International Association for the Reform and Codification of the Law of Nations. (1879). *Annual Conference Report of the London Meeting 1878*. London: n.p.

International Labour Office. (1919–1924). *Official Bulletin* I-VIII. Geneva.

Liu, Suhua (Ed.). (2015). *Qingji waijiao shiliao [Sources of the History of Foreign Relations During the Qing Period]*. Hunan: Hunan Normal University Press (Original work printed in 1934).

Martin, W.A.P. (1882). Traces of International Law in Ancient China. *Abhandlungen und Vorträge des fünften internationalen Orientalisten-Congresses, gehalten zu Berlin im September 1881*, 2 Vols. Berlin: A. Asher&Co, II.2, 71–78.

Naumann, Friedrich. (1917). *Der Kaiser im Volksstaat*. Berlin: Fortschritt.

Report of the Commission Sent by China to Ascertain the Condition of Chinese Coolies in Cuba. (1876). Shanghai: The Imperial Maritime Customs Press.

Report of the International Red Cross Committee of Shanghai, 1904–1906. (1906). Shanghai: n.p.

Richard, Timothy. (1916). *Forty-Five Years in China*. New York: Stokes.

Têng, Ssu-yü, & Fairbank, John K. (Eds.). (1979). *China's Response to the West: A Documentary Survey, 1839–1923*. Boston/MA: Harvard University Press.

Thomas, Albert (1924). Labour Legislation in China. *International Labour Office, Official Bulletin* VIII, 47–49.

Twiss, Travers. (1879–1880). Rapport. *Annuaire de L'Institut de Droit International* 3–4, 301.

Twiss, Travers. (1892). *The Law of Nations* (2nd edition). Oxford: Clarendon Press.

Die Verfassungsurkunde für das Kaiserreich Japan (Deutsche Übersetzung). (1890). Berlin: Carl Heymanns Verlag.

Wheaton, Henry. (1864). *Wanguo Gongfa* (W.A.P. Shimeng He, Dawen Li, Wei Zhang, and Jingrong Cao, Trans.). Peking: n.p.

Xi Jinping. (2013). Speech at Nazarbayev University, Astana, 7 September 2013. Retrieved December 11, 2018 from https://www.fmprc.gov.cn/mfa_eng/wjdt_665385/zyjh_665391/t1078088.shtml.

LITERATURE

Anghie, A. (2004). *Imperialism, Sovereignty and the Making of International Law*. Cambridge: Cambridge University Press.

Banno, M. (1964). *China and the West, 1858–1861: The Origins of the Tsungli Yamen*. Cambridge, MA: Harvard University Press.

Bayly, C. A. (2004). *The Birth of the Modern World, 1780–1914*. Oxford: Blackwell.

Benford, R. D., & Snow, D. A. (2000). Framing Processes and Social Movements. An Overview and Assessment. *Annual Review of Sociology, 26,* 611–639.

Carty, A., & Nijmann, J. E. (Eds.). (2018). *Morality and Responsibility of Rulers: European and Chinese Origins of the Rule of Law as Justice for World Order.* Oxford: Oxford University Press.

Carty, A., & Tan, J. (2018). Confucianism and Western International Law in 1900. Li Hongzhang and Sir Ernest Satow Compared: A Case Study of the Crisis of Russia in Manchuria (1900–1901). In A. Carty & J. E. Nijmann (Eds.), *Morality and Responsibility of Rulers: European and Chinese Origins of the Rule of Law as Justice for World Order* (pp. 434–453). Oxford: Oxford University Press.

Chang, H. (1987). *Chinese Intellectuals in Crisis—Search for Order and Meaning, 1890–1911.* Berkeley and London: California University Press.

Chang, J. (2014). *Empress Dowager Cixi: The Concubine Who Launched Modern China.* London: Vintage.

Chang, P.-y. (1968). The Constitutionalists. In M. C. Wright (Ed.), *China in Revolution: The First Phase 1900–1913* (pp. 143–184). New Haven and London: Yale University Press.

Ch'en, J. (1969). Introduction. In J. Gray (Ed.), *Modern China's Search for a Political Form* (pp. 1–39). London: Oxford University Press.

Cheung, E., & Fung, M. (2018). The Hazards of Translating Wheaton's Elements of International Law into Chinese. Culture of World Order Lost in Translation. In A. Carty & J. E. Nijmann (Eds.), *Morality and Responsibility of Rulers: European and Chinese Origins of the Rule of Law as Justice for World Order* (pp. 316–338). Oxford: Oxford University Press.

Chevrier, Y. (1989). Des réformes à la révolution (1895–1913). In M.-C. Bergère (Ed.), *La Chine au XXe Siècle. D'une révolution à l'autre (1895–1949)* (pp. 87–122). Paris: Fayard.

Chu, S. C., & Liu, K.-C. (Eds.). (1994). *Li Hung-chang and China's Early Modernisation.* Armonk, NY: Sharpe.

Cohen, P. E. (1987). *Between Tradition and Modernity: Wang T'ao and Reform in Late Ch'ing China.* Boston, MA: Harvard University Press.

Conrad, S. (2013). *Globalgeschichte. Eine Einführung.* Munich: C.H. Beck.

Covell, R. (1978). *W.A.P. Martin: Pioneer of Progress in China.* Washington: Christian University Press.

Eyffinger, A. (1999). *The 1899 Hague Peace Conference.* The Hague and London: Kluwer.

Eyffinger, A. (2008). Caught Between Tradition and Modernity: East Asia at the Hague Peace Conferences. *Journal of East Asia and International Law, 1,* 7–46.

Fairbank, J. K. (1968). A Preliminary Framework. In J.K. Fairbank (Ed.), *The Chinese World Order: Traditional China's Foreign Relations* (pp. 1–19). Cambridge, MA: Harvard University Press.

Habermas, J. (1991). *The Structural Transformation of the Public Sphere: An Inquiry into a Category of Bourgeois Society* (T. Burger, Trans.). Cambridge, MA: MIT Press.

Herren, M. (2004). *Internationale Organisationen seit 1865. Eine Globalgeschichte der Internationalen Ordnung*. Darmstadt: WBG.

Hill, C. L. (2013). Conceptual Universalization in the Transnational Nineteenth Century. In S. Moyn & A. Sartori (Eds.), *Global Intellectual History* (pp. 134–158). New York: Columbia University Press.

Hodgkin, H. T. (1923). *China in the Family of Nations*. London: George Allen & Unwin.

Hsü, I. C. Y. (1960). *China's Entrance into the Family of Nations: The Diplomatic Phase 1858–1880*. Cambridge, MA: Harvard University Press.

Kantorowicz, E. H. (2016). *The King's Two Bodies: A Study in Medieval Political Theology*. Princeton: Princeton University Press.

Käser, F. (2016). A Civilized Nation: Japan and the Red Cross, 1877–1900. *European Review of History, 23*(1–2), 16–32.

Kayaoğlu, T. (2010). *Legal Imperialism: Sovereignty and Extraterritoriality in Japan, the Ottoman Empire, and China*. Cambridge: Cambridge University Press.

Koskenniemi, M. (2001). *The Gentle Civilizer of Nations: The Rise and Fall of International Law 1870–1960*. Cambridge: Cambridge University Press.

Kuo, T-y, & Liu, K.-C. (1978). Self-Strengthening: The Pursuit of Western Technology. In J. K. Fairbank (Ed.), *The Cambridge History of China. Vol. 10: Late Ch'ing, 1800–1911, Part I* (pp. 491–542). Cambridge: Cambridge University Press.

Lei, Y. (2009). *Auf der Suche nach dem modernen Staat. Die Einflüsse der Allgemeinen Staatslehre Johann Caspar Bluntschlis auf das Staatsdenken Liang Qichaos*. Frankfurt/Main: Peter Lang.

Li, Y. (2016). Red Cross Society in Imperial China, 1904–1912: A Historical Analysis. *Voluntas, 27,* 2274–2291.

Liu, L. H. (1999). Legislating the Universal: The Circulation of International Law in the Nineteenth Century. In L. H. Liu (Ed.), *Tokens of Exchange: The Problem of Translation in Global Circulations* (pp. 127–164). Durham: Duke University Press.

Liu, L. H. (2004). *The Clash of Empires: The Invention of China in Modern World Making*. Cambridge, MA: Harvard University Press.

Martinez-Robles, D. (2016). Constructing Sovereignty in Nineteenth-Century China: The Negotiation of Reciprocity in the Sino-Spanish Treaty of 1864. *The International History Review, 38*(4), 729–740.

Meng, S. M. (1962). *The Tsungli Yamen: Its Organization and Functions*. Cambridge, MA: Harvard University Press.

Metzger, G. (2005). *Liang Qichao interkulturell gelesen*. Nordhausen: Bautz.

Metzger, G. (2006). *Liang Qichao, China und der Westen nach dem Ersten Weltkrieg*. Berlin: LIT.

Moyn, S. (2013). On the Nonglobalization of Ideas. In S. Moyn & A. Sartori (Eds.), *Global Intellectual History* (pp. 187–204). New York: Columbia University Press.

Mueller, C. (2018). 'And What Do We Know About China?' The International Labour Office, Albert Thomas and Republican China, 1919–1930. *Journal of the Royal Asiatic Society China*, 78(1), 101–122.

Muhs, R., Paulmann, J., & Steinmetz, W. (Eds.). (1998). *Aneignung und Abwehr. Interkultureller Transfer zwischen Deutschland und Grossbritannien im 19. Jahrhundert*. Bodenheim: Philo-Verlag.

Ng, R. (2014). The Chinese Commission to Cuba (1874): Re-examining International Relations in the Nineteenth Century from a Transcultural Perspective. *Transcultural Studies*, 2, 39–62. Retrieved from http://dx.doi.org/10.11588/ts.2014.2.13009.

Oberleitner, G. (2013). Humanitarian Law as a Source of Human Rights Law. In D. Shelton (Ed.), *The Oxford Handbook of International Human Rights Law* (pp. 275–294). Oxford: Oxford University Press.

Osterhammel, J. (2002). Gesellschaftsgeschichtliche Parameter chinesischer Modernität. *Geschichte Und Gesellschaft*, 28(1), 71–108.

Osterhammel, J. (2014). *The Transformation of the World: A Global History of the Nineteenth Century*. Princeton and Oxford: Princeton University Press.

Osterhammel, J., & Petersson, N. (2005). *Globalization: A Short History*. Princeton: Princeton University Press.

Paulmann, J. (1998). Internationaler Vergleich und interkultureller Transfer: Zwei Forschungsansätze zur europäischen Geschichte des 18. bis 20. *Jahrhunderts. Historische Zeitschrift*, 267, 649–685.

Paulmann, J. (2004). Grenzüberschreitungen und Grenzräume. Überlegungen zur Geschichte transnationaler Beziehungen von der Mitte des 19. Jahrhunderts bis in die Zeitgeschichte. In E. Conze et al. (Eds.), *Geschichte der internationalen Beziehungen* (pp. 169–196). Köln: Böhlau.

Pong, D. (1994). *Shen Pao-chen and China's Modernization in the Nineteenth Century*. Cambridge: Cambridge University Press.

Reeves, C. B. (1998). *The Power of Mercy: The Chinese Red Cross Society, 1900–1937*. Ph.D. thesis, MS Harvard.

Reeves, C. B. (2005). From Red Crosses to Golden Arches. China, the Red Cross, and The Hague Peace Conference, 1899–1900. In J. Bentley et al. (Eds.), *Interactions: Transregional perspectives on World History* (pp. 64–93). Honolulu: University of Hawai'i Press.

Rosanvallon, P. (1985). *Le moment Guizot*. Paris: Gallimard.

Rowe, W. T. (1990). The Public Sphere in Modern China. *Modern China, 16*(3), 309–329.

Smith, R. J. (1994). *China's Cultural Heritage, The Qing Dynasty, 1644–1912*. Boulder, CO: Westview.

Spence, J. D. (1990). *The Search for Modern China*. New York and London: Norton.

Stråth, B. (2008). Mitteleuropa: From List to Naumann. *European Journal of Social Theory, 11*(2), 171–183.

Sun, S. (2013). The Self-Strengthening Movement: Inevitable failure? In *From Climactic Destruction to Economic Revitalization: Commerce, Disease and War in Eurasia, 1200–1900*. Retrieved from http://history.emory.edu/home/documents/endeavors/volume6/endeavors-vlm-vi-sun.pdf.

Svarverud, R. (2007). *International Law as World Order in Late Imperial China: Translation, Reception and Discourse, 1847–1911*. Leiden: Brill.

Tao, T. (2018). Chinese Intellectuals' Discourse of International Law in the Late Nineteenth and Early Twentieth Centuries. In A. Carty & J. E. Nijmann (Eds.), *Morality and Responsibility of Rulers: European and Chinese Origins of the Rule of Law as Justice for World Order* (pp. 339–359). Oxford: Oxford University Press.

Troeltsch, E. (1922). *Der Historismus und seine Probleme. Das logische Problem der Geschichtsphilosophie*. Tübingen: Mohr.

Tsai, S.-s. (1983). *China and the Overseas Chinese in the United States, 1868–1911*. Fayetteville: University of Arkansas Press.

Wang, Y. C. (1966). *Chinese Intellectuals and the West, 1872–1949*. Chapel Hill: University of North Carolina Press.

Weber, M. (1951). *The Religion of China: Confucianism and Taoism*. Glencoe, IL: The Free Press.

Yin, Z. (2016). Heavenly Principles? The Translation of International Law in 19th-Century China and the Constitution of Universality. *European Journal of International Law, 27*(4), 1005–1023.

Yü, W.-t. (1981). *Die Deutsch—chinesischen Beziehungen von 1860–1880*. Bochum: Brockmeyer.

Zhang, X., Brown, M., & O'Brien, D. (2018). "No CCP, No New China": Pastoral Power in Official Narratives in China. *China Quarterly, 238*, 784–803.

Zhang, Y. (1991). China's Entry into International Society: Beyond the Standard of 'Civilization'. *Review of International Studies, 17*, 3–16.

Zhao, S. (2015). Rethinking the Chinese World Order: The Imperial Cycle and the Rise of China. *Journal of Contemporary China, 24*, 961–982.

CHAPTER 11

Port City on the Maritime Silk Road: Ningbo's City Branding Under the Theme of Intellectuals

Nancy Xiuzhi Liu

11.1 Introduction

The Belt and Road Initiative (BRI) put forward by the Chinese President Xi Jinping in 2013 is comprised of the land-based Ancient Silk Road Economic Belt and the oceangoing twenty-first Century Maritime Silk

This is part of the outcome of the project 'Ningbo City Branding under the Belt and Road Initiative' with the Seed-Corn Grant funded by the Institute of Asia-Pacific Studies (IAPS) at the University of Nottingham Ningbo China.

Nancy Xiuzhi is an Assistant Professor with a PhD. Her research interests primarily include media studies, sociocultural meanings of translation, translation of texts with culture-specific items, and didactic research into translation and interpretation. She is expanding her research into the broader context of contemporary Chinese studies.

N. X. Liu (✉)
School of Education and English, University of Nottingham Ningbo China, Ningbo, China
e-mail: Nancy.Liu@nottingham.edu.cn

© The Author(s) 2020
H. K. Chan et al. (eds.), *International Flows in the Belt and Road Initiative Context*, Palgrave Series in Asia and Pacific Studies,
https://doi.org/10.1007/978-981-15-3133-0_11

Road or Maritime Silk Road (MSR). Ningbo is one of the many cities and ports along the MSR that seeks to stand out through branding strategies. With the growth of numerous metropolises, cities make every effort to brand themselves in various themes to stand out and achieve socioeconomic development. A city, as defined by Friedmann (1986), has economic connotations of being a spatially and economically integrated social system in a given location or metropolitan region. The world's megacities inexorably attract and accumulate capital and labour, particularly talent, because of their cutting-edge development and never-ending opportunities. Historically, there have been no difficulties in the growth of such world cities as they always attract younger generations who represent the 'backbone' for development. However, Friedmann (1996) observed that while focusing on the urban nodes within these world cities, we must not forget other cities that are similarly linked into the global network, albeit in a more dependent position.

Comparatively speaking, second- or third-tier cities are less prominent on the global stage, although they are indispensable as a secondary force in fuelling and sustaining the growth of economy and society. At the same time, their less competitive positioning and more relaxed environment are attractive to millions of residents. Well-known megacities have well-defined 'positioning' to attract the public, particularly the younger generation. However, cities of smaller scale accommodate a bigger portion of the population in a less haphazard manner, as the case is in China. With constantly changing conditions and increasing competitiveness of rival cities worldwide, policymakers of cities constantly assess their cities' relative standing in the urban hierarchy when developing strategies to update their image, so as to attract new businesses, major events, tourists, and residents (Insch and Bowden 2016).

Alongside the escalation of global intercity competition and the adoption of attraction-oriented urban development strategies, academic research has focused more on understanding how cities acquire power and status as global cities. Henceforth, city branding has been investigated from various perspectives such as economic or societal gains, or multi-level governance, mostly for first-tier megacities (Insch and Bowden 2016; Lucarelli 2018; Ye and Björner 2018). However, what is lacking from the narrative is an evaluation of how the concepts of 'a strategic choice of a position for a brand (intended position)' and 'the resulting outcome (actual position)' (Urde and Koch 2014, p. 479) can be applied to second-tier cities seeking to enhance their reputations as global cities.

Relatively less attention is paid to second-tier, third-tier, or lower ranking cities (Insch and Bowden 2016). Furthermore, scarce attention has been paid to less competitive second- or third-tier cities. Thus, it is important to investigate how city branding strategies in second-tier cities work in rapidly urbanising countries, such as China. Under this context, the city of Ningbo situating on the MSR is of particular interest, with its impressive economic, occupational, demographic changes, and aspirational attempts to reposition itself as a global city, as it brands itself a 'city of intellectuals'. Thus, Ningbo has been specifically selected to investigate how city branding under one theme, with reference to its historical legacy, works or not. By examining city branding under a particular theme and its connections to urban policies in Ningbo, this study highlights Ningbo's experiences as reference for other Chinese cities and urban places worldwide.

This chapter proceeds as follows. The next section presents this study's theoretical framework, centred on city branding under specific themes. The subsequent section discusses Ningbo's strategic branding approach and the methodology used in this study. Next, Ningbo's case is analysed based on specific themes generated from the semi-structured interviews. The findings and discussions focus primarily on how city branding is manifested through the bottom-up approach, with intellectuals telling their own stories. The final section provides conclusions.

11.2 City Branding Under Specific Themes

City branding refers to the process of applying product-branding practices to cities in order to integrate and highlight a city's competitive advantages through persistent imaged identities, or brands (Kavaratzis 2007; Zhao 2010, cited by Zhao 2015). It is the 'purposeful symbolic embodiment of all information connected to a city in order to create associations around it' (Lucarelli 2012, p. 21). Kavaratzis and Ashworth (2005) expound that city branding is more difficult than product branding and marketing because of the complex nature of cities. A city is simultaneously a place of residence, a place of work, a destination to visit, and a place of investment opportunity. Therefore, a city's brand has to accommodate all stakeholders' demands in order to strengthen the city's overall competitiveness. Taking a city as a brand encompasses more stakeholders. As illustrated by Kavaratzis (2004, p. 63), adding branding to the list of developments brings marketing theory and practice closer to the nature and characteristics of places. A brand provides a basis for identifying and uniting a wide range of images intended for the city and the 'meanings' attributed to the city in one marketing message, the city's brand.

In communicating the image of a city, Kavaratzis (2004, cited in Ye and Björner 2018, p. 30) outlines three types of communication: primary, secondary, and tertiary communication. 'Primary communication' is described as unintentional, meaning that the city's actions, such as its landscaping, infrastructure development and behaviour, have communicative effects on the receivers. 'Secondary communication' is described as intentional communication that often takes place through established marketing practices, and 'tertiary communication' is related to 'word of mouth' and to communication by the media. City branding as a form of urban governance can be used strategically to stimulate and direct urban development and growth, applied to manage perceptions about places, and utilised to formulate unique city identities (Ye and Björner 2018). On the one hand, city branding provides a basis for developing policies to pursue economic development. On the other hand, it serves as a conduit for city residents to identify with their city (Kavaratzis 2004). Similarly, Zhao's study (2015) on the renovation of the ethnic group Bai's architectures found that public and private sectors both function in city heritage management towards city branding of Dali in Yunan Province. This has resulted in the renovation and revitalisation of historical buildings in the city.

Branding a city under a particular frame of reference is often the strategy of some cities in their primary communication or tertiary communication. For example, the City of London communicates its efficacy in financial systems; while New York City, labelled as the 'Capital City of the World' or the 'Big Apple', projects itself as having the most-sought-after rewards or accomplishments; and Paris, as the city of fashion; among others. Ningbo city historically has its frame of reference in intellectuality, besides port transportation. Intellectuality is defined 'in the sense of the desire to 'know' (Lloyd et al. 1984) in the context of learning, as one of the general connotations of the word. From a cultural perspective in the east, intellectuals are those knowledgeable personages who hold prestigious social status. From China's cultural tradition, particularly based on the 'Confucius heritage', being an intellectual is considered as achieving the supreme status in society above all others, as in the household saying 万般皆下品, 唯有读书高 (Intellectual is at the top of a society above all others). Similarly, Van Kham (2017) investigates the Vietnamese context, where for over four thousand years the Vietnamese people have paid more attention to those with wisdom and with well-founded intellects, and consider them as an intellectual resource for the nation. 'The intellectuals are acknowledged by the legal document and government policies as a critical factor for social development and for creating ideal conditions for the whole nation to overcome economic and social crises in the early 1990s' (Van Kham 2017, p. 660).

From a western perspective, a person can be an intellectual in terms of both critical thinking and research. An intellectual usually represents a persona that reflects on society and proposes solutions for its problems. Chomsky (1967) points out that intellectuals (as part of their responsibility) are capable of exposing the lies of governments and analysing actions to reveal underlying causes, motives, and often hidden intentions. They enjoy such privileges as access to information and freedom of expression and may seek the truth behind the veil of distortion and misrepresentation, ideology, and class interest. Given the different inference drawn from the term intellectual (between the east and the west), it is worthwhile to investigate the reason behind the branding strategies of Ningbo under such a theme.

11.3   Ningbo and Its City Branding

Ningbo, a city in the Yangtze River Delta (YRD), has been quite renowned and prosperous in garment making and port transportation with a long history of over 7000 years. In fact, it was more famous than Shanghai (before Shanghai grew from a small fishing village into a megacity). To date, its suit-making brands such as *Shanshan* and *Younger*, among others, are still the top brands in China. More importantly, it enjoys high prestige as a city with a tradition of profound learning. Ningbo was awarded the title of 'China's Leading Historical and Cultural City' by the State Council in 2010. It is located within one of the most developed regions of the YRD (away from the political centre of Beijing), which has proven to be the most dynamic economic zone in China. Its geographical location, being both at the mouth of the Grand Canal and open to the sea, has guaranteed Ningbo the exceptional advantage of being the starting point of the 21st Marine Silk Road's link to the outside world, as well as having access to inland towns upstream along the Grand Canal as illustrated in Fig. 11.1.

Moreover, Ningbo is rich in historical heritage and contemporary intellectuals. The library called *Tianyige* or One Sky Chamber is the most ancient private library in China's history, with a collection of 70,000 volumes of ancient books. Furthermore, the number of academicians born

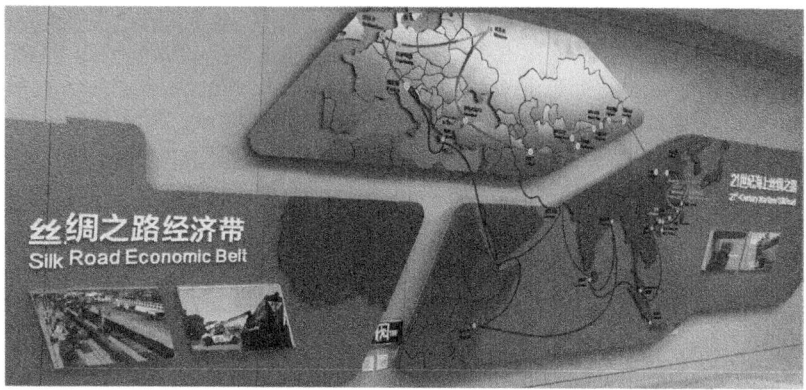

Fig. 11.1 Geographical Location of Ningbo Port in the twenty-first Century Maritime Silk Road (The picture was taken by the author during a field trip to Ningbo Port in 2018. The line at the top of the image is the Silk Road Economic Belt, while the lower line is the twenty-first Century Maritime Silk Road where Ningbo is the starting point, as highlighted in the circle)

in Ningbo that have been elected to the Chinese Academy of Sciences and Chinese Academy of Engineering is 150 to date, which is the largest number among all cities in the country. A park named Yinzhou Academician Park, covering an area of 62.8 hectares, is built in the southern CBD (Central Business District) area in Ningbo, where bronze statues of all the academicians stand high on a large platform. In 2017, the municipal government of Ningbo decided to promote the city under three themes, 'City of Intellectuals', 'City of Music', and 'City of Films' (书香之城, 音乐之城, 影视之城), and placed intellectuals in the most conspicuous position. According to *Ningbo Daily* (15 June 2017), branding the city under the three themes is meant to jointly promote Ningbo for its cultural attraction. At the 13th Session of the Central Party Committee of the city, the government decided to build the city into the 'Oriental Capital of Culture' on top of the biggest seaport.[1]

In fact, the position of Ningbo is rather cumbersome in the YRD between the megacity of Shanghai, which is directly administered under the central government, and Hangzhou, the capital city of Zhejiang. The

---

[1] http://zjnews.zjol.com.cn/zjnews/nbnews/201706/t20170615_4224853.shtml, accessed 12 December 2018.

city persistently aspires to enhance its economic competitiveness and out-perform others on various fronts. With the implementation of the BRI or the New Silk Road (an overland and maritime route connecting East Asia with Europe as proposed by the Chinese central government in 2013), Ningbo, sitting on one of the most developed zones in China, has cho-sen to brand the city in reference to intellectuals based on local strengths or historical traditions in order to attract more high-valued services and high-tech businesses. The local government of Ningbo resorted to this strategic plan, aspiring to enhance economic competitiveness and to out-bid its competitors like other cities in China, such as Guangzhou, as exam-ined by Ye and Björner (2018, p. 31).

To evaluate Ningbo's branding strategy, this study carried out semi-structured interviews with a bottom-up approach, letting intellectuals tell their own stories on whether this branding theme fits the city or how the city should be branded from their own perspectives. With this approach, we have carefully chosen our interviewees by categorising them into those who were born and grew up in Ningbo, those who chose to work in the city, and some international expatriates who have made Ningbo their home.

11.4 Research Methods

This study mainly used semi-structured interviews and qualitative the-matic analysis of the interviews. Interviewees were carefully selected from those involved in the bigger project called 'Ningbo City Branding under the BRI', wherein participants share their experiences and expectations based on their understanding of the city's branding (with a bottom-up approach). As explained by Sabatier (1986, p. 32), compared to the top-down approach, which is likely to overestimate the importance of gov-ernmental programmes, the bottom-up approach starts by identifying the network of actors involved in local areas and asking them to share their experiences related to planning or financing, and execution of relevant governmental and non-governmental programmes. The success or failure of city branding programmes depends on recognition and implementation from the bottom (the city residents) rather than from the local govern-ment officials at the top. Specifically, eight interviewees were chosen from a larger pool based on educational background (those with undergradu-ate degrees or above), being deemed to be intellectuals in the Chinese context. Another basis for the selection was the interviewees' life experiences so as to reflect diversified perspectives (i.e. some were born and grew up in Ningbo, others are young returnees, newcomers, as well as international personnel who work in the city).

For the bigger project, the main questions and discussions were about the interviewees' own life experiences in Ningbo and their viewpoints regarding the city's branding. For this study, some follow-up interviews with selected interviewees were conducted concerning the theme 'City of Intellectuals'. Towards the latter stage of the bigger project, other interviewees were asked more specific questions concerning their opinions about Ningbo's branding under the said theme.

All interviews were undertaken following the ethics regulation of the university and were conducted in public areas such as coffee shops or inside the University of Nottingham Ningbo campus. All interviews were recorded and transcribed, then analysed thematically. Thematic analysis, according to Braun and Clarke (2006), is the fundamental method for qualitative analysis due to its merit of flexibility that provides rich, detailed, yet complex accounts of data. The theme and subthemes in the next section were generated inductively in a bottom-up manner by focusing on the semantic content of the interviews. Summaries or quotations were used to elaborate the subthemes and to demonstrate the effects of the city branding strategies. The interviewees were anonymised as A, B, C, and so on, with dates of cited interviews listed after each direct quotation.

11.5   'The City of Intellectuals' from the Intellectuals' Perspective

11.5.1   The History and Modern Positioning of Ningbo

Ningbo city is deeply rooted in history, where the Hemudu cultural heritage dates back eight thousand years. It provides the earliest evidence that human culture of agrarian age originated along the Yangtze River besides the Yellow River basin. Another distinctive feature of the city is that it is the only city port that has never ceased developing in history starting from the Tang dynasty (618–907). Some cities either disappeared or their ports silted up for various reasons. Ningbo not only weathered history, but also sustained substantial growth (Gong 2017). Interest in this historical legacy is also shared by the interviewees.

Interviewee A was born and grew up in Ningbo. She completed her undergraduate education in Shanghai and worked as a lawyer in Ningbo. She thinks that Ningbo is well-known as an international port, and that Tu Youyou (who was born in Ningbo, is currently working at the China Academy of Traditional Chinese Medicine, and has won a Noble prize for her study of the treatment of malaria) has made Ningbo more famous. She also thinks that the city is well known for being an ancient (dating back to 4800 BC) site of the Hemudu culture, located 22 km northwest of Ningbo, all of which justify promoting the city under the theme of intellectuals. She thinks and sees that the city is developing at a very fast pace, with people rushing about their own business. She gets the impression that the promotion of the theme itself is not quite known to the general public, and that more work is needed in this regard.

Interviewee B is another local-born Ningbonese. He has deep love for his city. He thinks that the government did the right thing by promoting the city in connection to its history. He saw some measures taken in this regard. For example, the city has built the Corn Building (Book City is the official name of the building, but it is locally known as *yumi* building in Chinese because it is shaped like corn) at the three-river junction as a landmark of Ningbo, which is also officially called the Ningbo Fortune Centre. The building occupies one of the best locations in the city with the Book City by its side, which shows the city's effort and priority in this respect. However, this selling point was unsuccessful because most people in the city now pay more attention to doing business.

Interviewee C is a senior citizen born in Ningbo. He thinks the branding is highly appropriate. City people traditionally pay great attention to education. The city is one of the earliest cities that implemented the nine-year compulsory education. He said that 'investment in education from the city increases every year. For example, electronic borrowing is now possible at the city library' (9 October 2017).

11.5.2 Ningbo as a Port City

The city of Ningbo is also quite famous as the biggest seaport city in China, with Ningbo-Zhoushan Port having the second biggest throughput capacity in the world. Although the city, with a population of around 7.8 million (by 2015), is considered second- or third-tier in China, its fast development in terms of overall strength and technological upgrading is extremely noticeable in recent years, as it ranks first in Zhejiang

Province. In a national-level plan in June 2010, the State Council, in its development programme of the YRD, repositioned Ningbo as 'the base of advanced manufacturing and modern logistics, as well as an international port city' (Baidu 2018). This view also strikes a chord in some interviewees.

Interviewee D from another city belongs to the post-1980s generation. She started working in Ningbo after receiving her master's degree from the United Kingdom. She is aware of the city's historical connections to intellectuals in terms of the ancient library and the academicians. However, her co-workers from various departments at the port do not recognise the city's theme as 'the City of Intellectuals'. She stated that, 'the city has impressed me more with its atmosphere of doing business, making gains or losses, and the like' (8 June 2017). She thinks that if Ningbo is to be promoted as 'the City of Intellectuals', more activities, such as focused festivals or targeted task-forces should be organised. For example, she herself feels cut-off from the city's popular cultural gatherings, shows, matches, musicals, and others and thus, she usually visits Shanghai for entertainment during weekends.

Interviewee E returned to Ningbo after her post-doctorate study overseas. While she cherishes memories of her home town, she shares the younger generation's experiences/opinions of Ningbo that not enough has been done to highlight the city's cultural heritage. She thinks that by merely publicising a slogan with reference to intellectuals, the effect would be hard to measure and vague to achieve. Moreover, she questions the purpose of such a branding: whether it is to attract more tourists or to increase the number of residents, it is difficult to tell. The well-known branding theme '书藏古今, 港通天下' (A city with ancient and modern book collections, a port connecting the world) still enjoys quite popular support from the general public, which she feels captures the essence of the city with reference to both its ancient history and its modern port.

11.5.3   Ningbo from the Expatriates' Perspective

Ningbo enjoys the tradition of seafaring. This has been the attraction to foreign Jesuits and merchants throughout history. Although there is no official data on the number of international experts currently working in Ningbo, it is presumed to be more than any other second- or third-tier city in China, as can be inferred in the number of international schools in the city, which is around six (this number is quite big for a second- or third-tier city). The international schools are usually established in cities with fast economic development in order to cater to the needs of expatriates and sometimes Chinese scholars who have returned home.

Interviewee F is from Japan. She has worked and lived in Ningbo for twelve years. She thinks that Ningbo is improving on all fronts. When she arrived here, there was literally nothing around the area where she worked. She had to go into town for shopping or dining. She is particularly impressed by the friendliness of the people. She thinks that promoting Ningbo as a 'city of intellectuals' represents only one side. She said that 'the policymakers should not just hold on to the past. Ningbo needs to lead other cities in this regard, which means the Ningbo people need to develop and explore continuously' (19 June 2017). Honestly speaking, she does not know much about the current academic situation in Ningbo. She asked the rhetorical question: Do people think intellectual performance in Ningbo is better than Beijing or Shanghai? If yes, that's fine, but if not, why so? This can be a good starting point to explore. She personally felt that many international conferences are staged outside of Ningbo (e.g. Beijing, Shanghai, and others). Could the government seek different channels (not just internal but also external) to promote Ningbo as a city of intellectuals? How? These questions could help the city further explore the issue.

Interviewee G is an academic from New Zealand who spent ten years in Ningbo. Asked about how the city should be promoted to the outside world in terms of branding, he commented that the city is friendly. He thinks Ningbo is a vibrant city but not sophisticated like some big metropolises. He stated that 'Ningbo has a history of producing intellectuals; therefore, this should be taken into account. We should look to the past to move forward–building on what has been done before'. His understanding of claiming a 'city of X' is something very unique, unusual, and different, compared with any other cities. The residents are normally aware of their city's branding, not just the government; in other words, the residents need to embrace it. From the historical side of the city, he fully agrees that Ningbo occupies one of the strongest positions of being promoted as the city of intellectuals.

Interviewee H is another academic from Malaysia. He thinks that although Ningbo is famous in history as a city of intellectuals, this does not mean that the name can 'stick' forever. Given the fast pace of development in recent years, the theme of business is valued more by the people, rather than intellect. According to him, 'Entrepreneurial City' might be more appropriate for Ningbo. Because of the city's prosperity in the past as a port or cultural hub, it nurtured famous philosophers such as Wang Yangming.[2] Present-day materialism can very rarely cultivate such great thinkers. Universities are considered to be important sites of social interaction and intellectual exchange. If the city does want to promote itself as a city of intellectuals, it needs to interact more with educational institutions; not just higher education, but also schools at different levels because these are the places where intellectuals are generally nurtured.

11.6   Discussion on the Branding

As explained in the above interviews on branding the city of Ningbo as a 'City of Intellectuals', the interviewees, albeit their different backgrounds, share the common view that this branding can be representative of the city. This branding strategy captures the positive image and distinctive feature of the city that has been long nurtured in history. It integrates the identity and core values of local people, and that is why the branding is easily accepted by them, particularly the older generation. When people identify with the branding, they are likely to take action in harmony with policymakers. This is why from the outset of branding the city of Ningbo, the government has focused inextricably on the city's historical frame of reference. Of the 60 plus slogans promoting Ningbo (published in 2014), those focusing on its history and port account for about 70%, while the rest mostly refer to its booming business, habitable environment, or its people's benevolent spirit (Internet source 2014).[3]

From the policymakers' perspective, the label 'intellectual' may be more appealing as it connotes being well-educated and having an inquisitive and critical mind. According to Michalis Kavaratzis (2004), marketing the city is the objective of creating the city's image, which is the starting point for developing the city's brand. Successful branding means establishing a relationship between the brand and the consumer in a way where a close fit exists between the consumers' physical and psychological needs, and the brand's functional attributes and symbolic values (Hankinson and

---

[2] Wang Yangming (1472–1528) was a philosopher, writer, thinker, and strategist born in Zhejiang, who is famous for mental cultivation that features harmonization of knowledge and action (心行合一).

[3] http://www.jintang114.org/html/kouhao/2014/1105/17431.html, accessed 14 November 2018.

Cowking 1993). In this sense, Ningbo policymakers have made the right decision in branding the city by focusing on its historical ('intellectual') image as exemplified by its ancient library (large number of academicians). Effective branding can also stimulate tertiary communication such as word of mouth, people-to-people interactions and additional media coverage similar to the case of Guangzhou (Ye and Björner 2018).

However, with increasing worldwide competition, it is difficult for cities to 'stand out' in the markets they target. As pointed out by Insch and Bowden (2016), city brands face an inherent tension between achieving clear differentiation and seeking to appeal to multiple target groups. While communicating a distinctive benefit, a city's brand-positioning needs to be credible (i.e. anchored in reality). This relates to why the younger generation and overseas intellectuals who have not been in the city for too long tend to perceive the city as one that is more business-oriented and are less connected to its history that has a deeply rooted tradition of emphasising education. They tend to be less complacent (not identifying with the city's past history) and prefer that which more prominently captures the city's present characteristics. As such, the younger generation may look more to the 'excitement' in mega global cities, while overseas compatriots may look more to the hospitality of a city's inclusiveness. Therefore, if branding is not associated with some tangible outcomes for the city's stakeholders, such as improving habitability, economic vibrancy, and employment opportunities, city branding campaigns and incentives may end up achieving lacklustre effects for different social groups. In particular, positive demographic and economic outcomes for a city are associated with real and psychological positioning of the city brand (Insch and Bowden 2016).

Furthermore, the branding strategy under the theme, in the first place, shows no compelling evidence that it will provide a unique and distinctive position within this frame of reference. Particularly in the case of China, a country with long-standing history for thousands of years, cities with historical connections are numerous. It is essential that city branding campaigns raise the awareness of a city's strengths in the stakeholders' minds as direct economic benefits of city rebranding are difficult to quantify. In this context, nostalgia for the city's history is unlikely to have a significant impact, at least on some people.

Thus, policymakers need to design more specific contents under the branding. Clear measures need to go with the proposition so that the public is well-informed. Furthermore, detailed action plans need to be publicised and implemented to make people part of the branding process. It is encouraging that per the city government's website, to strengthen the city's branding, the government will build more libraries and purchase more books to encourage reading in public places, such as railway stations or bus stops. Nevertheless, providing access to resources is not enough, as demonstrated by the failure in building the 'Book City'. In this regard, concrete measures are needed so that the public may experience improvement in their cultural life. The slogan itself is rather superficial, with 'the City of Books' or 'the City of Scholars' primarily based on the 'signature image' of the ancient library and the large number of academicians. Being the 'City of Intellectuals' connotes more than this. However, this line of thinking raises more questions. Intellectuals generally have limited professional activities. According to Higgins (2011), 'the adjective "intellectual", used also as a noun, has become little more than a sociological label, indicating social rather than strictly intellectual status'. He claims that most human deeds are actually motivated merely by natural curiosity. People are in fact basically all made the same way. Therefore, being an intellectual is a pseudo justification, whereby the end justifies the means.

Moreover, the branding strategy does not mention the function of higher education. More integration of higher-education institutions with the local culture is called for in the implementation of the branding strategy. Altogether there are around ten universities and colleges in Ningbo, which is of a higher ratio in comparison with other cities of similar size in the country. Most of them operate independently, without much interaction with the local city. As far as the author is aware, international universities such as the University of Nottingham Ningbo China are interested in engaging in the city's development initiatives and being recognised as an integral part of the city. Such involvement will stimulate more tertiary communication such as word of mouth and people-to-people interactions, as well as additional media coverage (Ye and Björner 2018). One recent event has shown that the city does want to get universities involved in their various undertakings. This is the bidding by Ningbo to keep the title of 'the Top Civilised City' of the country for five consecutive years. (The word 'civilised' is a literal translation of the Chinese word *wenming* '文明', which has a very broad connotation in Chinese, on top of the meaning of civilisation in its historical sense. There is a long list of criteria to become a *wenming* city, including clean and safe environment, good behaviour of citizens in the public, high moral standards, among others.)

The city council sent out the call to universities in the hope that students and staff will contribute to this effort.

In an informal chat with the Chairman of the Association of Ningbo Film and Television Industry, the author has found that the other two branding strategies under the theme 'City of Film' and 'City of Music' have more concrete activities in place, such as building a film base in the nearby town of Xiangshan and organising a number of concerts or carnivals. However, such is not the case for the 'intellectual' theme, whereby it is being related more to the city's nostalgic history and modern version of scholars instead of actually initiating tangible measures to promote the city as such. On top of using the past as its frame of reference, what if the city brands itself to capitalise on being part of the globally connected clusters (with Shanghai and Hangzhou) within the YRD? Such branding may purposefully rebrand the city by communicating its strategic repositioning, while raising awareness of improvements in the city to targeted audiences and redirecting the city's growth. With the implementation of the BRI, five specific goals are generally identified: strengthening economic collaboration, improving road connectivity, promoting trade and investment, facilitating currency conversion, and bolstering people-to-people exchanges (Tharoor 2014). This is a good opportunity for fostering the growth of globally connected clusters such as the YRD. Although Ningbo did not make explicit its ambitions to brand itself as a leading global city, choosing to compete against such megacities as Shanghai and Hangzhou within the YRD (and perhaps even beyond) may not receive the desired outcomes that it wishes. As pointed out by Insch and Bowden (2016), while this effort represents an aspirational position, it could serve to limit its progress and competitiveness against these major rivals.

11.7 Conclusion

Overall, most people identify with the image of Ningbo being a place with intellectual achievements, rooted in its cultural background. That is to say Ningbo as a 'City of Intellectuals' itself has become the 'internal city' (Kavaratzis 2004, p. 63), the city of the mind. It is a much more inner-directed city, one that is concerned with social inclusion and exclusion, lifestyle, diversity, and multiculturalism. It is a place of complex, overlapping, and ambiguous messages. If we describe the 'internal city' as the subjective amalgamation of these ambiguous messages as perceived by the intellect (according to each individual's experiences and priorities), the two parallel cities exist simultaneously, overlapping and interacting. What is crucial for the management and marketing of the city is the point of interaction. This point of interaction is rather challenging for policy-makers to identify. Once this point is established, a message from the top can be conveyed to the citizens to make them feel part of the process.

Recently the author has learnt from some advocates that the first theme of the city be translated as 'The City of Literature', which may cap-ture the image of more literati tastes of Ningbo, nurtured through its history. However, they have failed to realise the fact that 'The City of Lit-erature' designation is part of the UNESCO Creative Cities programme, awarded in music, film, media, gastronomy, crafts and folk art, and design' (Hudson 2014). Such a title is extremely competitive and difficult to win. If the city decides to strive for such a title, it can be a rewarding effort as the title will capture the re-packaged image of the city by including a wider range of the arts (such as music and film-making) that is more appealing to young people. Although the city itself is not quite significant in these areas, given enough time and effort, it might develop as projected in a holistic manner so that newcomers may feel the cultural atmosphere within and outside of it.

However, given that geographical rivalries are inevitable with, for example, Shanghai or Hangzhou, Ningbo has to seek a new image to rebrand the city with realistic and tangible effects. In terms of attracting investors, tourists, or big events and talents, it is no longer appealing to focus on its ancient glory without recent achievement. Focusing more on its habitable environment and leisurely lifestyle (with some differen-tiation) might give Ningbo a competitive edge in its branding. Besides, greater involvement by institutions for higher education may strengthen Ningbo's competitiveness edge in today's highly interconnected world.

The study is limited to a small number of interviewees who have a background in higher education. More interviews of people with diverse background may be included in future research to reveal other findings and obtain additional evidence. In a similar vein, as stated by Insch and Bowden (2016, p. 49), regular in-depth research into stakeholders' per-ceptions and expectations of the city's brand is needed to assess credibil-ity and relevance in dynamic markets and to ensure the city possesses the assets and capabilities to protect its position.

REFERENCES

Baidu Encyclopedia. (2018). https://baike.baidu.com/item/%E5%AE%81%E6%
B3%A2%E5%8E%86%E5%8F%B2. Accessed 13 November 2018.

Braun, V., & Clarke, V. (2006). Using thematic analysis in psychology. *Qualitative Research in Psychology, 3*(2), 77–101. https://doi.org/10.1191/1478088706qp063oa.

Chomsky, N. (1967). The responsibility of intellectuals. *The New York Review of Books.* Retrieved October 12, 2017, from http://www.chomsky.info/articles/19670223.htm.

Friedmann, J. (1986). The world city hypothesis. *Development and Change, 17*(1), 69–83.

Friedmann, J. (1996). On the writing of 'the world city hypothesis'. *Scottish Geographical Magazine, 112*(2), 127–128.

Gong, Y. (2017). Talk on www.CNR.cn. http://tv.cnr.cn/zt/hsyzw/ydylsznxlft/20170123/t20170123_523524677.html. Accessed 13 Nov 2018.

Hankinson, G., & Cowking, P. (1993). *Branding in action: Cases and strategies for profitable brand management.* Auckland: McGraw-Hill Book Company.

Higgins, J. (2011). Pseudo-intellectuality and natural curiosity. *Heythrop Journal, 52*(2), 279–299. https://doi.org/10.1111/j.1468-2265.2010.00593.x.

Hudson, A. (2014). Industry: Seattle seeks UNESCO City of Literature designation. *Library Journal, 139*(8), 16.

Insch, A., & Bowden, B. (2016). Possibilities and limits of brand repositioning for a second-ranked city: The case of Brisbane, Australia's "New World City", 1979–2013. *Cities, 56,* 47–54.

Kavaratzis, M. (2004). From city marketing to city branding: Towards a theoretical framework for developing city brands. *Place Branding, 1*(1), 58–73.

Kavaratzis, M. (2007). City marketing: The past, the present and some unresolved issues. *Geography Compass, 1*(3), 695–712. https://doi.org/10.1111/j.1749-8198.2007.00034.x.

Kavaratzis, M., & Ashworth, G. J. (2005). City branding: An effective assertion of identity or a transitory marketing trick? *Tijdschrift voor economische en sociale geografie, 96*(5), 506–514. https://doi.org/10.1111/j.1467-9663.2005.00482.x.

Lloyd, J., Barenblatt, L., & Hogan, R. (1984). Intrinsic intellectuality: Its relations to social class, intelligence, and achievement. *Journal of Personality and Social Psychology, 46*(3), 646–654.

Lucarelli, A. (2012). Unraveling the complexity of "city brand equity": A three-dimensional framework. *Journal of Place Management and Development, 5*(3), 231–252.

Lucarelli, A. (2018). Place branding as urban policy: The (im)political place branding. *Cities, 80,* 12–21.

Sabatier, P. A. (1986). Top-down and bottom-up approaches to implementation research: A critical analysis and suggested synthesis. *Journal of Public Policy, 6*(1), 21–48.

Tharoor, S. (2014). *China's Silk Road revival.* https://www.project-syndicate. org/columnist/shashi-tharoor. Accessed 17 Nov 2017.

Urde, M., & Koch, C. (2014). Market and brand-oriented schools of positioning. *Journal of Product & Brand Management, 23*(7), 478–490. https://doi.org/ 10.1108/JPBM-11-2013-0445.

Van Kham, T. (2017). Social construction of public intellectuals in Vietnam: Current situation and possible changes. *Social Indicators Research, 132*(2), 659–679. https://doi.org/10.1007/s11205-016-1300-y.

Ye, L., & Björner, E. (2018). Linking city branding to multi-level urban governance in Chinese mega-cities: A case study of Guangzhou. *Cities, 80,* 29–37.

Zhao, Q. (2010). The interactive mechanism between city brand and city customers. *Modern Economic Research, 9,* 36–39.

Zhao, Y. (2015). 'China's leading historical and cultural city': Branding Dali City through public–private partnerships in Bai architecture revitalization. *Cities, 49* (Supplement C), 106–112. https://doi.org/10.1016/j.cities.2015. 07.009.

CHAPTER 12

Desertification and Its Prevention Along the Route of China's Belt and Road Initiative

Pengfei Li, Yuzhe Zang, Faith Ka Shun Chan and Juanle Wang

12.1   Introduction

President Xi Jinping of the People's Republic of China initiated the Belt and Road Initiative (BRI), also known as One Belt One Road, in October 2013 when he visited Kazakhstan (Wang 2013). It is the greatest international economic ambition of the PRC, to stimulate and

P. Li · Y. Zang
College of Geomatics, Xi'an University of Science and Technology, Xi'an, China

F. K. S. Chan (✉)
School of Geographical Sciences, University of Nottingham Ningbo China, Ningbo, China
e-mail: faith.chan@nottingham.edu.cn

J. Wang
Institute of Geographic Sciences and Natural Resources Research, Chinese Academy of Sciences, Beijing, China

F. K. S. Chan
Water@Leeds, School of Geography, University of Leeds, Leeds, UK

© The Author(s) 2020   271
H. K. Chan et al. (eds.), *International Flows in the Belt and Road Initiative Context*, Palgrave Series in Asia and Pacific Studies,
https://doi.org/10.1007/978-981-15-3133-0_12

encourage socio-economic development in a vast region covering over 65 countries in Asia, Europe, and Africa (*The Economist* 2016). This region accounts for 64% of the world's population and 30% of the world's Gross Domestic Product (GDP) (Huang 2016). The initiative was devised to reconfigure China's external sector in order to continue its strong growth. While infrastructure development plays a central role (Lechner et al. 2018), the BRI also fosters policy dialogue, unimpeded trade, financial support, and people-to-people exchange (Huang 2016). It has the potential of turning the underdeveloped 'Belt & Road' region into a new multinational vibrant economic pillar and contributing to economic policymaking by developing a new transnational economic model that benefits China and many countries that involves in the BRI.

Since the BRI was initiated, the policy has contributed considerably to the international cooperation within the region (Irshad et al. 2015; NRSCC 2015; Turgel et al. 2017). It promoted infrastructure development (Lechner et al. 2018) and international financial and trade cooperation, which was further accelerated by the establishment of the Asian Infrastructure Investment Bank (Yu 2017) and the Silk Road Fund (Fallon 2015). However, there are some uncertainties and difficulties associated with the BRI, particularly because of its potentially adverse impacts on the ecosystem, biodiversity, and environment (Lechner et al. 2018; Li et al. 2014). Within the BRI region, the topic of desertification in particular has been connected to the accelerating economic development. However, most of the BRI countries are located at the arid and semi-arid areas that are currently facing the risk of desertification.

The concept of desertification dates back to the 1920s when the extension of the West African Sahara into the Sahel zone was first observed (Kertész 2009). The term 'desertification' was first used to describe the change of productive land into a desert. In 1977, the Nairobi United Nations Conference on Desertification (UNCOD) was established following extremely arid periods in Sahelian Africa (Kertész 2009), and desertification was defined as the diminution or destruction of the biological potential of the land that could lead ultimately to the formation of desert-like conditions (UNCOD 1977).

In the 1990s, the definition of 'desertification' was further revised by the United Nations Environment Programme (UNEP) to 'land degradation' in arid, semi-arid, and dry subhumid areas resulting from various factors including climatic variations and human activities (D'Odorico et al.

2013; Helldén and Tottrup 2008). In terms of the definition, 'desertification' can be triggered by climate change and human activities including prolonged drought; soil erosion through water and wind; over-farming; deterioration of the physical, chemical, biological, or economic properties of soil; and loss of natural vegetation. Drylands support a population of over 2 billion people, 90% of which live in developing countries (D'Odorico et al. 2013). Dryland degradation costs developing countries 4–8% of their national GDP, and a relatively large fraction of drylands' population (about 135 million people in 1995) is at risk of episodic mass starvation due to land degradation (UNCCD 2011). As a result, desertification has become a substantial land degradation problem that seriously influences the arid regions of the world (Dregne 2002; Dregne and Chou 1992).

A large proportion of regions along the BRI are classified as drylands (Fig. 12.1) being subject to different levels of desertification induced and exacerbated by human interventions. These regions particularly include areas in Central Asia (Behnke 2008; Jin et al. 2012; Liu et al. 2004), North-western China (Wang et al. 2008), and Western Asia (Alvi 1995; Amin 2004; Bayram and Öztürk 2014; Darwish et al. 2004; El Shaer 2015; Haktanir et al. 2004). The BRI encourages improvements and

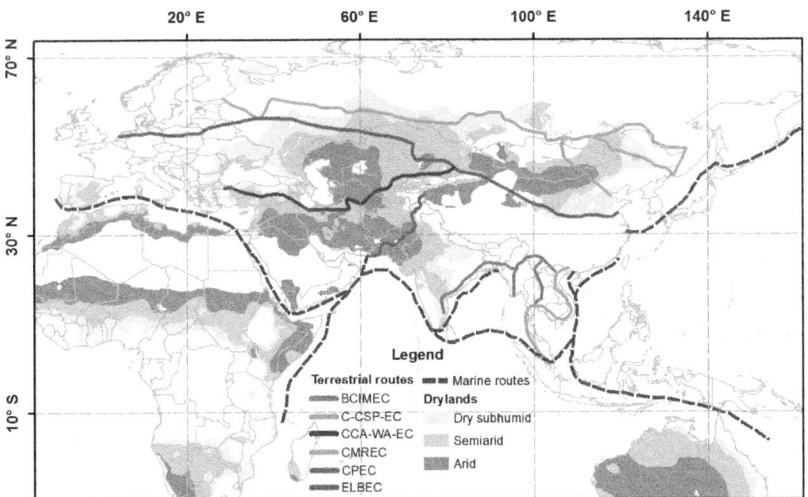

Fig. 12.1 BRI countries and spatial distribution of drylands along the BRI

expansions of existing road logistic systems (e.g. high-speed railways and multinational highways) across the economic corridors from East Asia to Europe, East Africa via Central Asia, South Asia, and West Asia. Further land use changes and deforestation is very likely to occur due to the rapid developmental pressure induced by the BRI, hence potentially exacerbating desertification in the region. Therefore, without responsive environmental management strategies to address desertification issues, it is likely that the desertification problem will be extensively magnified by the BRI.

Given that desertification is one of the most serious eco-environmental issues for some of the semi-arid and arid countries along the BRI (NRSCC 2015; Park et al. 2018), desertification control should be considered an essential part of the BRI to reduce the risk of potentially adverse effects of BRI measures and thereby secure the long-term success of the BRI. Comprehensive conservation measures are required to prevent and reduce the adverse effects of desertification in these BRI countries. However, such measures should be implemented based on a thorough understanding of desertification along the BRI countries, including its impacts and driving forces. Therefore, in this chapter, we systematically review the current state of desertification in the BRI countries, its driving forces, current identification methods, impacts, and contemporary measures to mitigate desertification. We suggest and discuss several existing and new solutions to control desertification derived from our comprehensive review of relevant grey literature (include scientific literature) and governmental documents.

12.2   The BRI

There are six economic corridors along the terrestrial routes of the BRI framework (NASMGC 2017). On land areas, the initiative focuses on jointly building a new Eurasian Land Bridge Economic Corridor (ELBEC) and developing the China–Mongolia–Russia Economic Corridor (CMREC), the China-Central Asia-West Asia Economic Corridor (CCAWAEC), and the China–Indochina Peninsula Economic Corridor (CIPEC) (Fig. 12.1). The intention is to accomplish this by taking advantage of international transport routes, relying on core cities along the 'Belt and Road' passages and using key economic industrial parks as cooperation platforms. At maritime (coastal) environment, the initiative proposed to focus on jointly building the China–Pakistan Economic Corridor (CPEC) and the Bangladesh–China–India–Myanmar Economic Corridor

(BCIMEC) for smooth, secure, and efficient transport routes connecting major sea ports along the 'Belt and Road' passages. Although the current number of countries involved in the BRI has been increasing, in this chapter, 66 countries were considered in eastern Asia, Association of Southeast Asian Nations (ASEAN), western Asia, southern Asia, central Asia, Russia and surrounding countries, and central and eastern Europe (Table 12.1).

Four out of the six corridors are facing drought issue, including CMREC, CCA-WA-EC, ELBEC, and CPEC (NRSCC 2015). Particularly affected countries include, for example, Kyrgyzstan, Mongolia, Pakistan, and Egypt, among others, all of which suffer from severe

Table 12.1 Countries involved in the BRI

Region	No. of countries	Country name
Eastern Asia	2	China, Mongolia
ASEAN	10	Singapore, Malaysia, Indonesia, Myanmar, Thailand, Laos, Cambodia, Vietnam, Brunei, Philippines
Western Asia	18	Iran, Iraq, Turkey, Syria, Jordan, Lebanon, Israel, Palestine, Saudi Arabia, Yemen, Oman, United Arab Emirates, Qatar, Kuwait, Bahrain, Greece, Cyprus, Egypt
Southern Asia	8	India, Pakistan, Bangladesh, Afghanistan, Sri Lanka, Maldives, Nepal, Bhutan
Central Asia	5	Kazakhstan, Uzbekistan, Turkmenistan, Tajikistan, Kyrgyzstan
Russia and surrounding countries	7	Russia, Ukraine, Belarus, Georgia, Azerbaijan, Armenia, Moldova
Central and Eastern Europe	16	Poland, Lithuania, Estonia, Latvia, Czech Republic, Slovakia, Hungary, Slovenia, Croatia, Bosnia and Herzegovina, Montenegro, Serbia, Albania, Romania, Bulgaria, Macedonia

drought effects due to a generally arid climate further enforced through environmental changes due to climate change (Fig. 12.1).

Moreover, there are also seven provinces within China, which are located on the major route of the BRI and are suffering from severe desertification issues. These provinces (Xinjiang, Ningxia, Inner Mongolia, Gansu, Shaanxi, and Hebei) are all located in the north-western and northern parts of China and encompass over 95% of desertified land in the country (Wang et al. 2008).

12.3   Desertification in the BRI

12.3.1   Current Desertification Situation and Possible Future Changes Along the BRI Route

Most of the BRI countries are landlocked countries with large-scale agricultural production that deepen the degree of desertification, both naturally and artificially. Thus, the desertification is widespread in BRI countries, which indicates that the situation in different areas have specific characteristic due to different geographical bases (Suocheng et al. 2015).

12.3.1.1   Eastern Asia

In Mongolia, 90% of the territory can be regarded as vulnerable to desertification. These areas are almost exclusively used as rangelands, supporting about 30 million heads of livestock and numerous populations of wild animals (Batjargal 1997). In China, desertification has occurred in regions around the Gobi areas and deserts because of mobile sand (sediments) caused by the cultivation of, and grazing by, livestock. The resulting adverse changes have been defined as land degradation characterized by wind erosion (Tao and Zhu 2003; Zhu 1998). Since the 1970s, the area affected by desertification reached its maximum during the 1970s to the early 1980s, then decreased continuously from the late 1980s to 2008 (Wang et al. 2008).

12.3.1.2   ASEAN

In south-eastern Asia and among the ASEAN countries, Vietnam is not designated as an arid or semi-arid country; however, some regions located in the central highland and the coastal areas are still at risk of desertification. Vietnam currently has more than 9×10^4 km^2 of barren land, accounting for 28% of the country's total land area, of which 7.5×10^4 km^2 are affected directly by desertification (VNA 2015). In Thailand, the desertification risk areas of the Pa Deng sub-district subdivided in low level, moderate level, and high level were 2.00, 9.14, and 0.79% of the total area, respectively. Forest areas and water bodies were considered as not being affected by desertification (Wijitkosum et al. 2013). Most areas (74.4%) in the Huay Sai area were at high risk of desertification in Northern Thailand, and the risk remained high (77.2%) in 2010. The areas classified as being at severe risk of desertification decreased at 4.2% per annum (Wijitkosum 2016).

12.3.1.3 Western Asia

According to the United Nations Development Programme (Biswas 1995), desertification is threatening about one-fifth of the Middle East and North Africa (MENA) region. In light of the global desertification assessment provided by Mamdouh (1999) assessed the desertification for the MENA region by considering the irrigated area as only slightly, or not at all, desertified, and assessing the proportion of rangelands desertified over 50% up to 85%. They found that approximately 48.6% of the land area in the Mashreq (Egypt, Lebanon, Palestine, Jordan, and Syria), 28.6% in the Nile Valley and the Horn of Africa, 16.5% in North Africa, and 9% in the Arabian Peninsula is endangered because of desertification. Among the MENA countries, Libya, Egypt, and Jordan are facing the greatest dangers; while in the Arabian Peninsula, Bahrain, Kuwait, Qatar, and the UAE are the most affected countries (El Shaer 2015).

In Bahrain, where locates in the outskirts of China-Central Asia-West Asia Economic Corridor (CCAWAEC) (HKTDC 2019; CSIS 2018), one of the major financial and transport hub in the Gulf Nations. Bahrain is one of the major spot in the twenty-first century Maritime Silk Road Initiative (MSRI) (Chaziza 2019). Most of the country's area has been found to be at risk of desertification (Thomas and Middleton 1994), and the aridification is likely to intensify and spread under current climate conditions (Elagib and Abdu 1997). In Turkey, around 109.1 km^2 are desert, and some 374.4 km^2 are prone to desertification and dishabituation, which may be accelerated in the future given a hotter, drier climate, has been projected for the region (Bayram and Öztürk 2014).

In Iran, dryland ecosystems cover more than 85% of land area, of which desertified and desert lands account for 3.4×10^4 km^2 (Pakparvar 1998). In the desertified area, 12% is classified as very severe, 81%, as severe, and

7% as moderately affected by desertification (Sepehr et al. 2007). In Iraq, over 92% of the land area has been subject to desertification, which is particularly prevalent in arable areas (Al-Saidi and Al-Juaiali 2013). Since 1981, the percentage has increased, especially since military operations have damaged both soil, plants, and had other negative consequences detrimental to the environment (Haktanir et al. 2004).

In Oman, where locates besides the China–Pakistan Economic Corridor (CPEC) and outskirts of the China-Central Asia-West Asia Economic Corridor (CCAWAEC) (HKTDC 2019), and the country is on the way becoming a major financial hub in the Gulfs of Oman. For example, China has currently investing over 25 projects for an industrial park that consists of logistic, energy, petroleum, and automobile sectors in Duqm, Oman (The Sirius Report 2018). However, Oman has extensive arid territories, which are subject to different levels of desertification. In extreme cases such as the AI-Bathina Region, severe degradation was found by Al-Balooshi and Charabi (2012). They reported that the degraded area rose from 343.85 km^2 in 2005 to 655.95 km^2 in 2010.

12.3.1.4   Southern Asia

In Afghanistan, less than 1% of the land lies within the protected areas, which means none of these land use areas are covered by the dwindling conifer forests. Moreover, one of the most threatening impacts arise from loss of soil (by erosion) and vegetation (by deforestation and de-vegetation), which contribute to desertification (NEPA 2008). As a result, around 5% of the country's land is vulnerable to desertification (Ahmadzai et al. 2008). In Bangladesh, no region can be termed as dryland. However, it does experience long spells of dry weather, and drought events are common over a region of 5.46×10^4 km^2 (Paul 1998; Shahid and Behrawan 2008). In India, the total area affected by desertification is 8.15×10^5 km^2, including 2.62×10^5 km^2 caused by water erosion and 1.78×10^5 km^2 by wind erosion, 1.76×10^5 km^2 vegetation degradation, and 9.47×10^5 km^2 of frost shattering (Ajai et al. 2009). In Pakistan, out of 7.96×10^5 km^2 of the country's land area, 6.24×10^5 km^2 are susceptible to desertification, as only 4.2% of the total land is under forests (Hussain and Irfan 2012). Moreover, most of the climatic models project a decrease in precipitation during the dry season and an increase during the monsoon season in southern Asia (Ahren and Dobler 2015), which implies higher land degradation risk in the future.

12.3.1.5   Central Asia

In Kazakhstan, over 75% of the land area is subjected to degradation and desertification; over 14% of pastures have reached an extreme degree of degradation or are completely degraded (Issanova et al. 2014). Hot spots of land degradation and desertification mainly occur in regions with unfavourable ecological conditions such as the Aral and Caspian Sea and the Lake Balkhash regions (Almaganbetov and Grigoruk 2008).

12.3.1.6   Russia and Surrounding Countries

In Russia, desertified areas, areas experiencing desertification, and areas threatened by desertification were found to occupy about 1,250,000 km² (Kust et al. 2011). Desertification processes on the territory of Armenia became more pronounced under recent conditions of socio-economic crisis and blockade. About 80% of the country's territory is affected (MNP 2002; Susanne Khachatryan 2013). Georgia's arid and semi-arid regions, mainly including the south-eastern part of the country, are especially sensitive to desertification. The catastrophic development of desertification processes begins, as precipitation is less than 200 mm (Davitashvili et al. 2009).

12.3.1.7   Central and Eastern Europe

In Europe, desertification processes affect approximately 10% of the total land area (Rubio et al. 1998). This is particularly the case for Mediterranean, Central, and Eastern European countries. In Serbia, there are three so-called Sands: the Deliblato Sands, Subotičko-Horgoška Sands, and Golubačka Sands. These areas emerged due to desertification and drought. The area under sand amounts to 344 km² (Gajić and Đeković 2005). Drylands in Romania cover 40% of the agriculture land, mainly in the South, South East, and East of Romania (Lupu et al. 2010). Since 1901, Romania has seen in every decade one to four extremely droughty/rainy years. Because of climate change, an increasing number of droughts became increasingly apparent, especially after 1981 (Mateescu et al. 2013). Besides, Romania has been ranked among the top seven countries in Europe that would be strongly impacted by aridity in the next few years, with an anticipated rise of average annual temperatures by as much as 5°C due to climate change (Peptenatu et al. 2013).

12.3.2   Driving Forces of Desertification in the BRI

The causes of desertification are mainly attributable to climate aridification and human interventions (El Shaer 2015). In some regions, the desertification is mainly attributed to worsening climate conditions. For example, in Negev, Israel, the desertification was traditionally attributed solely to the Arab tribes that conquered this region in the seventh century A.D. However, evidence suggests that a climate moister than the present prevailed in the Negev region from ca. 100 B.C. to ca. 300 A.D. This climate slowly became more arid and reached a critical level around 500 A.D. (Issar and Tsoar 1987). The desertification in Bahrain has also been connected to climate variability (the Bahrain Islands are located entirely within the arid and semi-arid zones of the earth), periodic droughts, and persistent aridity exacerbated by inappropriate land and water use and degradation of the vegetation by the local population (Thomas and Middleton 1994). Desertification in Kuwait results primarily from the combined influences of climatological and geological processes, with intensive human activities (e.g. Gulf War) in sandy areas accelerating these processes (Al-Awadhi et al. 2003). Dry conditions in the early Holocene in central Asia are closely related to decreased water vapour advection due to reduced wind speeds of the westerly winds and less evaporation upstream from the Mediterranean, Black, and Caspian Seas in boreal winter (Jin et al. 2012). A great risk of desertification in Armenia is due to an existing arid climate marked by sporadic mountainous terrain, scarce vegetation, frequently recurring droughts, devastatingly heavy precipitation, all combined with millennia of human utilization of the ecosystem (Susanne Khachatryan 2013).

In some other regions in Asia, the desertification is dominated by human activities. For example, in the dry zone of Myanmar, population pressure and overgrazing were major factors that contributed to the overall degradation of the environment (Tun 2000). Desertification in Turkey is generally caused by incorrect land use, excessive grazing, forest fires, urbanization, industry, soil erosion, salinization, and uncontrolled wild type plants picking (Çetin et al. 2007). The different ecosystems in Lebanon are mainly threatened by deforestation, overgrazing, urban development, road development, bad agricultural techniques, and excessive use of chemical products, over-hunting, and industrial development (Haktanir et al. 2004). In Pakistan, the desertification is mainly due to unsustainable land management practices (Anjum et al. 2010), further aggravated by scarcity of water, frequent drought, flash flood, and extreme climatic conditions (Hussain and Irfan 2012). In Tajikistan, desertification is due to steep slope and overgrazing; unfortunately, the current policies on soil erosion prevention and relevant measures are lacking, thus desertification is occurring in pasture zones and areas (Nekushoeva and Akhmadov 2008).

In many regions, desertification is a result of the interactions of different factors. In China although the classifications of desertification (e.g. the main form of desertification normally refers to 'sandy' desertification, which changes soil stability) are now nearly consistent, the causes are still being disputed (Wang et al. 2008). For instance, Wang, Chen, et al. (2005), Wang, Dong, et al. (2005) have proposed that desertification in the Mu Us and Otindag deserts and their adjacent regions caused by climate change, and this hypothesis is supported by archaeological evidence. On the contrary, others have argued that human activities were responsible (Wang et al. 2008). In Mongolia, climate conditions and human activities are both considered to be important factors for desertification (Batjargal 1997).

In Iran, the causes of desertification involve climatic factors, population pressure, over-exploitation of water resources, and overgrazing. These factors often interact in contributing to desertification. For example, adverse climatic conditions may prevent the continuation of previously sustainable levels of water use, leading to over-exploitation of the resource; and secondary salinization may develop in association with irrigation (Wang, Chen, et al. 2005). In Georgia, desertification occurrence depends on complex interactions among many factors, including a decrease in precipitation coupled with soil erosion by wind and the drying up of water resources through increased regional temperatures. In addition, many areas also suffer from land degradation due to over-cultivation, overgrazing, deforestation, and poor irrigation practices (Davitashvili et al. 2009).

12.3.3 Research Methods for Desertification Identification

The progress of desertification may be evaluated by several means, for example, by direct observation and measurement, and mathematical models (Ladisa et al. 2012; Rubio and Bochet 1998). Typically, the evaluation of desertification risks combines both the environmental conditions and physical characteristics of the location and land use patterns in the area.

In terms of the modelling approach, the Mediterranean Desertification and Land Use (MEDALUS) model was employed to investigate the extent of land degradation, land use changes, and desertification risk in the Huay Sai area, Thailand, from 1990 to 2010 (Wijitkosum 2016), and to map the desertification in Kashan, Iran (Zehtabian et al. 2005) and Larestan, Southern Iran (Sepehr et al. 2007). The Centre for Ocean–Land–Atmosphere Studies applied Global Climate Model (GCM) modelling to investigate the impact of, and mechanisms for, biosphere feedback in the grassland of Mongolia and Inner Mongolia (Xue 1996). A risk assessment model based on a Leopold matrix was applied to assess risks of desertification for the Binh Thuan province (Vietnam) (Hai et al. 2013).

The use of remote sensing provides a wide array of opportunities and advantages for monitoring desertification, in that it provides large-scale, repetitive, and accurate coverage. More detailed information on data requirement and availability for remote-sensing-based land degradation and desertification in the Mediterranean basin has been given by Sommer (Dragan et al. 2005; Sommer 2001). Geographical information system can be used to evaluate water erosion, wind erosion, vegetation degradation, and range utilization as desertification indicators, which is efficient in desertification assessment and mapping (Grunblatt et al. 1992). A spatial analysis using remote sensing and geographical information system techniques was performed to assess the desertification risk for Pa Deng sub-district, adjoining Kaeng Krachan Natural Park, Thailand (Wijitkosum et al. 2013). Two images of NOAA-AVHRR and SPOT vegetation data acquired in November 1992 and 2000 were used to assess desertification and changes of agricultural lands in Egypt. A supervised classification of the two images was carried out using the maximum likelihood technique (Shalaby et al. 2004). The Advanced Spaceborne Thermal Emission and Reflection Radiometer and Envisat Advanced Synthetic Aperture Radar (ASAR) were used to map desertification in semi-arid coastal areas, southern Vietnam (Anh et al. 2006).

There are also several studies investigating desertification based on a combined analysis of several contributing factors. For example, Šarapatka et al. (2010) evaluated the land degradation threat for the Czech Republic based on an overlay analysis of individual degraded areas with their weights being assigned in ArcView Spatial Analyst GIS environment. Perčec Tadić et al. (2014) developed a drought vulnerability for Croatia, consisting of a complex combination of the geomorphologic and climato-logical inputs (maps) that are presumed to be natural factors that modify the amount of moisture in the soil. The first version of the vulnerability map developed from the slope map, solar irradiation, and coefficient of the variation of precipitation is updated by inclusion of optional param-eters: soil types and land cover classes. Food and Agriculture Organiza-tion of the United Nations (FAO)/UNEP proposed a system of criteria for the evaluation of desertification status (Dregne and Boyadgiev 1983). The matrix contains data on plant cover, water and wind erosion, and salinization. However, Verón et al. (2006) criticized the matrix from sev-eral perspectives, particularly the subjective nature of the data (Kertész 2009). Li et al. (2013) developed a desertification classification and grad-ing system for grassland of Ningxia province, China, based on fieldwork and expert review.

12.4 Impacts of Desertification in the BRI (Possible Impacts)

Within the BRI countries, desertification has been found to affect regional climate, economic development, and environmental security. In terms of the GCM modelling work conducted by Xue (1996), the desertification of grasslands in Inner Mongolia and Mongolia had a significant impact on the simulated climate. During the past 40 years, the observed rainfall has decreased in northern and southern China but interestingly increased in central China and the Inner Mongolian grasslands, while northern China has become warmer. The simulated rainfall and surface temperature differ-ences between the desertification integrations and grassland integrations are consistent with these observed changes.

It was estimated that the annual average income foregone in the MENA region due to desertification was $1.98 billion. The estimated costs for rehabilitation are about $8 billion per year, or $160 billion for a 20-year programme of anti-desertification measures in the region (Nasr 1999). Al-Saidi and Al-Juaiali (2013) found that the cost of combating desertification is around $10.3 billion to $20.5 billion in Iraq. This huge cost affects present and future economic situation and slows down further development. It was estimated that the cost of soil degradation in Syria is equivalent to about 12% of the value of the country's agricultural output or about 2.5% of the total GNP (Haktanir et al. 2004).

In Iraq, desertification has had several consequences, including loss of productive lands and their conversion to barren lands, increase in the surface of sand dunes in addition to their mounting negative effects, diminishing forms of biota, increase in air pollution and sand movement, and increasing pressure on groundwater (Haktanir et al. 2004). Major issues related to desertification in Bangladesh include: (i) deterioration of the natural resources, adversely affecting the socio-economic condition and livelihood support systems; (ii) reduction of irrigation potential; (iii) diminishing food security base of human beings and livestock; (iv) scarcity of drinking water, depletion of groundwater, interference with spacing of tube well, including hand tube well, and shallow and deep tube well; (v) health and nutrition status of the population, arsenic contamination in groundwater, contamination due to disposal of waste and inadequate sanitation; (vi) reduced availability of biomass for fuel; (vii) loss of biodiversity; and (viii) impoverishment, indebtedness, and distress sale of assets of production (DOE et al. 2005). Land degradation has decreased productivity by 30–40% in the highland areas of Kyrgyzstan, and by 40–60% in Tajikistan (Gringof and Mersha 2006). Kazakhstan's arable land has lost up to 20–30% of its humus, and approximately 30% of the pastureland vegetation (6.5×10^5 km^2) has degraded (Gringof and Mersha 2006).

12.5   Solutions and Policy Advice to Mitigate Desertification

There have been some control countermeasures and policies developed to mitigate desertification in the BRI countries. For example, in Mongolia, a 'National Plan of Action' has been implemented to combat desertification (Batjargal 1997). In Iran, a national plan to combat desertification was ratified in 2004 to emphasize community participation (Amiraslani and Dragovich 2011). In Afghanistan, an attempt has been made to establish a basic land and natural resource policy and regulatory framework (NEPA 2008). In Ningxia, China, a region-wide grazing ban, together with other ecological engineering measures, has been implemented to mitigate desertification and promote the restoration of grassland vegetation (Li et al. 2013). However, these contemporary measures need further improvement.

For example, as Batjargal (1997) suggested, the national plan of Mongolia should pay more attention to a continued functioning mechanism of interaction among agriculture, animal husbandry, forestry, water resources management, and industry. In Iran, current measures still face challenges, including questions of how to manage existing desertified areas as well as taking into account potential future problems associated with rapidly depleting groundwater supplies and a predicted reduction in the plant growth period accompanying climate change (Amiraslani and Dragovich 2011).

In Afghanistan, existing efforts need to consider wider aspects of social development that include stakeholders at the national level and more fully engage vertically provincial and local governments that are directly involved in natural resource management, as well as the communities themselves (NEPA 2008).

Many of the BRI countries are still lacking a national plan to combat desertification, although the need for such strategies has been widely acknowledged, and researchers have suggested the priorities of the strategies. In Kuwait, a national strategy or an action plan to combat the desertification should be placed on: (1) policies, regulations, legislations, and reinforcements; (2) education; (3) national field management of the ground; (4) control measures for sand encroachment (conservation and protection of areas); and (5) water management (Al-Awadhi et al. 2003). In Saudi Arabia, an education-oriented extension programme for the training of the farming community is a basic need and can play a significant role in minimizing the extent of desertification (Amin 2004).

For Sri Lanka, there are short-term steps and solutions for reducing desertification that will provide food, increase the peasants' income, and provisionally relieve the pressure to clear forests for Chena (an important cause for desertification). As the final strategy to suppress the emerging signs of desertification in the 'Dryland Zone', attempts should be made to declare sandy and alkaline soil stretches as 'nature reserves' and prohibit any wilful damage to plants standing on them (Tennakoon 1980).

In Nepal, detailed information on spatial inventory on land degradation and its consequences are still rarely available. To deal with its problems, an integrated approach addressing the physical, biological, and socio-economic aspects of the processes of land degradation should be implemented. In addition, community participation, utilization of local knowledge of people, and cooperation among interdisciplinary agencies are suggested for effective management (Paudel et al. 2009).

In Pakistan, some actual measures have been taken, such as sustainable land management, soil and water conservation, afforestation, and rehabilitation of degraded land, combined with practices that include assessments and monitoring activities such as repetitive high-resolution satellite images, delineation and mapping of affected areas, remote sensing, and GIS. These measures are likely to be suitable strategies for combating desertification in Pakistan (Anjum et al. 2010).

In addition to the above, all the BRI countries should carry out in-depth collaboration to combat desertification. In fact, a cooperation framework has been developed among the BRI countries to fight against desertification on 10 September 2017. The framework was set up on the sidelines of the thirteenth session of the 'Conference of the Parties' (COP13) to the United Nations Convention to Combat Desertification (UNCCD). The framework will help members cooperate on financing, information sharing, training, and learning from each other through example projects (Zhang 2017).

Moreover, the UNCCD is also an important platform for the BRI countries to jointly fight desertification. It is increasing its efforts to create awareness about ongoing programmes and projects, such as those on soil and water management, climate extremes, food security, and poverty alleviation. It is also stimulating concerted efforts of communities to incorporate the UNCCD policies into national development strategies. One example is 'Cyprus', which attempts to establish appropriate links and synergies between groups of people and to build up tightened partnerships at the national and international levels, especially for transboundary geographical aspects (Van Cotthem 2006).

Here, we suggest that China and other BRI-involved countries located in (semi-)arid areas take this opportunity to collaborate with the UNCCD closely to further develop and implement cross-boundary transnational policies to reduce drought impacts, improve water resource management, and restrict deforestation in order to mitigate and prevent desertification processes.

12.6   CONCLUSION

In this chapter, we introduced desertification and its prevention along the BRI countries. The chapter was organized into three parts:

i. Current situation, possible future changes and driving force of desertification in the BRI region and the corresponding research methods for identifying and assessing desertification,
ii. The impact of desertification in relation to the sustainable development of the BRI countries, and
iii. Solutions to address and mitigate desertification from a perspective of sustainable development based on an analysis of the desertification and existing solutions of the BRI countries.

This review reveals that the BRI countries have been experiencing different levels of desertification, which deserve increased attention in the future. The driving forces of desertification in BRI countries are varied, covering human activities and droughts. The assessment or identification of desertification is mainly dependent upon the modelling approach, remote sensing, and relevant measures; while a more in-depth research investigating the processes and mechanisms of desertification via field measurements and modelling approach is still desirable in the future.

The BRI countries are likely to suffer from more severe desertification in the future under the context of global warming and more intensive human interventions under the BRI framework. Some BRI countries have adopted regional/national control countermeasures for desertification, while there are many countries still lacking such strategies. More importantly, contemporary measures are subject to drawbacks and a framework, such as the one established on 10 September 2017 on the sidelines of COP13 to the UNCCD, which is urgently needed to further enhance the collaboration among BRI countries towards desertification conservation.

Acknowledgements We would like to express our best gratitude for Dr. Fabian Fassnacht (Karlsruher Institut für Technologie [KIT]) for reviewing and providing suggestions to improve this book chapter. This work is supported by the National Natural Science Foundation of China (grant number NSFC41850410497; NSFC 41807063), the Ningbo Municipal Bureau of Science and Technology (grant number 201401C5008005).

REFERENCES

Ahmadzai, H., Kakar, F., Rashidi, M., Suarez, P. G., Ameli, O., & Hartman, A. F. (2008). Scaling up TB DOTS in a fragile state: Post-conflict Afghanistan. *International Journal of Tuberculosis and Lung Disease, 12*(2), 180–185.

Ahren, B., & Dobler, A. (2015). Regional climate projections. In N. Sharma & W. Flügel (Eds.), *Applied geoinformatics for sustainable integrated land and water resources management (ILWRM) in the Brahmaputra River Basin.* New Delhi: Springer.

Ajai, R. R., Arya, A. S., Dhinwa, P. S., Pathan, S. K., & Raj, K. G. (2009). Desertification/land degradation status mapping of India. *Current Science, 97*(10), 1478–1483.

Al-Awadhi, J. M., Misak, R. F., & Omar, S. S. (2003). Causes and consequences of desertification in Kuwait: A case study of land degradation. *Bulletin of Engineering Geology and the Environment, 62*(2), 107–115.

Al-Balooshi, A., & Charabi, Y. (2012). *Assessment of land degradation in Al-Bathina Region, Oman.* Paper presented at the International Geographical Congress, University of Cologne, Cologne, Germany.

Almaganbetov, N., & Grigoruk, V. (2008). *Degradation of soil in Kazakhstan: Problems and challenges.* Netherlands: Springer.

Al-Saidi, A., & Al-Juaiali, S. (2013). The economic costs and consequences of desertification in Iraq. *Global Journal of Political Science and Administration, 1*(1), 40–45.

Alvi, S. (1995). Climatic changes and desertification in some regions of the Middle East. *GeoJournal, 37*(4), 483–488.

Amin, A. (2004). The extent of desertification on Saudi Arabia. *Environmental Geology, 46*(1), 22–31.

Amiraslani, F., & Dragovich, D. (2011). Combating desertification in Iran over the last 50 years: An overview of changing approaches. *Journal of Environmental Management, 92*(1), 1–13.

Anh, H., Williams, M., & Manning, D. (2006). *Remote-sensing monitoring of desertification using ASTER and ENVISAT ASAR: Cast study at semi-arid area of Vietnam.* Paper presented at the International Symposium on Geoinformatics for Spatial Infrastructure Development in Earth and Allied Sciences.

Anjum, S. A., Wang, L.-C., Xue, L., Saleem, M. F., Wang, G.-X., & Zou, C.-M. (2010). Desertification in Pakistan: Causes, impacts and management. *Journal of Food, Agriculture and Environment, 8*(2), 1203–1208.

Batjargal, Z. (1997). *Desertification in Mongolia.* RALA Report, *200*, 107–113.

Bayram, H., & Öztürk, A. B. (2014). Global climate change, desertification, and its consequences in Turkey and the Middle East. In K. Pinkerton & W. Rom (Eds.), *Global climate change and public health* (Vol. 7, pp. 293–305). New York: Humana Press.

Behnke, R. (Ed.). (2008). *The socio-economic causes and consequences of desertification in central Asia.* Dordrecht, Netherlands: Springer.

Biswas, P. (1995). Food: Stock, import and price. *Dhaka Cour, 11*(34), 9.

Çetin, S. C., Karaca, A., Haktanır, K., & Yildiz, H. (2007). Global attention to Turkey due to desertification. *Environmental Monitoring and Assessment, 128*(1–3), 489–493.

Chaziza, M. (2019). *Gulf nations and Xi Jinping's BRI.* https://www.weeklyblitz.net/oped/gulf-nations-and-xi-jinpings-bri/. Accessed 2 Nov 2019.

CSIS. (2018). *China's Belt and Road is full of holes.* CSIS Briefs Report. https://www.csis.org/analysis/chinas-belt-and-road-full-holes. Accessed 2 Nov 2019.

Darwish, T., Khawlie, M., Faour, G., Masri, T., Shaaban, A., & Bou Kheir, R. (2004). *Land degradation in Lebanon: Vulnerability of soil resources to desertification.* Paper presented at the United Nations/Islamic Republic of Iran Regional Workshop.

Davitashvili, T., Khantadze, A., & Kutaladze, N. (2009). Droughts and desertification problems on the territory of Georgia. *Reports of Enlarged Session of the Seminar of I* (Vol. 23, pp. 14–19). Vekua Institute of Applied Mathematics.

DOE (Department of Environment), MOEF (Ministry of Environment and Forest), GPRB (Government of the Peoples Republic of Bangladesh), & IUCN (The World Conservation Union Bangladesh Country Office). (2005). National action programme (NAP) for combating desertification in Bangladesh, Bangladesh.

D'Odorico, P., Bhattachan, A., Davis, K. F., Ravi, S., & Runyan, C. W. (2013). Global desertification: Drivers and feedbacks. *Advances in Water Resources, 51,* 326–344.

Dragan, M., Sahsuvaroglu, T., Gitas, I., & Feoli, E. (2005). Application and validation of a desertification risk index using data for Lebanon. *Management of Environmental Quality: An International Journal, 16*(4), 309–326.

Dregne, H. (2002). Land degradation in the drylands. *Arid Land Research and Management, 16*(2), 99–132.

Dregne, H., & Boyadgiev, T. (1983). *Provisional methodology for assessment and mapping of desertification.* FAO/UNEP (Food and Agriculture Organization of the United Nations, United Nations Environmental Program), Rome.

Dregne, H., & Chou, N. (1992). Global desertification dimensions and costs. In H. Dregne (Ed.), *Degredation and restoration of arid lands.* Lubbock: Texas Tech University.

The Economist. (2016, July 2). Our bulldozers, our rules. *The Economist.*

Elagib, N. A., & Abdu, A. S. A. (1997). Climate variability and aridity in Bahrain. *Journal of Arid Environments, 36*(3), 405–419.

El Shaer, H. M. (2015). Land desertification and restoration in Middle East and North Africa (MENA) region. *Sciences in Cold and Arid Regions, 7*(1), 7–15.

Fallon, T. (2015). The New Silk Road: Xi Jinping's grand strategy for Eurasia. *American Foreign Policy Interests, 37*(3), 140–147.

Gajić, G., & Đeković, V. (2005). Land degradation in Serbia and Montenegro and official frameworks in the function of combating desertification. *Glasnik Šumarskog fakulteta Univerziteta u Banjoj Luci* (4), 77–90.

Gringof, I., & Mersha, E. (2006). Assessment of desertification, drought and other extreme meteorological events. In S. Gathara, I. Gringof, E. Mersha, K. Sinha Ray, & P. Spasov (Eds.), *Impacts of desertification and drought and other extreme meteorological events* (pp. 12–29). Geneva, Switzerland: World Meteorological Organization.

Grunblatt, J., Ottichilo, W., & Sinange, R. (1992). A GIS approach to desertification assessment and mapping. *Journal of Arid Environments, 23*(1), 81–102.

Hai, L. T., Gobin, A., & Hens, L. (2013). Risk assessment of desertification for Binh Thuan Province, Vietnam. *Human and Ecological Risk Assessment: An International Journal, 19*(6), 1544–1556.

Haktanir, K., Karaca, A., & Omar, S. (2004). The prospects of the impact of desertification on Turkey, Lebanon, Syria and Iraq. In A. Marquina (Ed.), *Environmental challenges in the Mediterranean 2000–2050* (Vol. 37). Dordrecht, Netherlands: Springer.

Helldén, U., & Tottrup, C. (2008). Regional desertification: A global synthesis. *Global and Planetary Change, 64,* 169–176.

HKTDC. (2019). *The Belt and Road Initiative.* HKTDC Research. http://china-trade-research.hktdc.com/business-news/article/The-Belt-and-Road-Initiative/The-Belt-and-Road-Initiative/obor/en/1/1X000000/1X0A36B7.htm. Accessed 2 Nov 2019.

Huang, Y. (2016). Understanding China's Belt & Road Initiative: Motivation, framework and assessment. *China Economic Review, 40,* 314–321.

Hussain, Z., & Irfan, M. (2012). Sustainable land management to combat desertification in Pakistan. *Journal of Arid Land Studies, 22,* 127–129.

Irshad, M. S., Xin, Q., & Hamza, A. (2015). One Belt and One Road: Dose China-Pakistan economic corridor benefit for Pakistan's economy? *Journal of Economics and Sustainable Development, 6*(24), 200–207.

Issanova, G., Saparov, A., & Ustemirova, A. (2014, October 9–10). *Soil degradation and desertification processes within Kazakhstan.* Paper presented at the The 4th International Conference "Ecology of Urban Areas 2014", Zrenjanin, Serbia.

Issar, A., & Tsoar, H. (1987). *Who is to blame for the desertification of the Negev, Israel.* Paper presented at the Proceedings, IAHS Symposium.

Jin, L., Chen, F., Morrill, C., Otto-Bliesner, B. L., & Rosenbloom, N. (2012). Causes of early Holocene desertification in arid central Asia. *Climate Dynamics, 38*(7–8), 1577–1591.

Kertész, Á. (2009). The global problem of land degradation and desertification. *Hungarian Geographical Bulletin, 58*(1), 19–31.

Kust, G., Andreeva, O., & Dobrynin, D. (2011). Desertification assessment and mapping in the Russian Federation. *Arid Ecosystems, 1*(1), 14–28.

Ladisa, G., Todorovic, M., & Trisorio Liuzzi, G. (2012). A GIS-based approach for desertification risk assessment in Apulia region, SE Italy. *Physics and Chemistry of the Earth, Parts a/B/C, 49*, 103–113.

Lechner, A. M., Chan, F. K. S., & Campos-Arceiz, A. (2018). Biodiversity conservation should be a core value of China's Belt and Road Initiative. *Nature Ecology and Evolution, 2*, 408–409. https://doi.org/10.1038/s41559-017-0452-8.

Li, J., Yang, X., Jin, Y., Yang, Z., Huang, W., Zhao, L., et al. (2013). Monitoring and analysis of grassland desertification dynamics using Landsat images in Ningxia, China. *Remote Sensing of Environment, 138,* 19–26.

Li, Z., Wang, J., Zhao, Z., Dong, S., Li, Y., Zhu, Y., et al. (2014). Eco-environment patterns and ecological civilization modes in the Sile Road Economic Zone. *Resource Science, 36*(12), 2476–2482. (in Chinese with English abstract).

Liu, A., Liu, Z., Wang, C., Niu, Z., & Yan, D. (2004). *Monitoring of desertification in central Asia and western China using long term NOAA-AVHRR NDVI time-series data.* Paper presented at the Geoscience and Remote Sensing Symposium, Toulouse, France.

Lupu, A. B., Ionescu, F. C., & Borza, I. (2010). The phenomenon of drought and its effects within Romania. *Research Journal of Agricultural Science, 42*(4), 102–109.

Mamdouh, N. (1999). *Assessing desertification and water harvesting in the Middle East and North Africa: Policy implications.* ZEF Discussion Papers on Development Policy. Bonn, Germany.

Mateescu, E., Smarandache, M., Jeler, N., & Apostol, V. (2013). *Drought conditions and management strategies in Romania.* Initiative on "Capacity Development to Support National Drought Management Policy" (WMO, UNCCD, FAO and UNW-DPC) Country Report.

MNP (Ministry of Nature Protection of the Republic of Armenia). (2002). National action programme to combat desertification in Armenia. Yerevan.

NASMGC. (Cartographer). (2017). *The major routes and the economic corridors of BRI.*

Nasr, M. (1999). *Assessing desertification and water harvesting in the Middle East and North Africa: Policy implications.* ZEF Discussion Papers on Development Policy.

Nekushoeva, G., & Akhmadov, H. (2008). Desertification and sustainable agriculture development of Tajikistan. *The International Archives of the Photogrammetry, Remote Sensing and Spatial Information Sciences, 37*(B8), 887–890.

NEPA. (2008). Afghanistan's environment 2008. Afghanistan: National Environmental Protection Agency of the Islamic Republic of Afghanistan, United Nations Environment Programme.

NRSCC. (2015). *The Belt and Road Initiative ecological and environmental conditions.* Beijing: National Remote Sensing Center of China, Ministry of Science and Technology of the People's Republic of China.

Pakparvar, M. (1998). *Desert research and control desertification in Iran.* Paper presented at the New Technologies to Combat Desertification. In Proceedings of the International Symposium held in Tehran, Iran 12–15 October 1998 organized by the United Nations University, Ministry of Jihad-i-Sazandagi, Government of the Islamic Republic of Iran, Forest and Range Organization.

Park, C.-E., Jeong, S.-J., Joshi, M., Osborn, J., Ho, C.-H., Piao, S., et al. (2018). Keeping global warming within 1.5 °C constrains emergence of aridification. *Nature Climate Change, 8,* 70–74. https://doi.org/10.1038/s41558-017-0034-4.

Paudel, P. P., Devkota, B. D., & Kubota, T. (2009). Land degradation in Nepal: A review on its status and consequences. *Journal of the Faculty of Agriculture, Kyushu University, 54*(2), 477–479.

Paul, B. K. (1998). Coping mechanisms practised by drought victims (1994/5) in North Bengal, Bangladesh. *Applied Geography, 18*(4), 355–373.

Peptenatu, D., Sîrodoev, I., & Pravalie, R. (2013). Quantification of the aridity process in south-western Romania. *Journal of Environmental Health Science and Engineering, 11*(1), 5.

Perčec Tadić, M., Gajić-Čapka, M., Zaninović, K., & Cindrić, K. (2014). Drought vulnerability in Croatia. *Agriculturae Conspectus Scientificus, 79*(1), 31–38.

Rubio, J., & Bochet, E. (1998). Desertification indicators as diagnosis criteria for desertification risk assessment in Europe. *Journal of Arid Environments, 39*(2), 113–120.

Rubio, J., Recatala, L., & Andrew, V. (1998). European desertification. *WIT Transaction on Ecology and the Environment, 31,* 3–16.

Šarapatka, B., Bednář, M., & Novak, P. (2010). Analysis of soil degradation in the Czech Republic: GIS approach. *Soil and Water Research, 5*(3), 108–112.

Sepehr, A., Hassanli, A. M., Ekhtesasi, M. R., & Jamali, J. B. (2007). Quantitative assessment of desertification in south of Iran using MEDALUS method. *Environmental Monitoring and Assessment, 134*(1–3), 243–254.

Shahid, S., & Behrawan, H. (2008). Drought risk assessment in the western part of Bangladesh. *Natural Hazards, 46*(3), 391–413.

Shalaby, A., Ghar, M. A., & Tateishi, R. (2004). Desertification impact assessment in Egypt using low resolution satellite data and GIS. *International Journal of Environmental Studies, 61*(4), 375–383.

Sommer, S. (2001). *Assessment of data requirement and availability for remote sensing based land degradation and desertification monitoring in the Mediterranean basin.* Paper presented at the Enne, G; Peter, D.; Pottier, D. Desertification convention—Data and information requirements for interdisciplinary research. European Commission, Alghero.

Suocheng, D., Zehong, L., Yu, L., Guangyi, S., Huilu, Y., Juanle, W., et al. (2015). Resources, environment and economic patterns and sustainable development modes of the Silk Road Economic Belt. *Journal of Resources and Ecology, 6*(2), 65–72.

Susanne Khachatryan, A. K. (2013). *The modeling of natural socioeconomic factors of desertification and its particularity for the Republic of Armenia.* Paper presented at the The 3rd International Geography Symposium-GEOMED 2013.

Tao, W., & Zhu, Z. (2003). Study on sandy desertification in China—1. Definition of sandy desertification and its connotation. *Journal of Desert Research* (3), 374–384 (in Chinese with English Abstract).

Tennakoon, M. (1980). Desertification in the dry zone of Sri Lanka. *Perception of Desertification,* 4–33.

The Sirius Report. (2018). *Oman is a key regional partner in the Belt and Road Initiative.* https://www.thesiriusreport.com/geopolitics/oman-china-bri. Accessed 2 Nov 2019.

Thomas, D. S., & Middleton, N. J. (1994). *Desertification: Exploding the myth.* Hoboken, NJ: Wiley.

Tun, T. (2000). Greening the dry zone of the Myanmar. *Myanmar Forestry Journal, 34*(1), 8–14.

Turgel, I. D., Vlasova, N. Y., & Xu, Y. (2017). Economic links between Russia and China: from cross-border to interregional cooperation (The case of Sverdlovsk region and Heilongjiang province). *R-Economy, 3*(3), 149–160.

UNCCD. (2011). *Global drylands: A UN system-wide responses.* United Nations Environment Management Group, UN.

UNCOD. (1977). *Round-up, plan of action and resolutions.* Nairobi, Kenya: United Nations Conference on Desertification.

Van Cotthem, W. (2006). *Biodiversity and desertification on Cyprus—An important role for cooperation at all levels.* Paper presented at the Eco Forum 2006–World Environmental Day, Cyprus International Conference Centre Nicosia.

Verón, S., Paruelo, J., & Oesterheld, M. (2006). Assessing desertification. *Journal of Arid Environments, 66*(4), 751–763.

VNA. (2015). *Vietnam marks world day to combat desertification.* http://www.xinhuanet.com/english/2015-06/11/c_134318970.htm

Wang, X., Chen, F., Hasi, E., & Li, J. (2008). Desertification in China: An assessment. *Earth-Science Reviews, 88,* 188–206.

Wang, X., Chen, F. H., Dong, Z., & Xia, D. (2005). Evolution of the southern Mu Us Desert in North China over the past 50 years: An analysis using proxies of human activity and climate parameters. *Land Degradation & Development, 16*(4), 351–366.

Wang, X., Dong, Z., Yan, P., Zhang, J., & Qian, G. (2005). Wind energy environments and dunefield activity in the Chinese deserts. *Geomorphology, 65*(1-2), 33–48.

Wang, Y. (2013, September 8). *President Xi's vision for the future OBOR strategy.* CPC News.

Wijitkosum, S. (2016). The impact of land use and spatial changes on desertification risk in degraded areas in Thailand. *Sustainable Environment Research, 26*(2), 84–92.

Wijitkosum, S., Yolpramote, K., & Kroutnoi, L. (2013). *Desertification risk assessment in Pa Deng sub-district, adjoining area of Kaeng Krachan Natural Park, Thailand.* Paper presented at the The PSU Phuket International Conference. Price of Songkhanaklarin University, Phuket.

Xue, Y. (1996). The impact of desertification in the Mongolian and the inner Mongolian Grassland on the regional climate. *Journal of Climate, 9*(6), 2173–2189.

Yu, H. (2017). Motivation behind China's 'One Belt, One Road' Initiatives and establishment of the Asian Infrastructure Investment Bank. *Journal of Contemporary China, 26*(105), 353–368.

Zehtabian, G., Ahmadi, H., Khosravi, H., & Rafiei Emam, A. (2005). The approach of desertification mapping using Medalus methodology in Iran. *Desert, 10*(1), 51–60.

Zhang, J. (2017, September 11). *Belt and Road countries in joint fight against desertification.* Xinhua News Agency.

Zhu, Z. (1998). Concept, cause and control of desertification in China. *Quaternaryences, 18,* 145–155.

International Flows in the Belt and Road Initiative: The Future

David O'Brien, Faith Ka Shun Chan and Hing Kai Chan

The Belt and Road Initiative (BRI) is a game changer on many levels. As a demonstration of the economic and political status of China, an announcement that it has retaken its place among the leading nations of the world, it is a clear statement of intent. It will have profound and long-lasting ramifications across much of the globe and has the potential to impact directly in the lives of a majority of the world's population. It may indeed herald a new Chinese century in which much of the old-world

D. O'Brien (✉)
Faculty of East Asian Studies, Ruhr-University Bochum, Bochum, Germany
e-mail: David.OBrien@ruhr-uni-bochum.de

F. K. S. Chan
School of Geographical Sciences,
University of Nottingham Ningbo China, Ningbo, China
e-mail: faith.chan@nottingham.edu.cn

H. K. Chan
Nottingham University Business School China, University of Nottingham
Ningbo China, Ningbo, China
e-mail: hingkai.chan@nottingham.edu.cn

© The Author(s) 2020   295
H. K. Chan et al. (eds.), *International Flows in the Belt and Road
Initiative Context*, Palgrave Series in Asia and Pacific Studies,
https://doi.org/10.1007/978-981-15-3133-0_13

order is swept away. It is certainly ambitious enough to give the impression that this is the path China is on. It is also increasingly clear that China will both define the BRI and be defined by it. This volume has sought to explore some of the complexity that this entails and has, through a wide-ranging analysis, attempted to go beyond rhetoric and headline in order to understand what this vast project may mean for humanity.

The BRI is still in an early form and it will take on meaning as it develops. It is a narrative and many actors will seek to control that narrative in the years to come. Much will be written in seeking to understand its impact. Where this book has contributed is in exploring the BRI as a flow of ideas, of people, politics, and business and how these flows have been shaped by history. For long periods China has closed itself off from the world, sealed into various ideological battles that saw this once stable and mighty land decay and crumble. But this is no more, China today has thrown open the gates and seeks to reclaim its historical legacy as a great civilization. Its leader Xi Jinping is the most powerful China has known since Chairman Mao. He has consolidated his authority to such an extent in the People's Republic that it increasingly seems politics in China operates through his will alone. BRI is his creation and the strength of Xi and of China will be measured in what it achieves for China.

This is a grand globalization strategy which seeks to fundamentally alter the current status quo, a status quo China believes has been created by the 'Western world' to exploit it and to take advantage of its weakness. China is no longer weak and it believes the road back to the position it believes to be its destiny that of great power lies through this initiative.

Yet as with other narratives of rejuvenation and civilization, BRI runs of the risk of becoming as much about division as common purpose. China struggles when it comes to telling its story, and with great power tensions increasing with the United States the battle for the control of narrative may be as important as the battle for the control of resources. Much has been written of the 'Thucydides Trap', the idea that war between a rising power and an established power is inevitable, since the term was coined by Graham Allison in 2017.

The BRI may indeed prove central to this, for good or bad. Another area explored in this volume is the impact BRI may have on Chinese Russian relations, currently at an historic high. BRI brings a huge Chinese influence into Russia's backyard and while it seems for now that Russia is happy to continue its close partnership, the historical precedence of the Great Game is surely relevant and possible indicator of trouble ahead.

From the historical to the current day the authors in this collection have attempted to situate our understanding of this project in the past, the present, and future. In doing so it has explored both the international, the national, and the local. This is an attempt to understand how this project will for better or worse change the world.

One of the most striking aspect of BRI is that the PRC has adopted some of the imperial rhetoric of the Silk Road in its discursive framing of the initiative. While the Chinese Communist Party would strongly refute that this is a colonial project and indeed has gone to great lengths to reassure its neighbours that BRI is a mutually beneficial solution to developing their economies in partnership, there are undoubtedly historical echoes here. As the chapters contained in this volume have demonstrated the potential for conflict resulting in these flows is very real. This is as true today as it has been historically.

We emphasize the importance of addressing history, geography, and environmental issues in the BRI strategy. These perspectives are influential, immensely complex and multi-scaled in the BRI. Through the chapters in this book, we defined BRI and the dimensions and implications from business, politics, history, geography, and its impacts and drivers. We further address the modern history by digesting the background, connections, and influences of China and Western world (e.g., Europe), though such phenomenon can lead us to rethink the future BRI strategy on trades, international cooperations, transnational legislations, etc., which are important put into consideration.

Furthermore, the BRI attracts investments and talents to cities, we project many cities will be grown and transformed into larger cities and some of them will become megacities and metropolitans. City's branding and future urban planning contexts are equally important driving cities that engaged with BRI forward, in terms of creating further social-economic activities, business developments, marketing, infrastructures, social well-being, etc., these perspectives are essentially required driving cities growing sustainably long-term. We also rethink and purpose the range of impacts on different components of the environmental impacts particularly in the Belt's region that mostly consist of arid and semi-arid (dryness) areas, we definitely believe many of these areas and cities will be grown and developed under BRI, to bring decent economic growth, wealth, and prosperous living style to people.

Similarly, we envisage that there will be a substantial impact on environmental systems, such as enlargement of desertification exacerbate by large-scale deforestation, de-vegetation, urban developments, and urbanization, these damages could be particularly affected on highly sensitive environmental or ecological protected areas that align on current proposed BRI economic corridors (which projected to construct transnational highways and railways links that connects China with South East Asia, South Asia, Middle East and Eastern Europe). Environmental, economic and sociopolitical drivers will influence BRI development and impacts. In addition, we provided in-depth discussions and thoughts on transnational large-scale of socio-economic-political, history and environmental and addressing the potential impacts of BRI.

Understanding these characteristics and according impacts of BRI on the social-economic, history and environmental perspectives are able to devise policy and plans for addressing its impacts to ensure a long-term sustainable development that benefits our next generations across nations. At this stage, it is difficult to ensure the project scale, as the projected impacts may be over-estimated, but that also gives us an opportunity to establish better policies collectively to move things in positive direction.

We have found that recent BRI policy briefs and published guidelines have stood up on the importance of transboundary multi-nations and using various scale (spatially and financially) approaches to implementing and undertaking this policy. However, at the moment there are yet to have detailed information for practitioners and policymakers, we believe stakeholders and policymakers in China and recipient countries should find this book useful in debates about how these challenges we raised in business, history, geography and environmental issues and impacts (of BRI) should be understood and managed better.

The complexity of the BRI and the conflicts mentioned above can be facilitated with a good business tune. After all, business, and hence economic, benefits generated by the BRI can leverage political and social tensions and even instability. Compromises can be reached via a good negotiation process in order to lead to a win-win or even multi-win situation. That said, how to balance the driving forces from different patrons is far from easy. Various chapters in this volume attempt to define the BRI economics and integrated market from a business perspective. The insights from the definitions can reshape the flow of business activities that will help compliment the benefits generated by the BRI. If different parties can see their pay-off transparently, the chance to reach such compromises is definitely higher.

To ease the aforementioned negotiation process, transparency and connectivity, which is the main widely publicized objective of the BRI, plays an irreplaceable role. Innovation in cross-border transportation systems can smoothen the flows of physical goods and make the transactions simpler. But innovation or innovative technologies are still required human operations so developing human capability is equally important to advancing technological innovation. More importantly, these talents involved in the BRI activities should equip with appropriate political sense due to the complexity of the BRI. We hope that the BRI can raise the standard, both technologically and human capital-wise, of the globe.

The strength of this collection is that it brings together scholars from a very broad range of disciplines who explore these issues from multiple perspectives, from the macro to the micro and in doing so demonstrate that the impact of this enormous project will be felt keenly across a vast area for years to come. There is no doubt that BRI has the potential to significantly alter the current equilibrium, what this volume has attempted to do is demonstrate how this can happen in the most unexpected and unintended ways.

Flows of course can never be just one way and this volume has demonstrated how China, while attempting to control the flow of money, influence and power can also expect to meet with unexpected blockages and backlashes. The transformative potential of BRI is clear, what is also clear is that the movement and flow of ideas has the potential to insight opposition and resistance. In seeking to create a new world order in which China plays *a* or indeed *the* dominant role, a role legitimized in by its own understanding of itself as a mighty civilization brought low by hostile foreigners, China runs the risk of coming into direct conflict with others ideas and flows. At the time of writing, as we approach the 70th anniversary of the founding of the People's Republic of China. For the BRI to succeed, China will need to persuade those through which it passes that the prosed 'win-win' situation does not, as the joke goes, mean China wins twice.

CPI Antony Rowe
Eastbourne, UK
May 18, 2020